The Hudson Valley and Catskill Mountains

AN EXPLORER'S GUIDE

The Hudson Valley and Catskill Mountains

AN EXPLORER'S GUIDE

JOANNE MICHAELS & MARY-MARGARET BARILE

Second Edition

The Countryman Press
Woodstock, Vermont

Library of Congress Cataloging-in-Publication Data
Michaels, Joanne, 1950–
The Hudson Valley and Catskill Mountains: an explorer's guide /
Joanne Michaels and Mary-Margaret Barile—2nd ed.
p.   cm.
Includes index.
ISBN 0-88150-363-0 (alk. paper)
1. Hudson River Valley (N.Y. and N.J.)—Guidebooks.
2. Catskill Mountains Region (N.Y.)—Guidebooks.
I. Barile, Mary.   II. Title.
F127.H8M52   1996
917.47'30443—dc20
95–39154
CIP

Maps by Mike Henkle
Text design by Glenn Suokko
Cover design by Ann Aspell
Cover photograph of stone house in Tillson,
by Phyllis McCabe
Published by The Countryman Press
    P.O. Box 175, Woodstock, Vermont 05091
Distributed by W.W. Norton & Company, Inc.
    500 Fifth Avenue, New York, NY 10110
Printed in the United States of America

Dedication

This book is dedicated to the memory of Ralph Barile
who kept us going when we had given up hope.
We loved him.

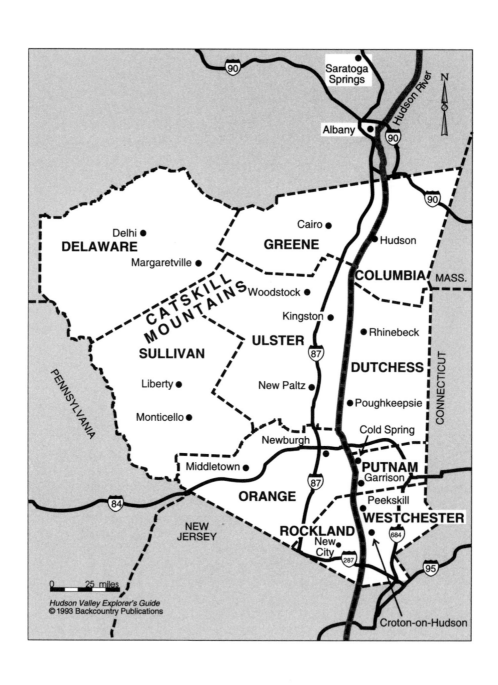

Hudson Valley Explorer's Guide
© 1993 Backcountry Publications

Contents

A Note to the Reader

No entries for any of the establishments appearing in the *Explorer's Guide* series have been solicited or paid for.

Please note two things: The prices cited in the book are those available at press time in 1996 and do not include the state and county rooms and meals taxes, which vary from 6 to 8 percent. We have tried to note the addition of a 15 percent gratuity where applicable. Increases are possible.

Smoking: Most bed & breakfasts are now smoke-free, and several have nonsmoking rooms, as do larger restaurants. If this is of importance to you, ask when you call for reservations.

The price rating system is simple. For entrées in the *Dining Out* and *Eating Out* sections:

$ means $10 and under
$$ means $10–20
$$$ means above $20.

For inns and bed & breakfasts (per person):

$ means $55 and under
$$ means $55–$75
$$$ means above $75.

Acknowledgments

It is never possible to thank everyone who helps a book of this kind come to life; for every person we mention there were a dozen more behind the scenes who answered questions, sent out brochures, provided suggestions, and opened their homes. Many people gave us their opinions and the names of their favorite spots, based on years of growing up and living in their respective towns. They probably didn't realize at the time how helpful they were. These friendly folk got us off the beaten track, where we discovered restaurants, back roads, and a fishing hole or two that we probably never would have found on our own. So this book, aside from being what we hope is the very best guide to the area, is also a valentine to all the people in the Hudson Valley and Catskills.

Introduction

During the years we worked as editors of a regional magazine covering the Hudson Valley and the Catskills, we realized that there was no guidebook available for tourists or local residents who traveled for a day, a weekend, or on an extended journey through this diverse region. We wanted to share the beauty and history of this area, which includes more than a dozen counties and parts of counties, some the size of entire states.

When people think of the Hudson Valley and the Catskills, many of them imagine mysterious mountains where Rip Van Winkle slept and the Headless Horseman rode, or lush valleys where bobcats roamed, or even brash hotels, where the entertainment and the food never stopped. True, these are part of the region's story, but after traveling thousands of miles on back roads and main roads, in snow, fog, sun, and rain, we know that the area has so much more to offer: It is a treasure trove of history, with jewellike scenery and colorful, independent people.

Because there is so much to see and do here, we chose to include only what we considered the "best" of the region—whether it was food, inns, views, or history. At historic sites or places of interest, we looked for tours or unusual exhibits. At hiking and fishing spots, we checked to see if the areas were attractive and accessible. In the case of restaurants, inns, hotels, and B&Bs, we looked for distinctiveness, quality, cleanliness, and courtesy. We traveled the area in all seasons, talked to hundreds of people, and visited nearly every site. In some cases, if we couldn't experience a place ourselves, we talked to experts whose judgment we relied on, so you are getting the recommendations of the "best" people as well.

There are many different types of travelers, and this book offers a large number of places for visiting and dining. We have tried to select sites that will please people of all ages, all backgrounds, all purses. Some places are free, others expensive, but all are the best.

We have to emphasize, however, that some of the dollar ratings will have changed between the time this book was written and the time it appears in your bookstore. We also must point out that lunches may cost considerably less than dinners, that single rates may be higher or lower, depending on the establishment, and that special rates are available for some historic sites. (One suggestion: Senior citizens should always inquire about special rates, discounts, and free passes. They will often be pleasantly surprised.) Please accept the numbers as guides only. If a site or restaurant does not appear in this book, this omission does not reflect a negative review. Perhaps we didn't know about it, or it may recently have opened, or we may just have missed it. Tell us about it, so that future editions of this guidebook will be as complete and as accurate as possible. Suggestions and complaints should be sent to us care of PO Box 425, Woodstock, NY 12498.

All the sites included in this book are within a day's drive of New York City, and many are a few hours by car from Boston and Philadelphia. The book is arranged by county, beginning with the chapters on counties on the west side of the Hudson River, heading north to Albany and Saratoga, and continuing with the counties south of Albany on the east side of the Hudson. You can plan a day trip or a week-long vacation, as the spirit moves you. You can be where the action is or utterly alone. You can eat crunchy apples and creamy goat cheese, hike scenic mountains, canoe icy rivers, or just take a walk. The climate is temperate, the views are extraordinary, the people are friendly.

Many places of interest are seasonal, as are the outdoor activities, but there are sites open year-round throughout the region. (Of course, not every county offers the same activities, so don't be surprised to find dozens of farms in one area and only one or two somewhere else.) We strongly suggest—in these days of budget cuts and financial adjustments at museums and galleries alike—that you call ahead and check on schedules if you are taking a long trip.

The Hudson Valley and the Catskills have something to please everyone—from auctions to zoos, clog dancing to ballet. There are secrets worth discovering by bicycle, on foot, or from a hot-air balloon. We just hope you set aside plenty of time to explore our favorite region. And remember to send us your suggestions—we want you all to enjoy your visit to our home.

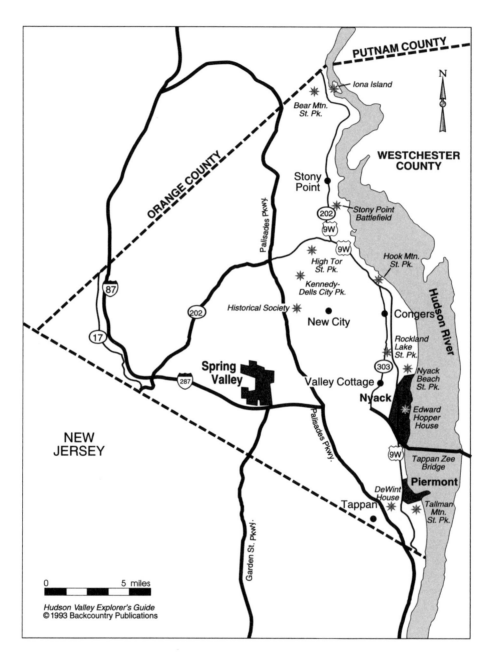

Rockland County

Rockland County

Only 176 square miles in size, Rockland County packs a lot into its area. It seems that everywhere you look in Rockland there is a park, from the tiny vest-pocket squares of green in towns and villages to the great spaces of Bear Mountain. Only 30 miles north of New York City, Rockland has saved many of its forests, wetlands, mountains, and historical sites from development. Wealthy patrons, civic leaders, and citizen activists joined forces to prevent Bear Mountain and High Tor from becoming a prison site and a quarry, respectively. Today the fruits of those early environmental battles are seen and enjoyed by all. Hundreds of miles of hiking and biking trails wind through estuarine marshes, along the Hudson River, and up and over dramatic peaks. Lakes and streams teem with wildlife, and plant lovers will delight in the explosion of color and scent that mark the spring wildflower season. Stony Point Battlefield, the mountaintop meadow where American troops defeated the British Redcoats, is almost as it was more than 200 years ago. In small towns and villages throughout the county, houses have been preserved with such care and such a sense of history that visitors feel as if they have stepped back in time. While touring Rockland you will hear again and again the names of those who made history and are still remembered in ceremonies and festivals throughout the county: George Washington, Benedict Arnold, John André, and even Captain Kidd!

GUIDANCE
Rockland County Tourism (914-638-5122), 11 New Hempstead Road, New City 10956.

GETTING THERE
Rockland is accessible from the NYS Thruway; watch for the Nyack and Bear Mountain exits.

MEDICAL EMERGENCY
Helen Hayes Hospital (914-947-3000), Route 9W, Haverstraw; **Nyack Hospital** (914-358-6200), North Midland Avenue, Nyack.

VILLAGES

Nyack. Located off the NYS Thruway; follow signs to the village. First settled by the Nyack Indians, who moved there from Brooklyn, Nyack soon became home to the Dutch, who began to farm the region. When steamboats arrived, making river travel easier, Nyack became a center for shipping and boatbuilding. The town is now known as an antiques and arts center, home to dozens of shops that offer the finest furniture, jewelry, crafts, and artwork.

To see Nyack's charming architectural heritage (the less adventurous may want to purchase walking tour maps at any of the local bookstores), begin at South Broadway near the Nyack Public Library, one of the libraries built with funds from the Carnegie Foundation at the turn of the century. Next to the library is a Queen Anne–style house, with a tower and fine shingle work. Heading north at 46 South Broadway, Couch Court is an unusual late-19th-century building that sports a towerlike cupola. The Presbyterian Church was built in 1838 in the Greek Revival style, in which columns and symmetry were used in an effort to capture what was considered the ancient purity of Greece. Down the street a little farther, look for the Tappan Zee Theatre, built when movies were silent and vaudeville shows were the rage. Across the street the Reformed Church has a clock tower that dates back to 1850. On Burd Street a plaque on the bank tells a little of the history of Nyack. On North Broadway you'll see the Congregation of the Sons of Israel, founded in 1870. A side trip down and around Van Houten Road (it turns into Castle Heights) runs past riverfront homes and offers a magnificent view of the Hudson. Continue your drive up North Broadway, passing magnificent mansions and lovely 18th-century homes, to Hook Mountain State Park.

The village of Nyack (914-353-2221 for information) sponsors special events throughout the summer and fall, including art and antiques street fairs, wacky boat contests, a Septemberfest, a Halloween parade, and other happenings.

Tappan. The local government here was the first in New York State to establish by ordinance a historic district, with the result that a walk down Main Street in Tappan will reveal many 18th- and 19th-century structures. The Tappan Library, a frame house dating from the mid-18th century, boasts a restored Colonial garden. John André was imprisoned in the Yoast Mabie Tavern, built in 1755, although Washington's instructions were that André be treated civilly. Just beyond the tavern, look for the Killoran House, a town house built in 1835 with the bricks taken from a dismantled church. In the middle of Main Street, where it meets Old Tappan Road, the Village Green was the site of the public stocks and the liberty pole, depending on the mood of the townspeople at the time. The nearby Reformed Church of Tappan stands on the site where André was tried and convicted of spying. Although André requested that he be shot as a soldier, the tribunal ordered him hanged as a spy, since to do otherwise would have been to cast doubt upon his guilt. In the nearby burying grounds you will find many old tombstones. Farther up the road is the Demming-Latelle House, best known as the home of the man who manufactured the first canned baby food.

TO SEE

Edward Hopper House and Hopper House Art Center (914-358-0774), 82 North Broadway, Nyack. Open Saturday and Sunday 1–5. Donation suggested. The American realist painter Edward Hopper was born in Nyack in 1882 and as a youth spent much of his time in the village. Several of his paintings feature local landmarks. When he died in 1967, Hopper was buried in the Oak Hill Cemetery. His boyhood home was rescued from demolition not long after his death, and today it is a community arts and cultural center. Exhibits have included works by Hopper and other American painters, and concerts are given in the gardens of the Hopper House each summer. The site also sponsors a local garden tour.

HISTORIC HOMES

DeWint House National Shrine (914-359-1359), 20 Livingston Avenue, near Oak Tree Road in Tappan. Open year-round; call for hours. Free. Constructed in 1700 of Holland brick and sandstone, the DeWint House boasts the pitched roof and tile fireplace common in well-to-do Dutch homes of the period. Although the house is important architecturally, it is best known as George Washington's headquarters and as a shrine to Washington's participation in the fraternal organization known as the Masons. It was also here that Washington stayed the day the British spy Major John André was hanged, and it is recorded that Washington asked that the shutters to his room be closed, the same shutters that cover the window today. When the house was purchased by the Masons, the owner said family tradition held that several of the items in the house were there at the time of Washington's visits, including a hat rack, andirons, and a flintlock gun. Today the house offers a look into Washington's day-to-day life during the war, along with the story of his participation in the Masons. A small carriage house museum also contains period artifacts and exhibits, and trees around the site have been marked with identification tags. Don't miss the largest weeping willow tree in the country—34 feet in circumference and almost 150 years old. A self-guided walking tour of Tappan is also available at the carriage house.

HISTORIC SITES

Historical Society of Rockland County (914-634-9629), 20 Zukor Road, off New Main Street in New City. Hours of the gallery and house vary with the season; call for information. Admission fee. This society offers both history and art to visitors, along with year-round special events. Changing exhibits in the gallery feature works by local and other artists. The house is well known for its demonstrations of open-hearth cooking. Special events usually include a candlelight tour, a dollhouse exhibit, an ethnic festival, and an antiques fair. The shop offers a nice selection of local publications and maps.

Rockland Center for Holocaust Studies (914-356-2700), 17 South Madison Avenue, Spring Valley. Closed on national and Jewish holidays; call for hours. Visitors to this small museum will be humbled and moved by powerful images of the Holocaust and the strength shown by its survivors. A permanent exhibit examines the history and effects of the Holocaust, while videos and artwork bring home the personal horrors of this period. There is a research library for public use.

Stony Point Battlefield (914-786-2521), located on Park Road, off Route 9W, Stony Point. Open late April through October, Wednesday through Saturday 10–5; Sunday 1–5. Closed Monday and Tuesday, except Memorial Day, Independence Day, and Labor Day. Free. When George Washington felt he had to demonstrate that American troops were determined to stand up to the superior British forces in the Hudson Highlands, he sent in General "Mad Anthony" Wayne to prove the point. In July of 1779 Wayne led the elite troops of the Corps of Light Infantry in an attack on the British at Stony Point. During a midnight raid the Americans routed the British from their beds and challenged their reputation as an invincible fighting force. A walking tour of the battlefield today takes visitors through a wildly beautiful park where remnants of British fortifications still survive. Trails are marked with plaques explaining the battle, and you will pass the Stony Point Lighthouse, which was used for more than a century to aid ships on the Hudson. The museum offers a slide show that depicts events leading up to the battle and is accompanied by exhibits and original memorabilia illustrating the tactics and strategies that brought victory to the Americans. Dogwoods bloom along the paths, and special events, like military encampments and holiday celebrations, are held in the spring.

TO DO

BICYCLING

Both Bear Mountain State Park and Harriman State Park offer a number of challenging bike routes. However, both of these areas can get extremely congested on weekends. You might want to try Rockland Lake and Tallman State Park, which have paved bicycle paths. Another option is Nyack Beach State Park, located off Route 9W with access from Broadway in Upper Nyack. This park runs along the river, and the paths are flat with fine views of the Hudson. Hook Mountain State Park also has biking paths with scenic views of the Hudson. To get there, take North Broadway in Nyack east; the park is located at the end of the road.

FARM STANDS AND PICK-YOUR-OWN FARMS

Even though Rockland County is small, you can still discover some terrific outlets for local fruits and vegetables.

Cropsey Farm (914-634-1545), 230 Little Tor Road, New City. Open year-round, Cropsey Farm is a fully stocked stand that even has a holiday shop.

Dr. Davies Farm (914-268-7050), Route 9W, Congers (open year-round),

and Route 304, Congers (open May through November). You can pick
your own apples in the fall and then select from a wide variety of berries, pumpkins, plums, and other goodies at the farm stand.

Duryea Farms (914-356-1988), 101 Ackertown Road, Monsey. Open April
through October, and December. Pick your own plump, red strawberries,
juicy apples, and orange pumpkins in season; select a local tree at
Christmastime.

The Orchards at Conklin (914-354-0369), South Mountain Road, Pomona.
Open year-round. You can harvest your own fruits on weekends and pick
a pumpkin at Halloween.

Schimpf Farms (914-623-2556), 13 Parrot Road, West Nyack, has a roadside market from mid-July through Thanksgiving.

Van Houten Farms (914-735-4689), Sickletown Road, Pearl River, is
open April through Halloween and even has pony rides (fee charged)
for the kids.

Van Ripers Farm (914-352-0770), 121 College Road, Suffern, is open until Thanksgiving. You can pick raspberries in season or select from a
wide variety of fruits, vegetables, and bedding plants.

FISHING

The state parks allow fishing, but you will have to check with them for their
individual regulations and restrictions. Fishing is also allowed in the
Ramapo River, which has a long trout season. Route 17 has parking
areas, and the waters north of Ramapo are considered good fishing
spots. On Route 202 near Suffern, watch for the Mahwah River and the
parking areas along its bank. Minisceongo Creek has good fishing from
the Rosman Bridge upstream to the Palisades Mountain Parkway Bridge.

HIKING

Almost every park has hiking trails that wind through the woods and in some
cases over mountains. Some unusual trails, set up to commemorate the
American Revolution, also provide ways to get to know local history.
The 1777 Trail, the 1777 E Trail, and the 1777 W Trail—known collect-
ively as the **Bicentennial Trails**—are all under 3 miles in length.
Located in Bear Mountain and Harriman State Parks, you can find the
trails on Route 9W, 1 mile north of Tomkins Cove. Look for the diamond-
shaped white blazes with red numbers. This is also the starting area for
the **Timp-Torne Trail,** a 10-mile hike that offers spectacular views
down the Hudson River all the way to New York City. The trail ends at
the Bear Mountain Lodge.

The shorter **Anthony Wayne Trail**—a 3-mile loop marked with
white blazes—can be found along Seven Lakes Drive in Bear Mountain State Park, near the traffic circle. Another popular trail is the **Pine
Meadow Trail,** which begins at the Reeves Meadow Visitors Center
on Seven Lakes Drive.

If you want to climb Bear Mountain, take the **Major Welch Trail**
from the Bear Mountain Inn.

Buttermilk Falls Park, in Nyack, has trails from the parking lot to the falls themselves, lovely in early spring.

Kennedy Dells Park, Main Street, 1 mile north of New City (watch for signs), was once part of film producer Adolph Zukor's estate. Along with hiking trails, there is also a trail for people with disabilities.

Shorter walks may be taken in **Betsy Ross Park,** Tappan; **Tackamack North** and **Tackamack South** Parks, Clausland Mountain Road, Blauvelt; and along the **Erie Trail,** which runs from Sparkill to Grandview along abandoned railroad tracks.

GREEN SPACE

Bear Mountain State Park (914-786-2701). Take the Bear Mountain exit off the Palisades Parkway or Routes 6 and 9W. Open daily year-round; parking fee charged Memorial Day to Labor Day. Part of the vast Palisades Interstate Parks System, Bear Mountain shares almost 54,000 acres with its neighbor, Harriman State Park. Noted on maps since the mid-18th century, Bear Mountain has been known as Bear Hill, Bread Tray, and Bare Mountain (presumably because of a bald peak). Once the site of Revolutionary War Forts Clinton and Montgomery, the area the park now covers was slated to become the home of Sing Sing Prison until public outcry and political pressure persuaded the state to change its plans early in the 20th century. Since then a parkway system has made the park accessible to the hundreds of thousands who visit each year, and several lakes add to the park's outdoor appeal. Visitors to the park will find a four-season outdoor wonderland featuring a wide program of activities and special events, including swimming, fishing, min-

Bear Mountain Bridge over the Hudson River

iature golf, hiking, boating, sledding, and cross-country skiing. At the Trailside Museum, Nature Trail, and Zoo, located next to the Bear Mountain Inn (watch for signs), exhibits and programs describe the Native American, military, and natural history of the area. (There is even an exhibit of mastodon remains!) Open daily 9–5 year-round. Admission is free. The self-guided trail is the oldest continuously run trail in the country. The short trail also features a unique zoo, with wildlife in natural settings, including a beaver lodge (which has been cut away for easy viewing), a reptile house, and trees, shrubs, and plants with identification tags. On into the park visitors may want to bike or drive along the scenic interpark roads or rent a paddle- or rowboat at one of the lakes. (Canoes are subject to an inspection.) Three lakes—Welch, Sebago, and Tiorati—have swimming, picnicking, and other recreational areas, and special events are scheduled throughout the year at the Bear Mountain Inn and in the park. In the past there have been winter holiday fairs, orienteering meets, crafts and ethnic festivals, professional ski jumping competitions, even stargazing nights.

Crystal Run Environmental Education Center (914-425-3663), 681 Chestnut Ridge Road, Chestnut Ridge. Open daily; call for a list of special events. Admission charged for some events. The nature programs offered at this 110-acre site include maple syrup making, cider pressing, honey harvesting, and more. There are workshops and tours (by appointment for individuals or groups), and the center also has a farm stand on the site in summer.

Hook Mountain State Park and **Nyack Beach Park.** To reach Hook Mountain State Park, take North Broadway, in Nyack, east to the end; follow signs. To reach Nyack Beach Park, take Route 9W from Broadway. Both parks are open daily, dawn to dusk; free. Hook Mountain was once referred to by the Dutch as Verdrietige ("tedious") Hook because of the winds that could change rapidly and leave a boat adrift in the river. The area was also a favorite campground of Native Americans because of its wealth of oysters. For modern visitors the park provides a place to picnic, hike, and bike and enjoy scenic views of the Hudson. An annual hawk watch is held every spring and fall, and the park is said to be haunted by the ghost of the Guardian of the Mountain, a Native American medicine man who appears during the full moon each September and chants the ancient harvest festival. Nyack Beach is open for swimming, hiking, and fishing; the views of the river are outstanding, and there are cross-country ski trails available in winter.

Piermont Marsh and **Tallman State Park** (914-359-0544), Route 9W in Sparkill, near Piermont, north of Palisades Interstate Parkway, Exit 4. Piermont Marsh can be reached through Tallman State Park by following the bike path or from the Erie Pier in the village of Piermont. Admission fee. This nature preserve covers more than 1000 acres of tidal marsh, mountains, and river and is considered one of the most important fish breeding areas along the Hudson. Wildflowers, such as the spectacular rose mallow, abound in portions of the marsh, and this is a prime bird-watching area in all seasons. The area along the marsh is a marvelous place to view the river, and a hike up the mountain offers a spectacular panorama for photographers. Tallman State Park is a wonderful place to spend a summer day—along with the natural wonders, the park has complete recreational facilities, including bike paths, a swimming pool, tennis courts, and hiking trails. There are even some human-made ponds that have become homes for many varieties of reptiles and amphibians; ironically, the ponds were to have been part of a tank storage area for a large oil company earlier in the century. Today, especially in the spring, the ponds hum with the sounds of frogs, and the woods come alive with birdcalls.

Rockland Lake State Park (914-268-3020), Route 9W, Rockland Lake exit, Congers. Open daily year-round, although the Nature Center is closed October through May. Use fee. Another jewel in the crown of the Palisades Interstate Parks System, this popular recreation area is located at the base of Hook Mountain. The lake was once the site of an ice farm, which provided a harvest of pure, clear ice for nearly a century before the advent of modern refrigeration. The park is a wonderful place to explore—in addition to hiking, you can enjoy swimming, jogging, fishing, biking, boating, and golf. During the winter go ice skating on the lake or cross-country skiing and sledding on some of the challenging hills. At the Nature Center, you will discover live animals and exhibits, special-events programs throughout the summer, and guided tours along the wetlands walkway. Just outside the center are marked nature trails that run along a boardwalk and contain braille interpretation stops for the blind and visually impaired. Wildflowers and birds are particularly vibrant during the spring, but there are wonders to discover here any time of year.

LODGING

Bear Mountain Inn (914-786-2731), off Routes 9W, 9A, 9D, and 6, Bear Mountain 10911. ($$) Located in the heart of Bear Mountain State Park, the 75-year-old inn's rustic charm makes it a fine place to relax. The stone-and-wood building complements this panoramic spot, and all of the facilities of the park can be enjoyed as well. There are 60 guest rooms in the inn, all with private bathrooms. This is a large establishment in a public park, so it is best to visit off-season when the crowds have disappeared. Open year-round.

WHERE TO EAT

DINING OUT
Bully Boy Chop House (914-268-6555), 117 Route 303, Congers. ($$) Open for lunch Monday through Friday, noon–2:30; dinner Monday

through Saturday at 5, Sunday at 2. Specializing in steaks, chops, and seafood with an English touch, Bully Boy is renowned for its prime ribs, English pies, and Yorkshire pudding. There are seven dining rooms, with one of the less formal rooms overlooking a lovely duck pond and another elegant area decorated with rich red touches. Homemade scones are served with butter and honey. Children welcome.

La Capannina (914-735-7476), 606 South Pascack Road, Spring Valley. ($$) Open for lunch Tuesday through Friday, noon–2; dinner Tuesday through Saturday at 6. The site of this lovely French restaurant dates back to the early 1700s. Known as the Haring Homestead, after its 18th-century Dutch owners, the house is surrounded by 7 acres of beautiful grounds. Nearby the Old Pascack River roars over a dam, splashing through the glen below. The restaurant offers an extensive menu and wine list. Some of the house specialties are rack of lamb, Dover sole, and duckling with cherry sauce. Children are welcome. Call for reservations and detailed directions.

Chelsea on the Hudson (914-358-1973), 65 Main Street, Nyack. ($$) Open daily except Monday for lunch at noon; dinner Tuesday through Saturday at 5, Sunday at 3. Continental cuisine, with veal and seafood specialties. Eat lunch on the veranda and enjoy the romantic setting for a candlelight dinner. Reservations suggested; not recommended for children.

Freelance Cafe and Wine Bar (914-365-3250), 506 Piermont Avenue, Piermont. ($$) Open daily for lunch, noon–3; dinner from 5:30; Sunday brunch, noon–3. Right next to Xavier's, this informal eatery is a café at heart, with specialties like coconut shrimp in a sharp mustard sauce, grilled chicken salad with raspberry sauce, and tiramisu.

Giulio's (914-359-3657), 154 Washington Street, Tappan. ($$) Open for lunch Monday through Friday 11:30–2:30; dinner Monday through Friday 5–10, Saturday until 11; Sunday 2–9. Fine northern Italian cuisine is served in this 100-year-old Victorian house. There is a romantic candlelit setting at dinner and a strolling entertainer midweek and Friday evenings. Sample the Valdostana vitello (veal stuffed with prosciutto and cheese in a champagne sauce) or the scampi Giulio (jumbo shrimp sautéed with fresh mushrooms). Children welcome. Reservations suggested; proper attire recommended.

King and I (914-353-4208), 93 Main Street, Nyack. ($$) Open daily at 11:30 AM. Try the spicy, sophisticated flavors of Thai cuisine at this delightful restaurant. Chicken and vegetarian specialties are offered, and the decor is lovely. Try fried curry paste, shrimp simmered in coconut milk, or twice-cooked sliced chicken. The dishes range in spiciness from mild to dangerous. A unique dining experience.

La Maisonette (914-735-9000), 500 Veterans Memorial Drive, Pearl River. ($$) Breakfast (6:30–11:30), lunch (11:30–3), and dinner (5–10) daily. Located in the Pearl River Hilton, this elegant restaurant has a strong local following. The dining room overlooks the golf course, and the relaxing view futher enchances the gracious cuisine. Continental and American entrées include mushrooms filled with crabmeat and spinach, broiled tuna on eggplant, homemade bread, and luscious desserts (try their rich chocolate peanut butter pie). Reservations for dinner are suggested.

Marcello's (914-357-9108), 21 Lafayette Avenue, Suffern. ($$) Open for lunch Monday through Friday, noon–2; dinner daily 5–9:30. The chef-owner, Marcello, travels to Italy twice each year and brings back new ideas for the continually changing menu. Every dish at this elegant spot is cooked to order, and all pastas are homemade. The seafood ravioli and veal chop with sage are just a couple of the superb house specialties.

Old '76 House (914-359-5476), 110 Main Street, Tappan. ($$) Open daily except Monday for lunch at 11:30; dinner at 5. Located in a restored 1753 sandstone-and-brick house, this restaurant boasts beamed ceilings, fireplaces surrounded by Dutch tiles, and a real Colonial atmosphere. (Legend says British Major John André was imprisoned here during the Revolution.) The food is American and Continental, and entrées include veal Antoinette, steaks, and seafood.

Romolo's (914-268-3770), 77 Route 303, Congers. ($$) Open for lunch Tuesday through Friday 11:30–2:30; dinner Tuesday through Sunday at 5. There is a full range of Italian and Continental specialties here. The veal verbena is an interesting dish: veal with prosciutto, asparagus, and mozzarella cheese in a wine sauce. There are nightly salmon specials. This a good spot to try for fine casual dining.

The Turning Point (914-359-1089), 468 Piermont Avenue, Piermont. ($$) Open for lunch Monday through Saturday 11:30–3; dinner Monday through Sunday at 6; Sunday brunch at 11:30. Lunch menu served after dinner hours. Relax and enjoy a fine lunch, dinner, or brunch while listening to live music. The restaurant has been a hangout for movie companies, and it is a popular local spot. For dinner try fettuccine with goat cheese and sliced duck or poached salmon; 15 herbal teas and nearly 20 kinds of beer are listed on the menu. For Sunday brunch try buttermilk pancakes or French toast. Check the evening performance schedule—some well-known folksingers have appeared.

Wildflower Restaurant at Bear Mountain (914-786-2731), Route 9W, Bear Mountain. ($$) Open Monday through Saturday for lunch at 11, dinner at 5; open Sunday for brunch 11–3, dinner 5–9. Regional American cuisine and views of lovely Hessian Lake and the Hudson Valley. The time to come here is for Sunday brunch, when waffles with ice cream are served. Great lunch and brunch menu.

Xavier's at Piermont (914-359-7007), 506 Piermont Avenue, Piermont. ($$) Open Wednesday through Sunday for dinner at 6; Sunday brunch, noon–2:30. An intimate, elegant spot, this is a perfect place for people who enjoy fine dining. Continental cuisine has included roast pigeon with truffle sauce and fettuccine with fennel sausage and white grapes. For dessert try maple walnut soufflé, the house specialty. Not recommended for children.

A popular local spot, The Turning Point restaurant features live entertainment as well as hearty food.

EATING OUT

Big Pink Pasta (914-425-0534), 49–20 Spring Valley Market Plaza on Route 59, Spring Valley. ($) Open Monday through Saturday, noon–10; Sunday 4–10. This unassuming spot is right near Exit 14 of the NYS Thruway, and the restaurant is known for its incredible selection of pastas at bargain prices. A perfect spot for the kids.

El Bandito (914-425-6622), 27 East Center Avenue, Route 45, Spring Valley. ($) Open daily 11 AM–midnight. Strolling guitar players add to the fun atmosphere at this colorful Mexican eatery, where the portions are generous and the margaritas are first-rate.

Antiques browsing in Nyack

Good Times Restaurant (914-634-1790), 29 Third Street, New City. ($) Open for breakfast, lunch, and dinner 6:30 AM–10 PM; 3–10 PM on Sunday. Steak and seafood are the specialties of the house at this informal spot, which also offers a fine salad bar.

Khan's Mongolian (914-359-8004), 21 Route 303, NYS Thruway, Exit 12, Blauvelt. ($) Open daily for lunch and dinner. This is one of the better Mongolian barbecue restaurants we've tried. Choose your own ingredients and sauces and watch while the chef creates your meal right before your eyes. Don't miss this if you are traveling with children.

Mandarin Gourmet (914-352-9090), 212 Route 59, Monsey. ($) Open daily, noon–10. The Szechuan, Mandarin, and Hunan specialties are all particularly good.

Old Fashioned (914-358-8114), 83 South Broadway, Nyack. ($) Open daily for lunch and dinner at 11:30 AM. This chop house serves an eclectic menu, including shrimp feta over linguine, souvlaki, steamed clams, even spicy Buffalo wings.

Temptations (914-353-3355), 80½ Main Street, Nyack. ($) Open Monday through Saturday for lunch and dinner at 11 AM; Sunday at noon. The shop is open late on summer evenings. Those with a sweet tooth won't want to miss this café. There are scores of dessert selections in addition to a wide selection of ice creams, frozen yogurts, cappuccinos, and exotic coffees. The light menu features soups, quiches, salads, and sandwiches.

Texas Barbecue (914-735-6846), 150 Route 304, Pearl River. ($) Open daily 11:30–10 (till 11 on Friday and Saturday). This is the place to go in Rockland County for barbecued chicken and ribs. The chili is excellent and comes mild or red-hot, depending on your taste and your nerve!

SELECTIVE SHOPPING

In Nyack

Nyack has many shops that are worth a visit, and an entire day can be spent strolling the shopping district and enjoying the antiques and artwork on view. Most shops are open daily except Monday, but call ahead if you are planning to visit. The following shops are some of the highlights of the area, but there are many more with some great shopping.

Hand of the Craftsman (914-358-6622), 58 South Broadway, carries works from more than 200 artists and craftspeople and offers a unique selection of kaleidoscopes.

Beman Galleries (914-358-3344), 114 Main Street, specializes in fine 19th- and 20th-century art.

Christopher's (914-358-9574), 71 South Broadway, is a fine gift shop with all kinds of unique items.

Dawn's Early Light (914-358-0032), 14 South Broadway, has lovely imported laces and linens for the window, bed, and bath.

The Hudson Center for Photography (914-358-7701), 85 South Broadway, Nyack-on-Hudson Mall, offers contemporary photography exhibits and artwork.

My Doll House (914-358-4185), 7 South Broadway, has everything for the miniature doll furniture and doll lover.

Oh, You Beautiful Doll (914-354-6835), 37 South Broadway, specializes in dolls and accessories.

Squash Blossom (914-353-0550), 49 Burd Street, offers Native American jewelry and crafts.

Pickwick Book Store (914-358-9126), 8 South Broadway, stocks new, old, and rare books.

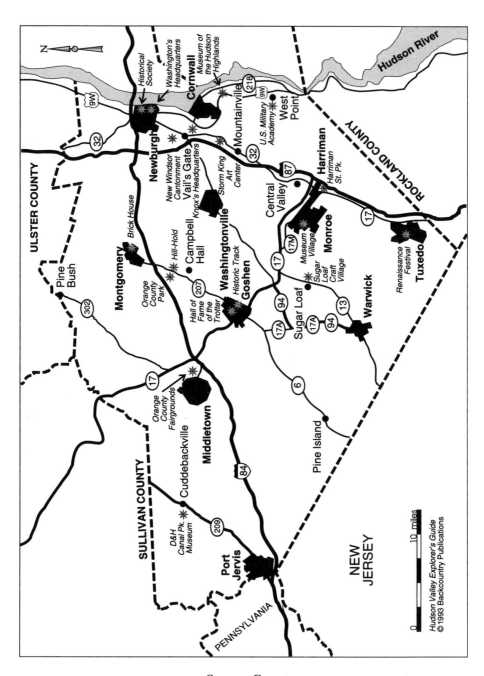

Orange County

Orange County

Visitors are reminded in every village and in every park in Orange County that this is a place that cherishes its history. Museums, restorations, and historic exhibits are everywhere, from the Native American displays in the Goshen Courthouse to the collection of military equipment at West Point. You can imagine the life of a Revolutionary War soldier as he waited out the bitter winters in a wooden hut, or watch as a costumed group of interpreters reenacts a battle that helped turn the tide of the American Revolution.

Orange County is also a place where the agricultural heritage of New York is still strong, a place where vegetable farming is a way of life for families and has been for generations. Stop at a farm and take home some just-picked peaches, or join in the fun at the Onion Festival. The Black Dirt area is a unique farming district where some of the best of New York's produce is grown, and a drive through the region in early summer gives new meaning to the word *bountiful*.

GUIDANCE
Orange County Division of Tourism (914-294-5151, ext. 1647), 30 Matthew Street, Goshen 10924.

GETTING THERE
Orange County is accessible from Exits 16 and 17 of the NYS Thruway, as well as from Route 17, which joins the Thruway at Suffern.

MEDICAL EMERGENCY
St. Luke's Hospital (914-561-4400), 70 Dubois Street, Newburgh; **Arden Hill Hospital** (914-294-4330), Harriman Drive, Goshen.

TO SEE

Hall of Fame of the Trotter (914-294-6330), 240 Main Street, Goshen. Open year-round, Monday through Saturday 10–5; Sunday, noon–5. Admission fee. Messenger and Hambletonian, pacers, trotters, standardbreds—all call to mind the speed and grace to be found on a trotting track, and the history and color of the sport can be discovered at this unique museum established in 1951. Trotters and pacers (trotters move their right front and left rear legs at the same time, while pacers move both legs on one side at the same time) have long been a part of American history: Such notable figures as George Washington, Abraham Lincoln, and Ulysses S. Grant spent time breeding and racing these swift horses. At the Hall of Fame of the Trotter, the history of the sport can be traced through dioramas, prints, exhibits, and statues displayed throughout the former Good Time Stables building. Galleries contain permanent displays of Currier and Ives prints, famous racing silks, and the amazing Hall of the Immortals, where dozens of small, lifelike statues recall the greatest men and horses of the sport. Restored stalls have full-sized replicas of horses and their equipment, while upstairs you can see the sulkies and sleighs the horses once pulled (it wasn't unheard of to drive a horse many miles, then race it, then drive it home to the farm). There is even a room that reproduces the interior of the clubhouse from the nearby Historic Track. The room is so well maintained that you expect to hear the rustle of programs and the voices of members discussing the best bet of the day. There are films and shows in the auditorium, as well as changing gallery exhibits throughout the year.

Historic Track (914-294-5333), located directly behind the Hall of Fame of the Trotter. The only sports facility in the United States that is a National Historic Landmark, the Historic Track has been hosting meets since the 1830s. Although the Grand Circuit races only visit here once a year, the track is used as a training facility, so you may be able to see pacers, trotters, and a local blacksmith at work, no matter when you visit. The track is such a local institution that some of the private boxes have been passed down in families for generations.

Museum of the Hudson Highlands (914-534-7781), The Boulevard, Cornwall-on-Hudson; take Route 218 east, turn onto Payson Road and follow signs. Open year-round, but hours vary so call for times. Donation suggested. Established in 1959 as a children's educational center, the Museum of the Hudson Highlands has expanded its natural history and environmental programs to include such special concerns as returning the bald eagle and peregrine falcon to the Hudson Valley and creating a detailed environmental "reference collection" of animals and plants from the region. Marked nature trails on the museum grounds wander through forests, glens, and even an unusual tall-grass prairie. The museum itself is a wonderful place for parents and kids to get to know the local environment and the creatures that inhabit it. The natural wing, with its high, vaulted ceilings and tall windows, houses an indoor minizoo, home to local snakes, mice, moles, turtles, owls, and crows, along with taxidermic mounts and a display depicting how local Native American tribes lived before the Europeans came. The Ogden Gallery shows the work of local artists. Throughout the year the museum hosts special events, which include exploration days, workshops, and nature walks. The museum has acquired a nearby farm and will expand its outdoor programs for the public.

Museum Village of Orange County (914-782-8247), Exit 129 off Route 17, Museum Village Road, Monroe (follow signs). Open May through December; hours vary with the season, so call ahead. Special events are held throughout the year; call for schedule. Admission fee. The daily life of preindustrial America has been preserved and re-created at this fascinating museum, comprising buildings and equipment moved to the site from other parts of the Hudson Valley. Set up like a small crossroads village, the museum is considered to have one of the largest sites devoted to the folk arts of everyday America. More than 35 buildings house crafts, equipment, and agricultural displays. At the blacksmith's shop, artisans hammer and pound hot metal into a door latch or horseshoe. The thump-thump of a foot-powered loom comes from the weaver's loft, where you may have a chance to try out the treadles yourself. In the newspaper office the master printer and the printer's devil (apprentice) are composing the weekly newspaper, and at the potter's workshop butter churns and mugs take shape on the wheel. Costumed guides answer questions, and photos, prints, and tools trace the history of Orange County. The museum is a favorite place for children, and special events, offered throughout the season, have included magic shows, cheese making, tinsmithing, kite flying, and square dancing. Every year there is a Civil War encampment, the largest in the Northeast, and it includes battles, camping demonstrations, and drills.

WINERIES

Three wineries in Orange County are open to visitors, but it is suggested that you call for their operating hours, since they vary widely throughout the year.

Brotherhood Winery (914-496-9101), Route 94, Washingtonville, is America's oldest winery and offers visitors a tour of the wine production facility and the cellars. There is a fee. A free tasting is included, and visitors can stroll the grounds and enjoy the special events, including concerts and shows in the summer.

Baldwin Vineyards (914-744-2226), Hardenburgh Road, Pine Bush, has tours and tastings as well as a gourmet café.

Brimstone Hill Vineyard (914-744-2231), Brimstone Hill Road, Pine Bush, has summer tours for visitors.

HISTORIC HOMES

Brick House (914-457-5951), take Route 17K into Montgomery and follow signs. Open May through October; Saturday and Sunday 10:30–4. Admission fee. A treasure trove of Early American furniture and decorative arts owned by the same family since 1768. Now run by the county, the house—a red Georgian mansion constucted with bricks imported from England—is considered one of the finest private homes built between New York City and Albany in the 18th century. It was a meeting site for Colonial officers during the Revolution, and many of the original furnishings are still intact. Pieces include a very rare 17th-century chest from Connecticut, fine crystal, Lafayette china (produced to honor the French hero), chairs that may have belonged to the Washingtons, and an Eli Terry shelf clock. Brick House is also the site of a large autumn antiques show.

David Crawford House Museum (914-561-2585), 189 Montgomery Street, Newburgh. Call for hours and holiday tour information. Admission fee. Maintained and run by the Historical Society of Newburgh Bay and the Highlands, Crawford House was built in 1830 and was modeled after a grand English country house. There are changing exhibits in the gallery and an annual celebration of landscape architect Andrew Jackson Downing's birthday. Visitors will enjoy the spectacular river views and the collection of pint-sized boats and ship models.

Hill-Hold and Brick House (914-457-5951), Route 416, Campbell Hall. Call for hours. Admission fee. Once a section of a 30,000-acre estate, the land Hill-Hold stands on was presented to William Bull, an English stonemason, as a wedding present in the early 18th century. His son, Thomas Bull, built the home. Fortunately for lovers of 18th-century architecture, later family members donated the house and most of its furnishings to the county. The large Georgian mansion is graced by elegant wood and stonework, with barrel-backed cupboards, paneling, and deep-silled windows. Rooms are furnished with many original Chippendale, Queen Anne, and Empire pieces. Two kitchens are still extant in the house: one in the basement and a newer one, added in 1800, in a separate stone wing. Like most manor houses of the era, Hill-Hold was also the center of a thriving farm. Surrounding the farmhouse are the original outbuildings, including the granary, barn, summer

The Brotherhood Winery's cellars

kitchen, wagon house, smokehouse, and, of course, the privy. On the working farm sheep, cows, chickens, and geese are tended. Children will enjoy the farm animals, and flower lovers should spend some time in the summer gardens. Also on the site is the Goosetown school, a one-room schoolhouse still used for educational programs on daily life in the 19th century.

HISTORIC SITES

Balmville Tree, Balmville, just past Route 9W in Newburgh. Make a right turn onto Chestnut Lane and a left turn at the end of the street. The tree is in the middle of the road. An odd treat but worth a visit. The tree has been standing since 1699 and has a trunk more than 25 feet in circumference.

Clove Furnace (914-351-4696), Route 17, Arden, south of Harriman. Admission fee. Open year-round Monday through Friday 8–noon and 1–5, weekends by appointment. Although not a very active site, it is an unusual one—a small museum devoted to the history of iron making in rural New York. The restored hot-blast furnace dates from 1854 and was used to produce artillery pieces during the Civil War. Exhibits outline the story of iron making and mining, and there are displays related to Orange County history. An enlightening stop for those interested in the commercial development of what was once a major industry in America.

Constitution Island and the Warner House (914-446-8676). Take Route
9W to West Point, enter the United States Military Academy gate, and
take the first right past the Hotel Thayer. The dock and a large parking
lot are at the end of the street. Open mid-June through late September;
Wednesday and Thursday at 1 and 2 only. Call for reservations—only
40 people per tour. Admission fee. To visit a Hudson River island, take
the boat from West Point to Constitution Island. There you will find a
17-room Victorian mansion, home to the Warner family from 1836 to
1915. The daughters, Anna and Susan, grew up on the island and were
best known for their writing; Anna wrote many hymns, including "Jesus
Loves Me," and Susan's *Wide, Wide World* was a best-seller. After their
father lost his fortune, the sisters stayed on in their home, living frugally
and teaching Sunday school courses to West Point cadets, who never
forgot the two spinsters. Their home is now a museum filled with their
original possessions. Also on the island are the remains of Fort Constitution, a Revolutionary War–era fort, and the Anna B. Warner Memorial Garden, which is particularly lovely in late June. The surrounding
Hudson is glorious anytime. If you visit the West Point cemetery, look
for the sisters' graves; they were buried not far from their beloved home.

Knox Headquarters (914-561-5498), Forge Hill Road, Route 94, Vails
Gate. Open Memorial Day through Labor Day; Saturday 10–5, Sunday
1–5; grounds open daily. Free. For several periods during the Revolution, the Ellison family's stone house served as headquarters for the
Colonial officers in the area. Generals Henry Knox, Horatio Gates, and
Nathanael Greene were only a few of the men who met in the house
and planned campaigns in the gracious rooms. Today it is furnished
with military camp beds and folding desks such as those that displaced
the Ellisons' fine 18th-century furniture. There is also a small plant
sanctuary on the grounds, dedicated to the memory of America's first
woman botanist.

New Windsor Cantonment (914-561-1765), Temple Hill Road, off Routes
32 and 300, Vails Gate. Open April through October; Wednesday
through Saturday 10–5, Sunday 1–5. Free. Washington's troops waited
out the last months of the Revolutionary War here in anticipation of an
announced cessation of hostilities. More than 10,000 soldiers, officers,
cooks, blacksmiths and their wives and other camp followers constructed the snug log cabins, outbuildings, and a meeting hall, and here
Washington quelled a mutiny of his troops, who resented Congress's
slowness with wages and pensions. After the war the buildings were
auctioned off for the lumber, and the land was unused until the state
acquired 70 acres and began restoration of the site.

A visit to the cantonment today provides a look into the everyday
life of Revolutionary soldiers. At the orientation center a slide show is
given on the history of the area during the war, and displays depict the
difficulties faced by both the troops and their leaders. One fascinating

display is of an original Badge of Military Merit, now known as the Purple Heart, which Washington presented to several soldiers. A walkway leads from the orientation center to the rebuilt parade grounds and buildings. Costumed guides go about their business, blacksmithing, drilling, cooking, and even entertaining (a fife player may be on hand). Although many of the buildings have been reconstructed from sketches that remain from the era, one was carted away and became an addition to a local house. There it remained for a century and a half, until its importance was realized and it was returned to the site. Just across the road, on the west side of Route 300, there is a small museum and re-created campground that illustrate the lives of the enlisted men during the war.

United States Military Academy (914-938-2638), located near Route 9W, just north of Bear Mountain State Park; follow the signs. The post is open year-round except major holidays; the museum is open daily at 10:30 except Christmas and New Year's. Admission is free, but there is a charge for a bus tour of the post. Situated on the bluffs overlooking the Hudson River, this is where the nation's army officers have been trained since 1802; where Benedict Arnold attempted to bring the British to power; where such distinguished cadets as Robert E. Lee, Ulysses S. Grant, and Douglas MacArthur once marched; and where undistinguished cadets like James Whistler and Edgar Allan Poe discovered other talents. Tradition is important at West Point, and tradition is what you will find here, from the Long Gray Line of cadets to the quiet cemetery and imposing stone barracks.

Visitors at the West Point Museum view World War I exhibits.

It is very difficult to see all of West Point in one visit—there are statues, museums, chapels, and points of interest everywhere you turn. But even if you can't stay overnight, use your time well and make your first stop the Visitors Center (914-938-2638) on Main Street near the Thayer Gate entrance. Maps, schedules of events, and a display and movie about the cadets' lives at the Point are available at the center, where you can also pick up the USMA bus tour, which leaves every 20 minutes and lasts nearly an hour. (The USMA grounds are open to visitors, although some areas may be off-limits at various times.)

The second stop on your tour should be the West Point Museum (914-938-2203), which is in Olmstead Hall, right next to the Visitors Center. The museum's holdings are among the largest in the world. Dioramas, permanent and changing exhibits, and thousands of artifacts are found throughout vast galleries, each with its own theme: the history of war, American warfare, weapons, the history of West Point. Visitors may see anything from a Stone Age hunting ax to the equipment used in Vietnam. Because the museum has so many collections, displays are changed frequently. Outside on the post itself, Trophy Point recalls the dead of the Civil War; there is also a 150-ton chain that was used to close off the Hudson River to British ships during the American Revolution. Although the attempt was unsuccessful, the chain represents the ingenuity that made America the victor. To the rear of the memorial is the Plain, the drilling area once used by Baron von Steuben to train and parade the troops. It is still used on Saturdays for full-dress parades by the cadets.

The Cadet Chapel is open to the public and contains stained-glass windows, the largest church organ in the world, and an overpowering sense of the men and women who worshiped there. Another restored section of the Point is Fort Putnam, which was used as a fortification in the Revolutionary War and now has exhibits on the lives of Revolutionary soldiers and a show about the battles fought in the area. It also offers a panoramic view of the surrounding mountains.

West Point is famous for its football games, played at Michie Stadium; tickets almost always have to be purchased in advance. Concerts are given throughout the summer at various sites on the post; most are free and include the West Point band. The concerts alone are well worth the trip.

Washington's Headquarters (914-949-1236), 84 Liberty Street, Newburgh. Take Route 17 from the NYS Thruway to downtown Newburgh; watch for signs. Open Wednesday through Sunday 10–4; call for schedule of special celebrations. Free. If Jonathan Hasbrouck's stone mansion set on a bluff overlooking the Hudson River could speak, it would say that Martha and George slept here, as did several aides-de-camp and personal servants. In fact, the end of the American Revolution was announced on the grounds. Construction began in 1750 but was not finished until 1782, when Washington's troops added a gun-powder laboratory, a barracks, a privy, and a larger kitchen. Washington remained here for nearly 1½ years, waiting for the British to leave New York under the terms of surrender. The house and grounds were acquired by the government in 1848 and became the first National Historic Site.

Visitors can see firsthand how Revolutionary armies lived and worked. The orientation center displays clothing, equipment, and memorabilia from the War of Independence, including a few of the first president's personal items. There are uniforms, field shovels, decorations, and even links from the chain that was stretched across the Hudson to deter the British. (For vision-impaired and blind visitors, a braille tour is available.) The story of the Revolution truly comes alive inside Hasbrouck House, where Washington is seen as a man who endured problems, boredom, and loss of the privacy that was so dear to him. (The house was owned by Tryntje Hasbrouck, a widow, who received notice of her eviction with a "sullen silence," or so history records.) Visitors are guided through the eight rooms in which Washington and his staff lived and worked. The dining room where George and Martha ate their meals still contains the original Dutch jambless fireplace, open on three sides. The plain bedrooms and offices are sparsely furnished, and a field bed with its tentlike covering speaks clearly of the winter cold, while bedrolls show that not everyone was fortunate enough to have a room. The grounds are well kept and offer wide views up and down the Hudson. Special events are held throughout the year and include kite flying days, Martha Washington's birthday celebration, military musters, and holiday tours.

SCENIC DRIVES

The term *scenic drive* in Orange County is almost redundant; there are so many well-maintained roads where the pace is unhurried and the views lovely that any drive around Orange is certain to please. Even the Thruway softens up a bit as it moves through the Harriman area—drivers can see deer at twilight and apple blossoms in the spring. Route 9W is an attractive road, but the section known as Old Storm King Highway, between West Point and Cornwall, is spectacular. For a lovely country drive past lakes and trees, start at Harriman and take Route 6 east across Bear Mountain State Park to the Bear Mountain Bridge; from there, 9W north offers vibrant Hudson River views on its way through West Point, Cornwall, and into Newburgh. Once in Newburgh, look for Route 32 around Cronomer Hill Park, a breathtaking sight in summer and fall. Another noted scenic highway in Orange County is Hawk's Nest Drive, Route 92, near Sparrow Bush. The road runs along the Delaware River for a short distance, but you can then follow Route 209 north to the Delaware and Hudson Canal Park (see *Green Space*). A

Storm King Highway

different type of view is found along Route 17A, which cuts through the rich Black Dirt farming area around Pine Island.

TO DO

BOAT CRUISES

One of the best ways to see the Hudson is from the river itself. **Hudson Highlands Cruises** (914-446-7171) offers daily cruises from Haverstraw Marina and West Point. Tours run daily May through October.

FARM STANDS AND PICK-YOUR-OWN FARMS

Because so much of Orange County is agricultural (in the Black Dirt area alone, more than 10,000 acres are under cultivation), you will find dozens of farm stands here. Some specialize in one particular fruit or vegetable, others offer a wide variety, but everything is as fresh as it gets.

The Pine Island area offers several top-drawer farm stands and pick-your-own farms. **Scheuermann Farms** (914-258-4221), Little York Road, off County Road 1, open May through December, and **Pine Island Farm Fresh Produce** (914-258-4071), Pine Island Turnpike, open year-round, both stock lots of local produce; **Kamarad Orchard** (914-258-4471), Newport Bridge Road, open September through November, lets you pick apples.

Applewood Orchards (914-986-1684), Four Corners, Warwick, open September and October, has a roadside stand with vegetables, but specializes in several varieties of pick-your-own apples. It also has wagon rides in-season, puppet shows, and a nature walk.

Ace Farms (914-873-1381), Highland Mills, 1.5 miles west of Route 32. Open year-round. Ace has a wide selection of fruits and vegetables, pick-your-own, and in autumn, hayrides and pumpkins. **Hodgson Farms** (914-778-1432), Goodwill Road, Montgomery, open May through Christmas, offers farm and greenhouse tours, along with pick-your-own berries, pumpkins, and flowers.

For a different type of farm, visit **Swissette Herb Farm** (914-496-7841), Clove Road, Salisbury Mills, which sells herbs and herb plants, dried spices, herbal and medicinal teas, and other herb-based products. Located off Route 94 in Vails Gate, the farm is open May through October, Tuesday through Sunday 1–5 or by appointment.

Farmers markets also bloom in Orange. The selection is often unique, and always special. The **Goshen Farmers Market** (914-294-7741) is held off Main Street in the main parking lot every Friday 10–7, May through November. The **Warwick Farmers Market** (914-986-2720) is held Sunday 10–3, July through October, at the South Street parking lot. The **Middletown Farmers Market** (914-343-8075) sets up Saturday 8–noon, late June through October, at the municipal lot on James and Depot Streets.

HIKING

Trails range from easy to advanced and offer views of river, woodlands, and meadows. The **Appalachian Trail** weaves through the southwest section of the county; call the Palisades Interstate Parks Commission (914-786-2701) for maps and specific trail information.

Black Rock Forest, Route 9W, north of West Point, has marked and unmarked trails that vary in length; hiking skill required.

Two other parks have trails of varying difficulty: **Schunnemunk,** Route 32 in Highland Mills, has six marked trails, the longest of which is 8 miles, and **Winding Hills Park,** Route 17K, Montgomery, has trails, a picnic area, and a nature study area.

Harriman State Park, Harriman exit, NYS Thruway, has hiking trails, swimming, and a variety of other outdoor activities.

SKIING

Thomas Bull Memorial Park Area (914-457-3000), Route 416, south of Montgomery. You can enjoy the small hill, with a vertical drop of 131 feet, complete with lift and snowmaking, or take a cross-country tour, skate across a lake, or slide down a sledding hill.

Mount Peter Ski Area (914-986-4992), on Old Mount Peter Road, Warwick, has a vertical drop of 400 feet, two chair lifts, and snowmaking capabilities. It is open daily, but call for hours.

Sterling Forest (914-351-2163), on Route 17A West in Tuxedo, is open daily and some evenings, has racing, four double chair lifts, and snowmaking.

Cross-country enthusiasts will want to call the **Ring Homestead Camp**

(914-361-3842) in Middletown for information on lessons and other adventure activities.

GREEN SPACE

Delaware and Hudson Canal Park (914-754-8870), just off Route 209 on Hoag Road, about 10 miles south of Wurtsboro in Cuddebackville; watch carefully for signs. The park is open year-round, with special events scheduled in the warmer months. The museum is open April through December; Thursday through Sunday, noon–4. Admission fee. This 300-acre park, a registered National Historic Landmark, recalls an era when coal, lumber, and other goods were moved from Pennsylvania to New York by a combination of water, mules, and backbreaking labor. Huge barges were often run as family businesses, with the crew consisting of parents and children. And there wasn't much room for profit: The barges moved at a leisurely 3 miles per hour. The park sponsors seasonal events that evoke life in old-time New York State. Demonstrations have included ice cutting, story evenings, nature walks, and even a silent film festival (the park was used by producer D.W. Griffith). The museum has exhibits about the canal and its people and is located in a restored blacksmith's house near the aqueduct. Tours of the towpath are offered Sunday afternoons; call for schedule.

Storm King Art Center (914-534-3115), Mountainville. Take the NYS Thruway to Exit 16; the center is off Route 32 North, on Old Pleasant Hill Road. Open daily April through November, noon–5:30. Admission fee. This 400-acre park and museum has one of the world's largest displays of outdoor sculpture. The permanent collection contains more than 130 works by 90 contemporary artists, including Isamu Noguchi, Louise Nevelson, Alexander Calder, David Smith, and Mark di Suvero. The surrounding landscape is lovely with a backdrop of Schunnemunk Mountain. Truly one of the impressive stops in the region.

LODGING

Cromwell Manor Inn (914-534-7136), Angola Road, Cornwall 12518. ($$$) This newly renovated inn is a historic country estate dating back to 1820. It is situated on 7 acres of woodland and gardens near West Point and Stewart Airport. The 14 rooms and suites (all with private baths) are beautifully decorated with period antiques. Many rooms have working fireplaces and Jacuzzis, and all are air-conditioned. A full breakfast is served in the country dining room or on the veranda. Step back in time without sacrificing modern amenities. Open year-round.

Dobbin's Stagecoach Inn (914-858-4300 or 1-800-336-5050), 268 Main Street, Goshen 10924. ($$) A former stagecoach stop, the inn is located in the middle of a country town, a few minutes' walk from shopping, dining, and the racetrack and museum. Four rooms with private baths; all rates include full breakfast. Open year-round.

Eddy Farm Resort (914-858-4300), Routes 42 and 97, Sparrow Bush 12780. ($$) Located on the banks of the Delaware River, this hotel has been taking care of guests for more than a century. When craftsmen took their logs down to Pennsylvania, they stopped at Eddy Farm; after the Civil War, families would visit from the city. A full-service resort, with an outdoor pool, two golf courses, a dance floor, and a restaurant (meals can be included and a B&B plan is offered). The hotel will arrange for rafting trips on the river and offers entertainment throughout the season, including an Irish cabaret. The resort is open May through October, and there are both private and shared bath arrangements available.

Gasho Inn (914-928-2387), Route 32, Central Valley 10917. ($$$) The history of the building began over eight centuries ago, when a defeated samurai clan fled to the mountains in Japan. There the warriors and their families developed a building style characterized by high arched roofs and strong wooden planks that were lashed and pegged together. Primarily known for its fine restaurant, Gasho also has overnight accommodations surrounded by lovely Japanese gardens, a pond, and teahouses. Use the two outdoor tennis courts at no extra charge. Twenty-five rooms with private baths; no breakfast is served. Open year-round.

Hotel Thayer (914-446-4731), United States Military Academy, West Point 10996. ($$) The Hotel Thayer reflects a long-ago period of grandeur, with many guest rooms overlooking one of the most scenic parts of the Hudson River—the Hudson Highlands. Although not included in the room rate, the dining room serves breakfast on the terrace, which offers an exquisite panoramic view of the Hudson Valley. The hotel is within minutes of the military academy's points of interest. Open year-round; reservations required, especially on special-events weekends at the academy.

Point of View Bed & Breakfast (914-294-6259), Ridge Road, RR2, Box 766H, Campbell Hall 10916. ($$) This establishment is adjacent to one of Orange County's most beautiful horse farms. Cozy, informal ambience coupled with spacious modern rooms, all with private bath, telephone, and cable TV. The owners, Elaine and Bill, have lived in Orange County for over 20 years and welcome both recreational and business travelers. Open year-round.

Ridgebury Inn and Hunt Club (914-355-4868), Ridgebury Road, Slate Hill 10973. ($$) An unusual establishment; guests are welcome to bring and board their own horses. The 1850s farmhouse has four rooms and a separate cottage and sits on 87 acres. Fishing is allowed in the pond, and hikers and cross-country skiers can bring their own equipment and make use of the 3.5 miles of trails. You can also rent bicycles, and if you come by train or bus, the hosts will pick you up at the station. The rates include a full gourmet breakfast. Four rooms share two baths.

Tara Farm Bed and Breakfast (914-294-6482), Kiernan Road, Campbell Hall 10916. ($$) The English owners are former innkeepers who now welcome guests to their 3-acre farm complete with horses, chickens, dogs, and cats. Guests are permitted to bring their own pets. A full, English-style breakfast with home-baked breads and muffins, sausages, and, of course, farm-fresh eggs is offered each morning. Two rooms available, shared bathroom. Open year-round.

Toulon Sapicourt Guest House (914-457-5770), 136 Clinton Street, Montgomery 12549. ($$) This elegant guest house is located in the historic section of town. The house itself has an interesting façade that will delight architecture buffs. The five guest rooms are furnished with antique French furniture, and a few rooms have fireplaces. All have private bathrooms. Breakfast is created according to your taste. Three restaurants are within walking distance of the guest house. No smoking or pets. Open year-round.

WHERE TO EAT

DINING OUT

Blue Heron (914-567-0111), 631 Route 17K, Montgomery. ($$) Open for lunch Monday through Friday, noon–2; dinner served daily from 6. The regional American fare here is great and the menu ranges from grilled chicken sandwiches and pizza to filet mignon and grilled salmon. Casual atmosphere; children are welcome.

Bull's Head Inn 914-496-6758), Sarah Wells Trail, Campbell Hall. ($$) Open for lunch Wednesday through Friday, noon–2:30; dinner Tuesday through Sunday from 5; Sunday brunch noon–3. Enjoy fine dining in a colonial atmosphere with many unusual American specialties. If you love garlic, make sure to order the baked garlic appetizer. Popular entrée selections include shrimp with four cheeses, filet mignon with peppercorn sauce, and pork tenderloin with fresh fruits.

C.D. Driscoll's (914-566-1300), 1100 Union Avenue, Newburgh. ($$) Open daily for lunch and dinner 11–11. This establishment offers live entertainment Thursday through Saturday evenings and is popular with jazz aficionados. The cuisine is American, although the spicy Mexican standards are very enjoyable. Not recommended for children on entertainment nights.

Catherine's (914-294-8707), 153 West Main Street, Goshen. ($$) Open for lunch Monday through Friday 11:30–2:30; dinner Monday through Saturday 5:30–9. Contemporary American cuisine featuring a variety of pasta and seafood specialties served in a comfortable country setting. The restaurant is housed in a historic building that dates back to 1869.

Château Hathorn (914-986-6099), 33 Hathorn Road, Warwick. ($$) Open for dinner Wednesday through Saturday 5–10; Sunday 3–8. Enjoy Continental cuisine with a French touch in a restored mansion dating back to the 1700s. The menu changes seasonally but the rack of lamb and chateaubriand are specialties of the house. For dessert try the coupe Denmark—melted Toblerone chocolate served over homemade vanilla ice cream and topped with fresh whipped cream.

Chianti (914-561-3103), 362 Broadway, Newburgh. ($$) Open for lunch Monday through Friday 11–2:30; dinner Monday through Saturday 4:30–9:30. Closed Sunday. Northern Italian and Continental cuisines are the specialties here. The pasta is homemade and there is an excellent wine list.

Cosimo's on Union (914-567-1556), Union & Orr, Newburgh. ($) Open daily 11:30–10 for lunch and dinner. The specialty here is the brick oven–baked, personal-sized pizza. There are dozens of toppings. Also available is a large selection of pasta dishes. The restaurant is very close to Stewart Airport. If you are traveling with children, this is a good choice.

Cornucopia (914-856-5361), Route 209, Port Jervis. ($$) Open for lunch Tuesday through Friday, noon–2; dinner Tuesday through Saturday 5–9, Sunday 1–7. Closed Monday. Reasonably priced Continental cuisine served in a casual atmosphere. The specialties are sauerbraten and Wiener schnitzel; excellent salad bar.

Elegant Peasant (914-355-4455), Route 284, Slate Hill. ($$) Open Thursday through Saturday for dinner from 5. The Victorian building that houses this restaurant is over 150 years old. The menu ranges from rack of lamb and roast duckling to steak au poivre and grilled salmon, all prepared to order by the chef-owner. A cozy, romantic spot; vegetarian and other special diet requirements are easily accommodated.

Flo-Jean Restaurant (914-856-6600), Routes 6 and 209, Port Jervis. ($$) Open for lunch and dinner Wednesday through Sunday, noon–10. Situated on the banks of the Delaware River, this establishment has been in business since 1929. The building was formerly used to collect tolls for the bridge. On the upper level the main dining room offers scenic views of the river, while the intimate Toll House lounge on the lower level is casual. The Continental cuisine is of good quality; children are welcome.

Gasho of Japan (914-928-2277), Route 32, Central Valley. ($$) Open daily for lunch at noon, dinner at 5:30. This authentic, graceful, 400-year-old farmhouse was dismantled in Japan, shipped to its present site, and reassembled. Gasho features hibachi-style fare: As you sit at heated steel-topped tables, Tokyo-trained chefs dazzle both eye and palate, preparing filet mignon with hibachi snowcrab, prime beef, and lobster tail before your very eyes. Shrimp, scallops, and eel are other specialties, and all dinners include soup, salad, vegetables, rice, and tea. After dinner, take a stroll through the Japanese gardens. Children welcome.

Il Cenacolo (914-564-4494), Route 52, Newburgh. ($$$) Open for lunch Wednesday through Monday, noon–2:30; dinner Thursday at 5, Friday and Saturday at 6, Sunday at 4. Fine food from northern Italy is the byword at this restaurant, based on an Italian supper room. Select from buffalo milk mozzarella with roasted peppers, spinach gnocchi with venison sauce, tuna steak in garlic and olive oil, and many different types of pasta. Save room for the homemade desserts and the excellent espresso. Not recommended for children; reservations required.

The Jolly Onion Inn (914-258-4277), Pine Island Turnpike. ($$) Open daily except Monday for dinner at 5; open Sunday at noon. A local tradition serving Continental cuisine, this inn is located right next to a large farm stand in the scenic farm region of Orange. There is an extensive doll collection on display.

John's Harvest Inn (914-343-6630), 629 North Street, Middletown. ($$) Open for lunch Wednesday through Friday 11:30–2:30; dinner Wednesday through Saturday from 5:30, Sunday 3–8. The Continental cuisine here is very good and the portions are hearty. The fresh seafood and veal dishes are specialties of the house.

Lake View House (914-566-7100), 205 Lakeside Road, Newburgh. ($$) Open daily except Tuesday; lunch (weekends only) noon–2:30; dinner 5–9:30. Watch the sun set over Orange Lake while dining at a restaurant in operation since 1899. The chef-owner specializes in traditional American fare. Hearty soups, salads, and sandwiches are served for lunch.

La Masquerade (914-294-6888), Route 17M, Goshen. ($$$) Open daily except Monday for lunch at 11:30, dinner at 5. The French and Continental cuisine here is first-rate, and the restaurant is housed in a restored, mid-19th-century building. Not recommended for children. Reservations are required on weekends and holidays.

North Plank Road Tavern (914-565-6885), 18 North Plank Road, Newburgh. ($$) Open Wednesday through Sunday 4–9:30. Traditional American favorites with a French accent. Enjoy live music with dinner.

Painter's Tavern (914-534-2109), Village Square, Route 218, Cornwall-on-Hudson. ($$) Open daily for lunch and dinner 11:30–10. Perfect for lunch or dinner. There are nightly dinner specials along with creative variations on burgers, sandwiches, and salads. The sun-dried tomatoes with cream pasta sauce is an excellent selection, and there are dozens of imported and domestic beers bottled and on tap. Children are welcome.

River House Restaurant (914-561-5255), Park Place, Newburgh. ($$) Open for lunch daily 11:30–4; dinner 5–10. Closed Monday and Tuesday January through March. Arrive by boat if you like at this Hudson River establishment; you can dock in one of the slips owned by the restaurant. Relax and enjoy all kinds of fresh seafood (crab legs, shrimp scampi, lobster) in a casual atmosphere.

Sugar Loaf Inn (914-469-2552), Kings Highway, Sugar Loaf. ($$) Open for lunch Tuesday through Saturday 11:30–3; dinner Tuesday through Sunday 5–9; Sunday brunch 11–3. Country dining in a Victorian setting amid plants and flowers. A nice place for lunch or drinks; the home-baked breads and desserts are especially good. The emphasis is on freshness, and the entrées are both classic and unusual. Summer diners may enjoy the garden tables. Children welcome.

Ten Railroad Avenue (914-986-1509), 10 Railroad Avenue, Warwick. ($$) Open for lunch Monday through Friday 11:30–2:30; dinner Monday through Saturday 5–10. Spanish and Italian cuisines are served here in a casual atmosphere; fish, pasta, and chicken specials daily. The chef suggests trying the paella if you enjoy that dish. Live music on Friday and Saturday evenings.

Warwick Inn (914-986-3666), 36 Oakland Avenue, Warwick. ($$) Open Wednesday through Saturday at 5 PM; Sunday at 1 PM. This 165-year-old mansion has been owned and operated by the Wilson family for the past 25 years. Original moldings, fireplaces, and antiques add to the cozy atmosphere. Roast prime rib and fresh roast turkey are served Friday through Sunday. Seafood specialties include baked stuffed shrimp, swordfish, and boiled stuffed flounder. Children welcome. Reservations suggested.

White House Inn (914-294-9795), Route 17M, Goshen. ($$) Open for lunch Tuesday through Friday 11–3; dinner Tuesday through Saturday 4–11, Sunday 1–8. Italian and Continental cuisines are prepared to order here. Try the veal bellanotte and the homemade pastas. The tempting desserts include raspberry cheesecake and Mississippi mud pie. The atmosphere is casual; the restaurant is housed in a restored Victorian mansion with a lovely fireplace.

Yobo Oriental Restaurant (914-564-3848), Union Avenue, Newburgh. ($$) Open for lunch and dinner daily 11:30–11. Fine Pan-Asian cuisine—hibachi steaks, Korean bulgogi, Indonesian sates, and regional dishes of China—under one roof. The dim sum is excellent; the sushi is the region's best. A popular and interesting dining experience. Children welcome.

EATING OUT

The Barnsider Tavern (914-469-9810), Kings Highway, Sugar Loaf. ($$) Open daily from 11:30 AM. This tavern has a beautiful taproom with handwrought beams and country decor and a glassed-in patio with a view of the Sugar Loaf crafts community. A crackling fire is always on the hearth in winter, and the menu of burgers, quiche, and other fine café foods makes this a nice stop for lunch. Children welcome.

Commodore's (914-561-3960), 482 Broadway, Newburgh. ($) Open daily at 9 AM, Sunday at 10 AM. An old-fashioned ice cream parlor and a favorite local dining spot. Commodore's has been in business for more than half a century and is famous for its handmade chocolates and ice cream confections. There are the usual delicious classics like marzipan and truffles, as well as Swedish fudge and almond bark. The fountain area serves simple lunches.

Hawk's Nest (914-856-9909), Route 97, Port Jervis. ($) Open daily at 11 AM; at 8 AM Saturday and Sunday in summer. A wonderful place for breakfast or lunch after canoeing on the Delaware River. The views are spectacular, and there are great pancakes, waffles, omelets, and ice cream; for lunch, chili and homemade soups are nice. The restaurant sits like a hawk's nest on the peak of the river gorge, 300 feet up, and on a clear day a stop here should not be missed.

SELECTIVE SHOPPING

ANTIQUES

The love of history found across Orange County extends to a love for antiques and collectibles, and there are many shops that cater to the connoisseur. Auctions are usually held on a regular basis, whether once a month or once a week. Estate sales may provide the antiquer and junker with everything from Persian rugs to eccentric collectibles. The best way to locate what's going on where is to check the classified listings in a local newspaper. Flea markets are another treat that spring up on warm weekends; look for markets that jumble together new and old, rather than just offering overstock and discontinued items. Most auctions and markets will not accept out-of-state checks; they will accept credit cards (sometimes), cash, and travelers' checks.

Old Red Barn Antiques and Auctions (914-754-7122), in Cuddebackville, has weekend auctions the first Saturday of the month. It also has a line of antiques and is open weekend afternoons.

New Windsor Auction Gallery (914-562-0638), Route 94, stocks fine paintings and sculpture; auction lovers will find what they want here.

CRAFTS

Sugar Loaf Crafts Village (914-469-4963). Take Exit 16 from the NYS Thruway to Route 17, and go west for 8 miles to Exit 127; follow the signs. Open 10–5 daily except Mondays year-round (open Monday holidays). Free. Once a bustling stagecoach and river stop, this area lost much of its trade when the railroads bypassed it in the mid 19th century. But in the last two decades, Sugar Loaf has regained its spirit. Home to dozens of craftspeople who live and work in many of the buildings along King's Highway and Wood's Road, the village is a terrific place to look for a special gift or add to a collection. You'll find hand-crafted rag dolls, stained glass, pottery, paintings, and jewelry. As befits an arts colony, there are fine crafts fairs and art shows throughout the year, as well as a fall festival and holiday caroling. The village is lovely, and it is an excellent place to spend an afternoon talking to the artists or watching them at work. Visitors will do lots of walking, and there is parking at either end of the village in well-marked lots.

FACTORY OUTLETS

If you ever get tired of seeing the beauty of Orange County, there is shopping, and plenty of it. Factory outlets have come a long way from the dingy shops of the past, and a stop at **Woodbury Common** (914-928-SHOP),

Route 32, Central Valley (open daily year-round, except major holidays), will prove this. There are more than 90 shops in this lovely Colonial-style mall, selling everything from shoes, clothing, crystal, sweaters, and watches to toys, wallets, and stockings. The mall also sponsors special events throughout the year, and there is a large food court.

Yarn and knitting wools are sold at **Montgomery Worsted Mills** (914-457-9241), 23 Factory Street, Montgomery, and wicker is sold at **Resnick Wicker Factory Outlet** (914-565-5115), 99 South William Street, Newburgh.

SPECIAL EVENTS

New York Renaissance Festival (914-351-5171, after June 1), Route 17A, Sterling Forest, Tuxedo; watch for signs. Open late July through mid-September, weekends only. Call for exact dates and hours. Admission fee. Knights and ladies, sorcerers and their apprentices, fools, varlets, bumpkins, and wantons all gather on the glorious grounds of Sterling Forest to re-create the lusty days of a merry English fair. The festival runs for eight consecutive weekends and presents a colorful, noisy look at a misty period of time somewhere between King Arthur and Shakespeare. Falconers show off the skills of their birds, opera and Shakespeare are presented at the Globe Theatre, Maid Marian flirts with Robin Hood, ladies dance beneath a maypole, and the extensive rose gardens are open for strolling. Craftspeople display and sell their wares (many belong to the Society for Anachronisms and stock things like chain-mail shirts), and the aromas of foods such as "steak on a stake" (turkey legs), mead, and cheese pie flavor the air. The living chess game, where 32 people/pieces cavort on a grassy playing field, is a wondrous sight. The actors play their roles throughout the entire festival, so authenticity combines with the personal touch. Kids adore the noise and action, and there is enough to see and do for every taste.

Orange County Fair (914-344-3377), Wisner Avenue fairgrounds, Middletown. Dates are usually mid-July to early August; gates open at noon. Admission fee. One of the oldest county fairs in New York State, this fair started as an agricultural display between 1818 and 1825. But local interest did not really begin to build until 1841, when the New York State Agricultural Society entered the picture. From then on, the fair was a hit. The 1841 extravaganza featured horses, cows, pigs, farm exhibits, and races; a visit to the fair today will turn up top-name entertainment, scores of food booths, thrill-a-minute rides, and some rather unique events, such as pig racing, where swift-footed swine dash for the purse—a cookie. Visit the lumberjack exhibition for a display of woodsmen's skills, and a log-rolling contest. Native American shows, stock car racing, and petting zoos are also on site, along with the finest local produce and livestock, and even an old-fashioned tent circus.

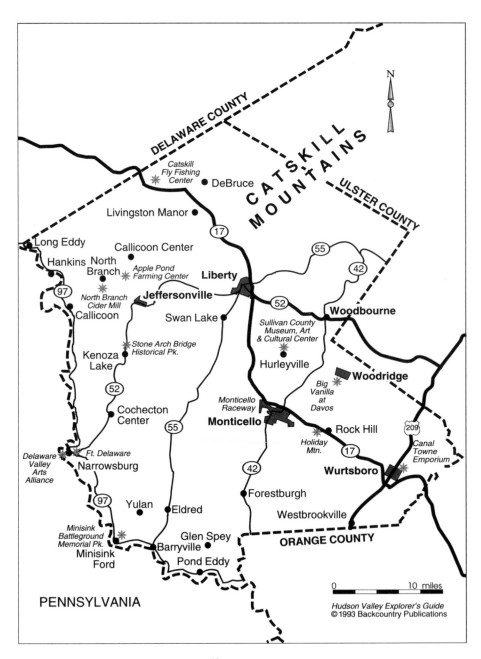

Sullivan County

Sullivan County

Only 90 miles northwest of New York City lies Sullivan County: 1000 square miles of outdoor paradise. Along the Delaware River, which snakes along the border and down into Pennsylvania, the rugged, untamed country is home to bald eagles. To the north, visitors will discover the charm of silvery lakes, lush forests, and narrow valleys where tiny villages nestle beside bubbling streams. Sullivan also offers some of the world's best trout fishing, and on opening day of the season—rain or snow—rods and flies are taken from basements and garages across the county in pursuit of the annual dream of catching "the big one." Only a small percentage of the county is considered agricultural, but there are dairy farms, pick-your-own fruit and vegetable markets, and organic farming centers. A drive through Sullivan County is a reminder that this area was the frontier not too long ago, a place where bears, bobcats, and the mysterious panther haunted the uneasy sleep of woodsmen and pioneers.

GUIDANCE

Sullivan County Office of Public Information (914-794-3000, ext. 5010), County Government Center, Monticello 12701.

GETTING THERE

Sullivan County is accessible from Route 17 or Route 209.

MEDICAL EMERGENCY

Community General Hospital (914-794-3300), Harris; **Grover-Herman Hospital** (914-887-5530), Callicoon.

TO SEE

Canal Towne Emporium (914-888-2100), located at the intersection of Sullivan and Hudson Streets in Wurtsboro. Open daily 10–5, March through December; closed Tuesday and Wednesday January and February. Free. Originally opened in 1845 as a dry goods establishment near the Hudson and Delaware Canal and now restored to its turn-of-the-century charm, this country store has received awards for historic preservation. The fixtures, furnishings, and equipment are all antiques, and include the first electric coffee mill ever used in the store, advertising prints, tins, and jars. Today the emporium sells fine furniture, handcrafted items, and decorative accessories as well as books. There is a restaurant next door.

Catskill Fly Fishing Center (914-439-4810), Main Street, Livingston Manor. Open daily late March through October, 10–4; November through March, Monday through Friday 10–1. Free. Fly-fishing enthusiasts will certainly find a lot to do in Sullivan County, where they'll find some of the best trout streams in the nation. Visitors should not miss this small but instructive museum located on Willowemoc Creek. The center offers a changing exhibit of fly-fishing equipment (such as rods, reels, and flies), memorabilia, and photographs. Special appearances by well-known anglers and craftspeople take place during the season, and the center will try to assist visitors with questions about local fishing.

North Branch Cider Mill (914-482-4823), Main Street, North Branch. Open daily mid-April through Christmas, 10–5:30. Free. This mill still uses a turn-of-the-century cider press and is the only mill licensed in the state of New York to produce hard cider. It's a great place to watch cider being made and even sample a glass. A well-stocked roadside stand sells apples and pumpkins in the fall and offers Christmas trees in November and December. Inside, the cider press thumps away, and the Mill Store is chock-full of locally made cheeses, baked goods, apple cider, and candy. There are baby animals outside in mild weather.

HISTORIC SITES

Apple Pond Farming Center (914-482-4764), Hahn Road, Callicoon Center (call ahead for detailed directions). Open year-round. Admission fee. Today most farms are run with advanced technology as older agricultural methods and theories are slowly being lost in an avalanche of computer information. But there are still many farmers who cherish the old ways and believe that if the land is worked well, it will yield a bountiful harvest. At the Apple Pond Farming Center, an educational center and working farm, visitors can judge for themselves the merits of organic farming practices and horse-drawn equipment. The farm is located on a rocky hillside with enchanting views of meadows, mountains, and valleys. Visitors can enjoy one of several different tours, which can include wagon rides, a sheepherding demonstration, beekeeping, haying, and logging. Sleigh rides may be arranged in winter. The farm is stocked with sheep, draft horses, goats, cows, and several incredible border collies, whose obvious dedication to the task of sheepherding is worth the trip. Founder Dick Riseling is a fascinating host, and since the farm also offers a well-respected apprentice program, you may find yourself visiting with students from across the country and around the world. Special activities like outdoor lamb roasts, spinning demonstrations, foliage drives, and draft-horse workshops are held throughout the year, but all activities here require advance reservations. A gift shop offers products made with farm produce. Don't expect a neat little restoration, and do expect to get a little mud on your shoes.

Fort Delaware Museum of Colonial History (914-252-6660), Route 97, Narrowsburg. Open Memorial Day weekend, weekends in June, and daily from late June until Labor Day, 10–5. Admission fee. Much attention is paid to the people who settled the main cities of New York, but those who decided to take on the wilderness are often forgotten. At the Fort Delaware Museum, the daily life of the wilderness settler is explored through exhibits, crafts demonstrations, and tours. The fort is a reconstruction of the original frontier settlement of Cushetunk on the Delaware River, with its stockades and stout log homes, which offered the only protection from hostile Native Americans and, later, English troops. The fort consists of a small settlement entirely surrounded by high log walls, or stockades. During the tour visitors see the blockhouses (where arms and ammunition were stored), settlers' cabins, a meeting-house, a blacksmith shop, a candle shed, a loom shed, and more. Outside the fort walls are a small garden planted with crops typical of the era and the stocks, which were used to punish minor infractions of the law. Costumed guides and staff members demonstrate skills and crafts from the period, including candle making, blacksmithing, and even weaponry. Special events are scheduled throughout the season, so your visit may include a show by Revolutionary soldiers, weavers, or cooks.

Minisink Battleground Park, Route 168, Minisink Ford. Open May through October, dawn to dusk. Free. One of the unusual and forgotten Revolutionary War battlegrounds in the region, this site offers visitors a chance to walk along trails that tell stories of both nature and combat. In July 1779 the area's most important historic battle took place when a group of American rebels were defeated by Mohawks in a massacre that took almost 50 lives. In an eerie postscript, the bones of the dead were not gathered and buried until more than 40 years after the battle, because the area was wilderness and not many people visited it.

Today the 56-acre park has three walking trails from which to explore its history and the surrounding natural setting. The clearly blazed trails have descriptive markers that tell the story of the area, and written trail guides can be picked up at the interpretive center. The Battleground Trail depicts the tactics and strategy of a woodland skirmish, and includes stops at Sentinel Rock, where the lone American defender was killed; Hospital Rock, where a rebel doctor lost his life while tending to his wounded charges; and Indian Rock, which legend says was set up to commemorate the dead. The Woodland Trail meanders through wetland, understory, second growth, and ferns. The map points out the trail's flora and describes some of the animal life you may encounter, such as fox, wood frogs, raccoons, and maybe even a bald eagle. On the Old Quarry/Rockshelter Trail, discover the logging, quarrying, and Native American histories of this section through trail markers. You may also want to plan a visit to the battleground in time for the small annual memorial service held each July 22 to honor those who fell there.

Roebling's Suspension Bridge. Look for the historic marker opposite the entrance to the Minisink Battleground. Built by the designer of the Brooklyn Bridge, this bridge on the Delaware River is the oldest of its kind still standing. The aqueduct was constructed because canal boats and logging rafts kept crashing into one another on the river; the aqueduct would actually carry the canal boats over the river itself. The aqueduct was turned into a bridge crossing in the late 19th century, and today it still carries traffic across to Pennsylvania.

SCENIC DRIVES

With more than 1000 square miles of countryside, just about any drive through Sullivan County will take you past exquisite views that change with the seasons: The earliest blush of spring may be enjoyed by driving along any back road or even on the Quickway (Route 17); summer is lush and lazy anywhere you turn; fall splashes the meadows and forests with color; and winter here can be lovely in spite of the cold.

If you want to travel the southernmost section of Sullivan County and see some spectacular river and mountain scenery, start your tour in Monticello. From there head south on Route 42 to Sackett Lake Road (you will go through a town called Squirrel Corners), and keep going south to Forestburgh Road, where you will make a right. This is the reservoir area of Mongaup Falls, a good spot to sight bald eagles. At Route 97, head west along the river drive known as Hawk's Nest; you will pass Minisink Battleground Park and Roebling's Suspension Bridge (see *Historic Sites*). At Narrowsburg, home of the Fort Delaware Museum (see *Historic Sites*), head north on Route 52 to Liberty, where you can pick up Route 17 back to Monticello.

A second drive, which will take you past some of the few remaining covered bridges in the county, begins at Livingston Manor (Exit 96 on Route 17). Turn onto Old Route 17 from the Vantran covered bridge, built in 1860 and one of the few existing bridges constructed in the lattice-truss and queen-post styles. Go back to Livingston Manor and follow the signs east from town along DeBruce Road to Willowemoc, which has a covered bridge that was built in 1860 in Livingston Manor, then cut in half and moved to its present site in 1913. From Willowemoc take Pole Road to West Branch Road, which leads into Claryville. The Halls Mills covered bridge, built in 1912, is on Claryville Road over the Neversink River. Head south from Claryville to Route 55, then west back to Liberty.

Another sight worth making time to see is Tomasco Falls, often called the Niagara of Sullivan County. These spectacular waterworks are enjoyable on a hot summer's day. Located off Route 209 in Mountaindale, there are daily tours of the area in July and August, Sunday tours in May, June, September, and October. Call 914-434-6065 for more information.

Other roads that offer scenic views include Route 209 and Routes

55 and 55A. Route 17, also called the Quickway, is the main north-south road through Sullivan County and provides access to most of the region's scenic areas.

TO DO

CANOEING AND RAFTING

Canoeists and rafters enjoy the Delaware's rapids and eddies from spring to fall. Both the Upper Delaware (from Hancock to Port Jervis) and the main section of the river (from Port Jervis to the Chesapeake) are used for canoeing and rafting, although there are sections that are particularly good for novices and the less adventurous. As with any other water sport, a few guidelines and suggestions will make your trip comfortable and safe; most rental agencies require that you know how to swim and that flotation gear be worn by anyone in a canoe or raft—it may look harmless, but the Delaware can reach depths of 15 feet! For your own comfort, take along sunscreen, lightweight sneakers, extra clothing, snacks, and a hat. If you go very early in the season, the water may be higher and colder than if you go in late July or August. The companies listed below rent equipment and canoes, and some offer a return trip to your starting point. Although you don't need to make a reservation, on busy summer and holiday weekends it may pay to call before you go. Rates are often lower midweek. The river is now managed by the National Park Service; for information call 717-729-7134, 717-685-4871, or 914-252-3947.

Cedar Rapids Kayak and Canoe Outfitters (914-557-6158), Barryville, has double and single kayaks, canoes, rafts, and tubes for rent; there also is a riverside restaurant where you can watch the fun.

Kittatinny Canoes (914-557-8611 or 717-828-2338), Route 97, north of Barryville, is one of the oldest operating canoe rental companies, and it has rafts, tubes, canoes, and kayaks. It also offers camping and special discounts (Mom and Dad float free on Mother's Day).

Landers Delaware River Trips (1-800-252-3925), Narrowsburg, has campgrounds and a motel for guests, in addition to full river equipment.

Upper Delaware Campgrounds (914-887-5344), Callicoon, has complete float and package trips for river rats.

Wild and Scenic River Tours (914-557-8783), Barryville, has adventure vacations for all ages and skill levels along with canoe and kayak rentals.

The following companies also rent canoes and tubes: **Jerry's Three River Canoe Corporation** (914-557-6078), Pond Eddy; **Red Barn Family Campground** (914-887-4995), Hankins; **Silver Canoe Rentals** (914-856-7055), Pond Eddy; **White Water Canoe Rentals** (914-557-8178), Barryville.

FARM STANDS AND PICK-YOUR-OWN FARMS

Nothing tastes like freshly picked fruits and vegetables that still have the blush of the sun and the field on them. Harvesting begins here in late spring with asparagus and berries and ends in late fall with pumpkins and apples, although some stands stock local eggs, maple syrup, and honey year-round. Hours vary with the season and harvest, so it is suggested that you call before you take a special trip. There are also lots of small, family-run farm stands that carry only one or two items and are open for only a few weeks a year; keep an eye out for these, too. They often have unusual selections or heirloom varieties. Whether you pick the produce yourself or buy from a roadside stand, the selection and quality in Sullivan County are excellent.

Apple Pond Farming Center (914-482-4764), Hahn Road, Callicoon Center, is an organic farm that sells a variety of fruits and vegetables at its roadside stand. Since they are off the beaten track, you may want to combine a tour of the farm (see *Historic Sites*) with a visit to the farm stand.

Bridge Farm (914-292-6299), Fox Mountain Road, Livingston Manor, has pick-your-own raspberries, strawberries, beans, peas, peppers, tomatoes, and pumpkins in season. They also have local maple syrup.

Diehl Farm (914-887-4935 or 887-5491), Gabel Road, Callicoon, is a well-stocked stand with a full range of local crops, from apples to eggs and dairy products.

The Fisher Farm (914-292-5777), Aden Road, Liberty, has only pick-your-own pumpkins and squash in the fall.

Maas Farm Stand (914-985-2686), Route 55, Grahamsville, has lots of pick-your-own peppers, eggplant, and squash, among many other crops.

Reinshagen Farm (914-583-4558), Swan Lake, Bethel (follow signs), has blueberries, strawberries, and even cucumbers for the picking.

Herbs are the specialty at the **Catskill Morning Farm** (914-482-3984), Youngsville, and vegetables and flowers are colorful crops; call for hours before you go. Eggs are extra special and organic at **Divine Gardens** (914-434-1176), Divine Corners, Loch Sheldrake, open April through September.

Sullivan County has a Down on the Farm Day each summer when self-guided driving tours of several local farms are offered to visitors. Call 914-794-3000, ext. 5010, for the next scheduled tour. Some farms also offer visitors the chance to select and cut their own Christmas trees; you can bring your own saw or rent one for the day. Dress warmly, bring rope to tie the tree to the car, and have a nice holiday! But remember, call ahead for directions, hours, and prices: **Theodore Nied** (914-482-5341), Jeffersonville; **Pine Farm Christmas Trees** (914-482-4149), Livingston Manor; **Winklestein Farm** (914-482-4976), Kenoza Lake; **Fred Weber Tree Farm** (914-557-8440), Yulan.

FISHING

Sullivan County is an angler's paradise. The famed Willowemoc and Beaverkill streams produce prize-winning trout each year, in addition to being recognized as the cradle of American fly-fishing. The Delaware

Fishing in Sullivan County

River offers its rich bounty to the patient angler, as do Mongaup Creek and Russell Brook. Then there are the icy lakes of the county, with such entrancing names as Kiamesha, Kenoza, Swan, and Waneta. There are hundreds of fine fishing areas in Sullivan County and too little space here to do them all justice. The following general information, however, will assist you in finding the perfect spot to enjoy a rocky stream, a sunny sky, and just maybe, a record catch!

The county's streams and rivers are famed for their brook, brown, and rainbow trout, but bass, pickerel, walleye, muskie, and shad are also plentiful. All streams on state land are open to the public; other streams often have public fishing rights through state easements, which are indicated by signs. New York State requires fishing licenses for people over 16, as well as special reservoir permits (call the New York City Board of Water Supply for application information). There are strict fishing seasons for certain species, and you could be in for a heavy fine if you disobey the law. The brochure you receive when you get your license should answer all your questions. Lake fishing is also popular in Sullivan, but there are separate use fees charged and some lakes are privately owned by hotels or resorts, so check on the site before you fish.

The Beaverkill is one of the best known trout streams in the world and may be reached from Roscoe, Livingston Manor, Lew Beach, Beaverkill, and Rockland. Fly-fishing tackle may be purchased in Roscoe at **The Beaverkill Angler** (607-498-5194), Broad Street.

Willowemoc Creek is found between Roscoe and Livingston Manor along Old Route 17; Mongaup Creek runs from Livingston Manor to

Mongaup Pond; the Neversink River is at Claryville on County Routes 19 and 15; and you can pick up the Delaware River at East Branch on Route 17.

Among the lakes are Kenoza Lake (Route 52, Kenoza Lake Village); Swinging Bridge Lake (Route 17B, Mongaup Valley); Swan Lake (Route 55, between Liberty and Kauneonga Lake); White Lake (junction of Routes 17B and 55); Waneta Lake (County Route 151 in Deckertown); Cable Lake (Route 17 northwest of Roscoe, end of Russell Brook); and Kiamesha Lake (Route 42, Kiamesha).

The Eldred Preserve (914-557-8316), Route 55, between Barryville and White Lake, has some restrictions on fishing for nonguests, so call ahead. They allow trout fishing (no license required) and bass fishing on their lakes by reservation of boat rentals only.

Those who enjoy the bracing thrills of ice fishing will want to check with the Sullivan County Office of Public Information (914-794-3000, ext. 5010) to find out when the King of the Ice Contest is scheduled and which ponds are open for ice fishing.

GLIDING AND SOARING

Wurtsboro Airport (914-888-2791), Route 209, Wurtsboro. Open daily, weather permitting. Established in 1927, this airport is home to the oldest soaring site in the United States. Soaring is done in sailplanes—motorless craft that are towed into the air and released. The pilot then sails the plane on the air currents before coming in for a landing. A 20-minute demonstration flight with a certified pilot can be arranged; if you enjoy the sport, flight instruction is available.

GOLF

The beauty of Sullivan County's farm country carries over to its golf courses. Many resorts have outstanding courses open to the public, but you should call to check on schedules.

Concord Hotel Golf Course (914-794-4000), Kiamesha Lake, is open from April to November, with the 18-hole Monster, the 18-hole International, and the 9-hole Challenger, along with full facilities.

Grossinger's Resort Hotel and Spa (914-292-9000), Grossinger's, has 27 holes of golf, a driving range and putting greens, and full facilities.

Tennanah Lake Golf (607-498-5502), Roscoe-Hankins Road, Roscoe, is open May through October and has package rates for guests who want to enjoy a lovely 18-hole course.

Villa Roma Country Club (914-887-4880), Callicoon, has a new, 18-hole course, a putting green, and full facilities.

Public courses include **Sullivan County Golf and Country Club** (914-292-9584), Route 52, Liberty; **Tarry Brae** (914-434-2620), South Fallsburg; and the **Lochmor Golf Course** (914-434-9079), Loch Sheldrake.

HARNESS RACING

Monticello Raceway (914-794-4100). Take Route 17 to Exit 104; follow signs. Open year-round, but days and hours vary, so call. Admission fee.

Soaring at Wurtsboro Airport

Recognized as one of the world's fastest 0.5-mile harness tracks, Monticello Raceway is home to many famous pacers and trotters. Because it is not as large as other harness tracks, Monticello has smaller crowds and plenty of parking. But the action at Monticello is just as heart-pounding, the crowds just as enthusiastic. The grandstand is glass-enclosed and the racing goes on rain or shine. There is exotic and pari-mutuel wagering, and the paddock is indoors. On special-events days, meet the drivers and their horses or enjoy a meal in Club Escoffier while watching the races from your table.

CROSS-COUNTRY SKIING

There are so many places to cross-country ski in Sullivan County that you would have to spend several winters here in order to try all the trails. Many local parks allow skiing for free, but often the trails are not groomed and there are no nearby rentals. At the large resorts, some trails are open for a fee to day visitors, but if you are uncertain of a hotel's policy, it is recommended that you call ahead; policies may also change from year to year.

Try the 160-acre **Town of Thompson Park** (914-796-3161), Old Liberty Road, 1.5 miles past Monticello Post Office; 110-acre **Hanofee Park** (914-292-7690), on Infirmary Road, off Route 52 East, in Liberty, where there are rentals, a trail fee, and a heated hut on weekends; and 260-acre **Walnut Mountain Park** (914-292-7690), Liberty, with rentals and a heated weekend trail hut.

Ski resorts open to the public include **Concord Resort Hotel** (914-794-4000), Kiamesha Lake, for downhill and cross-country skiing; **The**

Inn at Lake Joseph (914-791-9506), Forestburgh, for cross-country skiing; **Kutsher's Country Club** (914-794-6000), Monticello, for downhill and cross-country skiing; **The Pines Resort Hotel** (914-434-6000), Fallsburg, for downhill skiing with snowmaking and cross-country skiing; and **Villa Roma Country Club** (914-887-4880), Callicoon, for downhill and cross-country skiing, with night skiing and 100 percent snowmaking.

DOWNHILL SKIING

While downhill skiing in Sullivan does not revolve around huge resorts like Hunter or Gore, it does have a few centers that offer lots of fun for all ages. (See also *Cross-Country Skiing.*)

Davos (914-434-1000), Route 17, Exit 109 at Woodridge, has 23 slopes and trails serviced by nine lifts. Snowmaking capabilities (100 percent) keep the action going all season, and if you don't know how to ski or you need to rent equipment, the ski shop and school will provide. There is also a snack center with a view of the surrounding mountains, and a lodge where you can relax after a day on the slopes. Snowboarding and cross-country skiing are also available on site.

Holiday Mountain Ski Area (914-796-3161), Route 17, Exit 107 at Bridgeville, has both day and night skiing, 14 slopes, 100 percent snowmaking, and a vertical drop of 400 feet. The longest run is 3500 feet, and both beginners and advanced skiers enjoy the slope; cross-country skiing is allowed. A ski shop, snack stand, and trailer parking are all available, although a call ahead is recommended if you plan to stay the night.

GREEN SPACE

Stone Arch Bridge Historical Park, Route 52, Kenoza Lake. Open year-round. Free. This three-arched stone bridge, which spans Callicoon Creek, is the only remaining one of its kind in this country. Built in 1872 by two German stonemasons, the bridge was constructed from hand-cut local stone and is supported without an outer framework. Replacing an earlier wooden span that finally collapsed from the constant weight of wagonloads of lumber, the Stone Arch Bridge gained fame not only for its graceful design and unusual construction, but also for a bizzare murder that took place on or near it in 1892. A local farmer, believing that his brother-in-law had put a hex on him, convinced his son that only the brother-in-law's death could lift the curse. So the young man carried out the murder and dumped the body into the river. The case drew enormous publicity because of the witchcraft angle, and there have even been reports of a ghost appearing on the bridge. Today visitors fish from the banks, picnic on shore, or just walk through the 9-acre landscaped park and along the nature trails. Children will enjoy the small play area.

The Tea Garden (914-434-2330), Midwood Road, Loch Sheldrake. Open April 1 to October 31 daily except Monday, 11–5. Admission fee. This charming 6-acre garden has wooden bridges, benches, and gazebos and a riot of color in the summer months. Visitors should call ahead to get the garden's special-events program, which has included demonstrations of bonsai techniques, the Japanese tea ceremony, and Japanese gardening. Also on site is their landscape shop and a tearoom.

LODGING

Sullivan County is probably best known for the Catskills resorts that have flourished there for nearly a century. While some of the hotels, like the Concord, still welcome guests, others have shut their doors forever. But the region offers a very wide variety of bungalow colonies, resort hotels, and inns, which range from inexpensive to luxury. Be certain to call before you go, since the resorts can be booked well in advance of the summer months and winter holidays.

All Breeze Guest House (914-557-6485), Route 234, Barryville 12719. ($) This bed & breakfast will also serve dinner with advance notice, and it offers a nice getaway for families with children. There are ponds to swim in and fields and woods to walk and explore. The guest house is close to several of the rafting outfitters. There are four rooms and all have private baths. Open year-round.

Beaverkill Valley Inn (914-439-4844), Beaverkill Road, Lew Beach 12753. ($$$) This National Historic Site, built in 1893 and restored in recent years by Laurance Rockefeller, offers a perfect retreat for those who love the outdoors. Located within the Catskill Forest Preserve, near hiking trails and some of the best fishing anywhere, the inn also has tennis courts and an indoor pool. During the summer you can bike, hike, or fish; in the winter, cross-country ski. Twelve rooms with private baths; eight with shared facilities. Open year-round.

Bradstan Country Hotel (914-583-4114), Route 17B, White Lake 12786. ($$) This unique bed & breakfast features five comfortable suites with private baths overlooking beautiful White Lake. Also on the premises is a cabaret with live entertainment and a full bar. A gourmet breakfast is served, and special diets can be accommodated. Open year-round.

Clarke's Place in the Country (914-439-5442), Shandelee Road, Livingston Manor 12758. ($$$) A full country breakfast prepared by a professional chef is the specialty at this small but charming B&B. Three rooms with private baths are available all year, and there is a large, pine-paneled great room for guests, who will also enjoy the nearby swimming, canoeing, and fishing. There's a new hot tub for guests to relax in after a day filled with outdoor activities.

The Commodore Murray, 1830 (914-252-7220), 58 Fifth Street, Narrowsburg 12764. ($$) This three-story mansard-roofed mansion is right on the Delaware River. Visitors can even arrive by boat and dock here. There is swimming, fishing, white-water canoe rentals, and rafting to keep guests busy. Four rooms share two bathrooms. Enjoy a full breakfast while watching boats on the river. Pets are permitted; no children under 15. Open year-round.

Concord Hotel (914-794-4000 or 1-800-431-3850), Concord Road, Kiamesha Lake 12751. ($$$) This is it—one of the last of the great Catskills resorts, but updated with lots of entertainment and outdoor activities. There are 1225 rooms, as well as golf courses, indoor and outdoor tennis courts, health clubs, boating, horseback riding, and, for winter sports buffs, skiing, ice skating, and snowmobiling. A full children's program is offered, and adults will enjoy the big-name entertainers who brighten up weekends and holidays. Rates include three meals a day. Open year-round.

Dai Bosatsu Zendo (914-439-4566), Beecher Lake, Lew Beach 12753. ($$) This Buddhist monastery on 1400 wooded acres overlooking Beecher Lake, which at 2700 feet above sea level is the highest in the Catskills, is open to visitors. Harriet Beecher Stowe lived here for a time and is said to have written parts of *Uncle Tom's Cabin* here. There are no phones, televisions, or recreational facilities, but the rooms in the guest house are carpeted and comfortable. Some have fireplaces. The cost is exceedingly reasonable and includes three vegetarian meals daily. There are eight rooms, one with private bath; four more share two baths and three share one bath. This unique inn has been discovered as a relaxing getaway for stressed city dwellers. Not recommended for children. Open June through October; you must make reservations.

DeBruce Country Inn (914-439-3900), DeBruce Road, off Route 17 (Exit 96), DeBruce 12758. ($$) This inn, which dates from the turn of the century, is located within the Catskill Forest Preserve and on the banks of Willowemoc Creek. A restaurant serves three home-cooked meals a day, with Pilgrim pumpkin soup, stuffed trout, quail, and veal as some of the specialties. The Dry Fly piano lounge is the perfect place to unwind at the end of the day. Three suites have private bathrooms; 10 rooms share five bathrooms. Hot-spring spa, sauna, exercise room, outdoor pool. Open year-round.

Gabriel's Haven Bed & Breakfast (914-796-3456), 686 Cold Spring Road, Monticello 12701. ($$) This French country Victorian home has four cozy rooms to accommodate guests. A full gourmet breakfast is served, and box lunches and dinner will be prepared upon request. No pets or smoking. Open year-round.

The Guest House (914-439-4000), 223 DeBruce Road, Livingston Manor 12758. ($$$) This luxurious retreat is the perfect romantic getaway for those who want to rekindle a relationship. There are four rooms with private baths in the main house and three other rooms in cottages on the premises; one has a whirlpool bath surrounded by palm trees. A fully equipped fitness room is available and guests can book tennis lessons or a massage. Breakfast is served any time in the morning—or early after-

A picturesque lake in Sullivan County

noon. Located on Willowemoc Creek, with private fly-fishing. Open
year-round.

The Inn at Lake Joseph (914-791-9506), County Road 108, off Route 42,
Forestburgh 12777. ($$$) A 19th-century Victorian mountain retreat
nestled in the Catskills and surrounded by acres of forest, this inn was
built by a prosperous businessman who then sold the house to the Ro-
man Catholic Church, which used the inn as a retreat for Cardinals
Hayes and Spellman. A private spring-fed lake offers swimming, boat-
ing, and fishing. There are two tennis courts as well. This is a secluded

spot where every detail is attended to, making it one of the county's best inns. The dining room is open to the public by advance reservation only. The mansion has six fireplaces, and each guest room has a canopied bed, Persian rugs, lacy linens, and fine antiques. Eleven rooms with private baths. The carriage house is perfect for families, with its own library, TV, and stereo. Outdoor pool. Open year-round.

Kutsher's Country Club (914-794-6000 or 1-800-431-1273), Kutsher Road, off Route 42, Monticello 12701. ($$$) Since 1907 the Kutsher family has been running this resort. Although large (more than 400 rooms), an informal, homey atmosphere prevails. There is an 18-hole golf course on the grounds, and the indoor ice rink is open all year. The lake offers boating and fishing. Guests will enjoy indoor and outdoor pools, a health club, racquetball, tennis, and a full children's program. Rates include three meals a day. Open year-round.

Mountainview Inn on Shandelee (914-439-5070), Shandelee Road, Livingston Manor 12758. ($$) A 75-year-old building with a taproom and restaurant houses this family-owned and -operated inn. Guest rooms—each one is different—are furnished with period pieces, and some have canopied beds. The full breakfast includes homemade breads, jams, juice, and coffee. A lake is nearby for swimming, fishing, and boating, and there are cross-country ski trails. Eight rooms, all with private baths. Children welcome. No pets. Open year-round.

New Age Health Spa (914-985-7601), Route 55, Neversink 12765. ($$) A great place to stay, especially for those on special diets, since the menu features fresh fruits, vegetables, juices, and other healthy foods. The dining room is open to the public and serves inexpensive meals. Open year-round, daily at 8 AM.

Open Door Bed and Breakfast (607-498-5772), Old Route 17, Roscoe 12776. ($$) A Victorian country house furnished with antiques, this bed & breakfast also offers guests a chance to enjoy the mountain views from the veranda or gazebo. There are five bedrooms with private half-baths. Fishing, swimming, and hiking are nearby, and the local trout streams are famous. No children. Open year-round.

Stonewall Acres (914-791-9474), Glen Wild Road, Rock Hill, 12775. ($) Located on 13 private acres, this Victorian farmhouse has cottages for rent, one seasonal and one year-round. There are also two rooms available. The inn is near many recreation areas. Open year-round.

Villa Roma (914-887-4880), Villa Roma Road, Callicoon, 12723. ($$$) More than 215 air-conditioned rooms make this full-service resort a large one, but it has everything: fishing, swimming, golf, horse-drawn sleigh rides, and a decidedly Italian accent. All room rates, of course, include great food, and there's even a weekly Caesar's Night feast. Special events include children's programs, auctions, and rafting expeditions.

WHERE TO EAT

DINING OUT

Bernie's Holiday Restaurant (914-796-3333), Route 17, Rock Hill. ($$)
Open for dinner Monday through Saturday at 5, Sunday at 1; closed
Monday, October through April. The largest restaurant in Sullivan
County and also one of the best. Try visiting on Gourmet Friday for a
truly sumptuous meal. The specialties here are Chinese and American
cuisines, and the Cajun dishes are first-rate. Children welcome.

Dead End Cafe (914-292-0202), Route 17, Parksville. ($$) Open daily
except Tuesday at 4 for dinner, every night during summer. All kinds
of Italian fare are served here, with unusual seafood specials nightly.
There is live music on weekends and excellent espresso and cappuccino.

Eldred Preserve (914-557-8316), Route 55, Eldred. ($$) Open daily for
dinner at 5; limited hours off-season. The dining rooms here overlook
three stream-fed ponds stocked with rainbow, brown, brook, and golden
trout, as well as 2000 acres of unspoiled forest. Needless to say, the
specialty here is trout from the preserve's ponds. The fish is served many
ways, including smoked, and all baking is done on the premises. There
is also a 21-room motel and two private lakes open for boating and
fishing. Guests can enjoy the tennis courts and outdoor pool in warm
weather, ice fishing in winter. Children welcome.

Glen Spey Country Inn (914-856-8300), Glen Spey Road, Glen Spey.
($$) Open year-round Wednesday through Friday 4–9; Saturday, noon–
10; Sunday, noon–8. Decorated with brass chandeliers and American
art and antiques, this is a pleasant place to enjoy country dining. Specialties of the house include roast duck, filet of sole stuffed with scallops,
sirloin steak, and Cajun catfish. Children welcome.

House of Lyons (914-794-0244), Jefferson Street, Monticello. ($$) Open
Tuesday through Friday, noon–3; Tuesday through Sunday 5–9:30. The
specialties here are fresh seafood and prime rib, but the menu is huge
and offers a range of Continental cuisine. There are chicken wings and
burgers for children, who are welcome.

The Millbrook Inn (914-856-7778), Route 97, Pond Eddy. ($$) Open for
lunch and dinner Wednesday through Sunday from 11 AM. Fine coun-
try dining featuring a mix of American and European favorites. The
emphasis here is on freshness and the entrées are imaginative. A few of
the specialties are tidewater shrimp, maple walnut chicken, and game
pie. Children are welcome.

La Mingotiere (914-888-9912), Route 17, Wurtsboro Hills. ($$) Open in
season daily except Monday for dinner at 6; weekends only in winter. A
popular spot for lovers of fine French and Continental cuisine.

The 1906 Restaurant (914-887-1906), Main Street, Callicoon. ($$) Open daily for dinner 5–9; closed Wednesday in winter. Enjoy both traditional favorites and nouvelle cuisine specialties prepared by a Culinary Institute–trained chef. The Angus beef is popular, and so are the game dishes, which include venison, quail, and rabbit. All soups and desserts are made on the premises. Entertainment on weekends. Reservations suggested.

The Oak Table (914-439-3999), DeBruce Road, off Route 17, Livingston Manor. ($$) Open February 14 to January 2 for dinner: Wednesday through Saturday from 5; Sunday from 3. Fresh fish and seafood are the specialties. Tasty Continental and American cuisines are served here.

Old Homestead Restaurant (914-794-9873), Bridgeville Road, Monticello. ($$) Open daily year-round, for dinner at 4:30; closed Thanksgiving and Christmas. Enjoy country dining at an old stagecoach stop on the Cochecton–Newburgh Turnpike. The specialties here are steak and seafood, and all baked goods are made on the premises. There is an old covered bridge over the Neversink just outside. Children are welcome.

The Repast (914-888-4448), Sullivan Street, Wurtsboro. ($$) Open daily for lunch at 11; dinner Thursday through Sunday at 5; closed Thanksgiving, Christmas, and New Year's. This small, elegantly appointed Victorian restaurant features fine country fare. Lunch specialties include crêpes, baked Brie, and croissant sandwiches; for dinner, chicken with almonds and banana liqueur and prime rib have been among the selections. All breads and desserts are made in-house. Children are welcome at lunch, discouraged at dinner.

Tre Alberi (914-557-6104), Route 97, Barryville. ($$) Open every day except Wednesday for dinner 5–10. This restaurant serves the best northern Italian cuisine in Sullivan County. There are different pasta, fish, and poultry specials each day, and all are prepared to order. The desserts are made on the premises, and the chef-owner oversees their preparation. A worthwhile stop for those who appreciate fine dining.

EATING OUT

Frankie & Johnnie's (914-434-8051), Main Street, Hurleyville. ($) Open daily April through January, 11–11; closed in February and March. This reasonable Italian American restaurant specializes in steak, seafood, pasta, and pizza. It's a great spot for lunch or dinner if you're traveling with children.

Liberty Triangle Diner & Restaurant (914-292-7491), Old Route 17, Liberty. ($) Open 24 hours daily. A full range of diner fare is served here in addition to lobster and Chinese dishes. You can get a hot open roast beef sandwich or steamed dumplings.

Pete's Pub (914-932-8110), Route 52, Lake Huntington. ($) Open 10–10 daily except Tuesday. This family-style restaurant offers an array of old favorites like pot roast, beef stew, and lobster tails. On weekends there is a salad bar. The fare is simple and the portions are hearty. There are also steaks, pasta dishes, and burgers of all kinds.

ENTERTAINMENT

ARTS

Sullivan County has a long history of supporting the arts, and the cultural programs and shows that are offered throughout the region are some of the best in the state. **The Delaware Valley Art Alliance** (914-252-7576) is headquartered in the Arlington Hotel in Narrowsburg, which is on the National Historic Register. Its gallery is open year-round for exhibits and special events, so call for a schedule.

The Sullivan County Museum Art and Cultural Center (914-434-8044) in Hurleyville is open year-round and displays local historical material as well as the work of local artists.

THEATER

A summer stock theater housed in a 120-year-old barn can only mean fun, and that's what you'll have when you attend a performance at the **Forest-burgh Playhouse** (914-794-1194), RD1, Box 250, Forestburgh 12777. Drama, comedies, and musicals are all on the bill, and there is a dinner theater and cabaret format in the fall. Call for information and schedule.

Professional regional theater is brought to the Liberty area each summer by the **Liberty State Company** (914-292-5585) and to Highland Lake by the **Catskill Actors Theatre** (914-557-6523), which is located in the historic Bloomington Dutch Reformed Church (914-733-4809), also open for exhibits and shows.

SELECTIVE SHOPPING

Apollo Plaza (914-794-2010), Lower Broadway, Monticello. Open year-round; call for hours. There are more than 30 factory outlets and discounts shops located here, including Bass, Jonathan Logan, Corning, Van Heusen, and others. The mall is enclosed, and shops offer housewares, perfume, and refreshments in addition to clothing. **Mostly Books** (914-794-5070) is a *big* bookstore with lots of bargain books.

ANTIQUES

The search for treasures in Sullivan County can take you to a dusty little shop on a side road or into full-fledged auction barns where the prices are steep and the sales are fast. Many antiques shops are open all year, but some serve only the vacation crowds; call before you go to avoid disappointment. There are dozens of shops throughout the county, and the following is only a sampling of the wide selection.

Callicoon Flea Market (914-887-5411), Main Street, Callicoon, has everything from furniture to collectible pottery, along with reproduction furniture and decorative items.

Evelyn Baeyens Antiques (914-887-5367), Route 97, Callicoon, is open daily or by appointment from May through September.

Ace Trading Company (914-434-4553), Main Street, Hurleyville, has a wide selection ranging from antiques to odds and ends.

The Antique Palace Emporium (914-292-2270), 300 Chestnut Street, Liberty, has more than two floors of restored furniture and original collectibles.

Today's Pleasure—Tomorrow's Treasure (914-482-3690), 93B Hessinger-Lare Road, Jeffersonville, specializes in collectibles that are made today but in limited editions and established fields, such as Hummels and Precious Moments.

Memories (914-292-4270), Route 17 (Quickway), between Exits 98 and 97 (watch for signs), has a very large general line and has long been a popular stop with vacationers.

Auction-goers should watch for **Liberty Antique Warehouse** auctions (914-292-7450), Route 17 (Quickway), between Exits 98 and 97 (watch for signs). Announced in local newspapers, or call for a schedule.

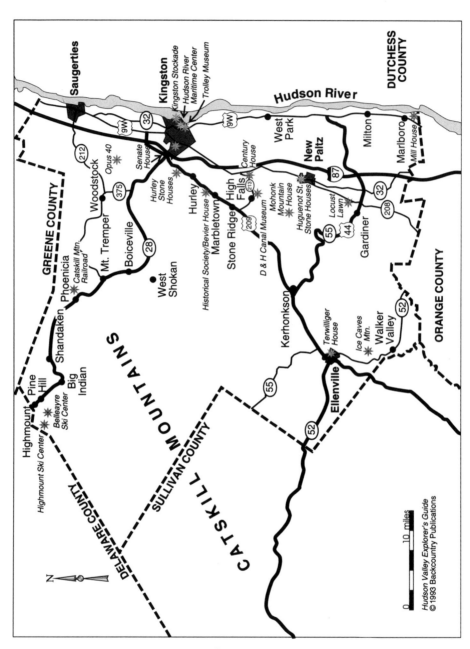

Ulster County

Ulster County

Both the Dutch and the English settled in Ulster County, drawn by the lush farmlands along the Hudson. Snug, well-built homes were constructed of stone, brick, and wood; many still stand and are open to the public. Ulster County was not always blessed with peace and wealth, however; it was the scene of conflict during the American Revolution, when the city of Kingston was burned by the British and spies were hanged in outlying orchards. But the area rebuilt itself through the years, and today Ulster is a study in contrasts. Businesses have settled alongside farms, and artists colonies thrive among boutiques. Dutch names of towns and lanes recall the past, while a thriving community of second-home owners and vacationers has brought different cultures to the region.

The outdoors offers excellent fishing, skiing, and hiking, and the mountains are still said to be haunted by the witches and goblins of centuries past. Ulster is mountainous, flat, river-lined, and forested by turns; there's enough here to keep visitors busy for another century or so. The region is easy to travel, with several major roads and enough byways to please every traveler. Bring a camera when you visit, because the seasonal changes in Ulster are dramatic and changing, with spring giving way to summer overnight, and winter making guest appearances as late as April!

GUIDANCE

Ulster County Chamber of Commerce (1-800-DIAL-UCO), Albany Avenue, Kingston 12401; **Ulster County Public Information Office** (914-331-9300), County Office Building, Box 1800TG, Kingston 12401.

GETTING THERE

Ulster County is accessible from NYS Thruway Exits 18, 19, and 20, and in the southern section of the county from Route 17. Bus service to the region is limited; the area is served by **Pine Hill Trailways** (1-800-225-6815).

MEDICAL EMERGENCY

Benedictine Hospital (914-338-2500), 105 Mary's Avenue, Kingston.

VILLAGES

Hurley. Take Route 209 south to Hurley and follow signs. Every July for one day only the historic stone houses are open to the public. Hurley Stone

House Day (call 914-331-4121 for information) is held the second Saturday in July; admission is charged for the tour. The village of Hurley was established in 1651 by Dutch and Huguenot settlers, who built wooden homes along Esopus Creek. After a short war with the Esopus Indians, which resulted in the burning of much of the settlement, the homes were replaced with stone structures, 25 of which are still standing. Hurley was a hotbed of activity during the Revolution, serving as the state capital when Kingston was burned, a resting place for troops, and a meeting place for spies. Later, Hurley was a stop on the Underground Railroad, the escape route for slaves fleeing to Canada, as well the home of abolitionist Sojourner Truth.

Visitors can still walk around the town and see the largest group of stone houses still in use in the country. Although the homes are open only one day a year, Hurley is worth a walk, and many of the buildings have historic markers that tell something of their history and lore. Along Main Street, look for the **Polly Crispell Cottage** (built in 1735), which was once used as a blacksmith shop. This house was also equipped with a "witch catcher"—a set of iron spikes set into the chimney, presumably to discourage witches (and birds) from flying in.

The **Jan Van Deusen House** became the temporary seat of New York's government in 1777, and a secret room was used to store important documents. The outer door is set off by the work of an early Hurley blacksmith, and a date stone is visible. Stop in at the **Van Deusen Antiques Shop,** which is now located in the back of the house.

Also on Main Street: the **Dumond House,** which was used to confine a convicted British spy before he was hanged across the road on an apple tree; the **Parsonage,** built in 1790; and the **Elmendorf House** (once the Half Moon Tavern), built in the late 1600s. A burial ground can be found between the Crispell and Elmendorf buildings. If you drive west on Main Street, follow the Hurley Avenue Extension and you will see several more stone buildings.

A corn festival, held in mid-August, celebrates the local sweet corn industry. Held on the grounds of the Reformed Church, the festival offers lots of crafts and lots of corn. Fresh ears of corn by the thousands are dished up with butter. There is corn chowder, corn bread with honey, entertainment, and good fellowship.

Woodstock. The town of Woodstock has long attracted creative people. Home to farmers and quarrymen for two centuries, the spring of 1902 brought new changes to the hamlet, when Ralph Radcliffe Whitehead, an Englishman schooled in the theories of John Ruskin, was searching for a place where an arts colony could be organized. With two friends as partners, Whitehead bought seven lush farms and formed a community called Byrdcliffe (a combination of his and his wife's names). Workshops for metalworkers, potters, and weavers were soon built, and over the years the colony has continued to attract artists and craftspeople.

During the 1930s folksingers discovered Woodstock; later, the town became a haven for beatniks, and then talents like Pete Seeger, Bob Dylan, Joan Baez, and Peter, Paul, and Mary discovered the inspiration Woodstock was famous for. In 1969, a concert actually held nearly 50 miles away on a farm in Bethel (Sullivan County) made Woodstock a legend in the world of rock music.

Today, the sometimes eccentric but never dull town is still a gathering place for talent of all types. The surrounding mountains create a dramatic backdrop for local galleries and shops. Woodstock's main thoroughfare is Mill Hill Road, which eventually becomes Tinker Street (according to legend, a tinker's wagon sank into the spring mud here, and the horse's harness bells can still be heard on quiet days). Just about everything in town can be reached by an easy walk. For parking, try the lots on Rock City Road or Tannery Brook Road. There is also a municipal lot near the town offices; watch for signs.

Kids will love **Woodstock Wonderworks,** an amazing playground designed by the town's kids themselves and built, under the guidance of an award-winning company, by the parents, youngsters, and townspeople. And if you get tired, sit on the village green and watch the colorful parade of people go by.

TO SEE

Delaware and Hudson Canal Museum (914-687-9311). Take Route 213 to High Falls; make a right onto Mohonk Road. Open May through October; hours vary. Free. This museum is dedicated to the history and lore of the great Delaware and Hudson Canal. Built in the early 19th century, the canal was used to ship coal from the mines in Pennsylvania to the factories of New York; later, cement was shipped south to be used in bridges and skyscrapers. The canal's designer was also responsible for the Erie Canal, and the locks, basins, and dams were engineering wonders of the era. In the museum, visitors find a miniature setup of the canal and its workings, and they can get a sense of what life was like on the canal boats used for the 6-day trips. While you are at the museum, take the self-guided tour of the locks (located across the road); along the tour you will see examples of stonework, snubbing posts, weirs, locks, and loading ships.

Shellbark Farm (914-626-5128), Route 209, Accord. Open April through October, Wednesday through Saturday 10–4; Sunday, noon–4. Admission fee. Shellbark Farm is a "living museum," modeled after a turn-of-the-century family farm; the land is worked by draft animals, the crops are heritage varieties, and rural arts and crafts are kept alive. Situated on Rondout Creek, the farm is named for the shellbark hickory trees that line the farm lane. Visitors can enjoy watching the farmhands guide the Ayrshire oxen or draft horses as they work in the market garden or bring in the hay and oats. Rare white wyandotte chickens scratch in the barnyard, and goats gambol in the pasture. Volunteers offer workshops and lectures throughout the season, and special events are held each year, including the Maple Festival and Pancake Breakfast, Spring Plow, Ice Cream Social, Cider Pressing, and Holiday Gift and Greenery Open House.

A.J. Snyder Estate Museum (914-658-9900), Route 213, Rosendale (watch for signs). Tours by appointment only from June through September. Admission fee. Children not permitted. This private home sits directly across from the Delaware and Hudson Canal. The house is open for tours, and the carriage house, with its fine collection of more than 20 antique sleighs and carriages, some dating from the 1820s, is a must-see. Phaetons, wagons, and cutters are all here and in beautiful condition. There are also the ruins of old cement kilns on the property.

Trolley Museum (914-331-3399), 89 East Strand, Kingston; follow Broadway south to its end, make a left, and watch for the signs. Open Saturday and Sunday, Memorial Day through Columbus Day, noon–5; open also on Friday in July and August. Admission fee. For anyone who remembers the ring of a trolley bell or the rolling ride of a self-propelled car, this museum offers lots of nostalgia. Housed in an old trolley shed along the Rondout, the museum offers displays and short rides on restored trolley cars.

Overlook Observatory (914-246-4294), West Saugerties Road between Saugerties and Woodstock. Hours by appointment; fee charged for classes. Both home and scientific workshop to astronomer Bob Berman, the observatory offers visitors a guided tour of the night sky with all its mysteries, quirks, and wonders, and outstanding instruments for viewing the heavens. Bob is a knowledgeable and enthusiastic guide.

Widmark Honey Farm (914-255-6400), Route 44/55 in Gardiner. Hours and times vary; call for schedule and a listing of special events. Admission fee (credited to any purchases). They offer bears and honey, but here the bears have been raised practically as family pets, and they will entertain you with their wrestling, climbing, and bicycling antics. A perfect outing for anyone with small children to amuse; adults will also enjoy the self-guided apiary tours and the honey tastings. There is a retail shop with local farm goods and, of course, many varieties of honey.

WINERIES

The Hudson Valley has become an important center of wine production in New York, and visitors are welcome to stop at many of Ulster County's wineries. They range in size from tiny "boutique" wineries to full-sized vineyards, complete with restaurants, bottling plant, and cellars. Wherever you go, however, you will find people who love their work and who are willing to share their expertise and wines with you. Some of the wineries offer formal guided tours, others just have a showroom and tasting area. You may want to call before you go—there are special events, concerts, and tours throughout the season, and hours may change when the harvest begins. Most of the sites are free, as are the tastings, but there may be admission charged to special events.

Woodstock Brewery (914-331-2810), 20 St. James Street, Kingston. Open year-round; call for hours. Beer lovers will want to stop by, tour this microbrewery, and sample one of the few beers made in the Hudson Valley. They produce a Hudson Lager and other fine-tasting brews, and visitors will learn a lot about the science and art of good beer.

Adair Vineyards (914-255-1377), Allhusen Road, New Paltz. Open daily May through December, noon–6. The vineyard has an old Dutch barn and offers tastings, tours, and picnics. The picture-perfect Ulster site looks as if unchanged through the centuries.

Baldwin Vineyards (914-744-2226), Hardenburgh Estate, Pine Bush, is located on a 200-year-old estate, where more than 40 acres of pastures, vineyards, and woodlands are open for strolling. Open daily June through December, weekends in winter and by appointment. Award-winning wines can be tasted (including a strawberry-flavored wine that tastes like summer), and lunch is served in their gourmet café overlooking the vineyards.

Benmarl Winery (914-236-4265), Conway Road, off 9W south of Marlboro. Open daily year-round. Visitors can enjoy guided tours, wine tastings, a stop at the gallery, or lunch in the Bistro, serving food à la France. Established in the early 19th century, the winery overlooks the Hudson River.

Brimstone Hill Vineyard (914-744-2231), Brimstone Hill Road, Pine Bush. Open year-round but call for hours; tours and tastings available May through October. French-style wines are the specialty, and the wineshop is also open for browsing.

Regent Champagne Cellars (914-691-7296), 200 Blue Point Road, Highland. Open weekends year-round, daily from March through December. They offer champagnes and cheese with their tastings, and special events include dances, tours, Oktoberfest, Christmas festivals, and concerts.

Rivendell Winery (914-255-0892), 714 Albany Post Road, New Paltz, specializes in chardonnay and is open every day, rain or shine, for tours and tastings. There are special events throughout the summer. They also have a retail shop on site. Call for detailed directions and events schedule.

Royal Kedem Winery (914-795-2240), Dock Road, Milton, is open May through December except Saturdays and Jewish holidays (call for hours). A tasting room is also located at 1519 Route 9W in Marlboro and is open all year. The winery produces a fine line of kosher wines, including honey and plum wine. There are a tour, a film, and tastings in the restored railroad depot that serves as the shop.

Windsor Vineyards (914-236-4440), 104 Western Avenue, Marlboro.

Walker Valley Vineyards

The wineshop and tasting room are open year-round here. New York and California wines and champagnes are stocked.

Smaller wineries that offer premium wines, tastings, and tours include **El Paso Winery** (914-331-8642), Route 9W, Ulster Park; **Magnanini Farm Winery** (914-895-2767), 501 Strawridge Road, Wallkill; **Walker Valley Vineyards** (914-384-6709), Oregon Trail, West Park; and **West Park Vineyards** (914-384-6709), Burroughs Drive, West Park.

HISTORIC HOMES

Bevier House (914-338-5614), 6 miles south of Kingston on Route 209. Open June through September, Wednesday through Sunday 1–5. Admission fee. Built in the late 1680s, this stone house now serves as headquarters of the Ulster County Historical Society, and it is a treasure trove of odd collections and memorabilia. Once a single-story Dutch farmhouse, much of the present structure was added during the last three centuries. Throughout the house you will see fine Hudson Valley Dutch and Victorian furniture, in addition to the tool and kitchenware collections, ceramic pottery from an early factory in Poughkeepsie, portraits, and decorative accessories. The Bevier House is not a very formal museum, and it has a great old-fashioned feel to it.

Huguenot Street's Stone Houses (914-255-1889), located on Stone House Street, off Route 32 in New Paltz. The street is open year-round; tours are offered late May through Labor Day, Wednesday through Sunday 10–4. Admission fee; Deyo Hall gallery and museum are free. In 1677 a group of 12 Huguenot men purchased almost 40,000 acres of land from the Esopus Indians and began the settlement that was referred to as "die Pfalz," after an area in the Rhineland Palatinate. By 1692 the original log huts were being replaced by stone houses, several of which still stand today as a result of the efforts of the Huguenot Historical Society. A trip to New Paltz offers a unique chance to see what life was like three centuries ago in upper-middle-class homes. The walking tour begins with **Deyo Hall** and **Grimm Gallery,** which were, respectively, a glass factory and private home before they were combined into the orientation center. Visitors here will see a large collection of local artifacts, including furniture, costumes, and portraits.

All the buildings are owned by the society, and many still have the original furnishings. At the **Abraham Hasbrouck House** (1692) the dark rooms include a cellar-kitchen, which was the heart of village social life, and a built-in Dutch bed. Other houses of the period include the **Bevier-Elting House,** which is distinguished by a long well-sweep and covered walk for the convenience of the ladies; the **Freer House,** with its mow door, which made it easier to move provisions into the attic; and the **Dubois Fort,** which is reputed to be haunted by a headless lady. Possibly the most interesting house is the **Jean Hasbrouck House,** which once served as a store and tavern. Downstairs there is a bar and grill (with the real grill, which could be pulled down to protect the bottles from thieves), as well as a jambless fireplace with its curtainlike decorations; upstairs, there is a massive brick chimney, the only one of its type in the United States. Several other buildings are also open to the public, including the reconstructed **French Church,** the Federal-style **LeFevre House,** and the **Deyo House,** a remodeled 17th-century home. There are two tours; the longer one may not be suitable for children, but it shouldn't be missed by anyone interested in history.

Hurley Patentee Manor (914-331-5414). Take Route 209 south to Hurley; follow signs to Old Route 209 and the manor house. Summer hours; call for tour information. Admission fee. This National Historic Landmark is a combination of a Dutch cottage, built in 1696, and a 1745 Georgian manor house. The manor was the center of the Hurley Patent, a 96,000-acre land grant that included the land between Woodstock and New Paltz and that today has been reduced to the 5 acres surrounding the house. The house is privately owned and has been restored to its original condition. The owners display many fine antiques from the 17th to the 19th centuries, including a chair once owned by Sir William Johnston and a desk with a secret drawer. The basement of the house has one of the few indoor animal pens still in existence and is also the display area for Hurley Patentee Lighting, a company that crafts handwrought reproduction lighting fixtures. The owners are friendly and well versed in local history, so don't miss out on their tour. Children will enjoy the attic museum in particular.

Locust Lawn, Terwilliger House, Little Wings Wildlife Sanctuary (914-255-1889), Route 32, outside of Gardiner. Open Memorial Day through September; hours vary at sites so call ahead. Admission fee. These three sites are within minutes of each other, and all are administered by the Huguenot Historical Society of New Paltz. Locust Lawn, a Federal-style mansion, was built in 1814 by Colonel Josiah Hasbrouck, a Revolutionary War veteran. The elegant white mansion still houses a fine collection of 18th- and 19th-century furniture and decorative arts, as well as several portraits by the American folk painter Ammi Phillips. Since Locust Lawn remained in the Hasbrouck family until the 1950s, when it was donated to the society, many of the original furnishings remain. Also on the site are outbuildings typical of a farm of that era, and visitors can see the carriage house, smokehouse, and slaughterhouse. One rare artifact found here is the great oxcart that was used to transport supplies to the beleaguered army at Valley Forge.

Down the road from Locust Lawn stands the Terwilliger House, built in 1738 and left almost untouched over the last two and a half centuries. This is a fine example of the architectural style used by the area's Dutch and French Huguenot settlers. Built of stone, with a center hall and great fireplace, the house has been furnished in the style of the era. Outside, visitors may follow a cleared path over the Plattekill Brook to a small graveyard where family members and their slaves were buried.

In the Little Wings Wildlife Sanctuary there are several nature trails to be explored, and more than 30 species of birds have been sighted on and near the refuge's pond. The magnificent wildflower garden is especially lovely in spring, when lady's slippers, Dutchman's breeches, and wake-robin bloom. Bring a picnic lunch and enjoy the afternoon.

HISTORIC SITES

Hudson River Maritime Museum and Rondout Landing (914-338-0071), located at the foot of Broadway in Kingston. Open May through December, but hours vary; call for special-events schedule. Admission

Mohonk Mountain House seen from Sky Top

fee. For almost two centuries, the Hudson River was a major water highway between New York and Albany. One of the ports of call along the way was the Rondout Landing in Kingston, once a bustling area of boatyards and rigging lofts that echoed with steam whistles and brass ships' bells. But when shipping on the Hudson fell into decline, so did the fortunes of the Rondout. Then, in 1980, the Hudson River Maritime Museum was opened with the goal of preserving the heritage of the river. The museum has since restored several riverside buildings as well as several historic vessels, and visitors can now see a working part of the Hudson's legacy. There is an exhibit hall that features shows on marine history. Outside there is an ever-changing display of river vessels, with the 1899 steam tug *Mathilda* and the cruise boat *Indy 7*. Visitors to the landing have also included the presidential yacht *Sequoia* and the sailing ships *Clearwater* and *Woody Guthrie*. Special weekend festivals are held throughout the year, including a Harvest Festival in October, a Shad Festival in May, sailing regattas, and tours to the Kingston Lighthouse.

Kingston Urban Cultural Park Visitors Center (914-331-9506), 308 Clinton Avenue, Kingston, with a satellite office at the Maritime Museum. Open daily except Tuesday year-round; call for tour information. Free. New York State has designated Urban Cultural Parks as the interpreters of urban settings of particular historic interest; Kingston's park is known for its importance in the history of transportation. The center is located in the Stockade area (once surrounded by walls of tree trunks 13 feet high) and offers orientation displays that cover Kingston from 17th-century Dutch settlement to the present. Directions for self-guided walking tours are available, and guided tours may be arranged by appointment. While uptown, you may also want to stop by the Volunteer Firemen's Hall and Museum, 265 Fair Street, open May through October, Friday and Saturday 10–4. The museum is in an old firehouse where antique fire apparatus, memorabilia, and period furniture are on display.

Mohonk Mountain House (914-255-1000), 6 miles west of New Paltz. Take Route 299 west over the Walkill River, turn right at the Mohonk sign, then bear left and follow the road to the gate. Open year-round; call ahead for skiing and hiking information and special-events weekends. Use fee is charged. When Alfred and Albert Smiley built this resort in 1869, they were determined to preserve the surrounding environment and offer gracious accommodations to visitors from the city. Guests here could hike the nearby Shawangunks, take a carriage ride around the manicured grounds, or enjoy the carefully tended flower beds. There was a lake for ice skating, as well as croquet lawns; the hotel itself was furnished in the best of the Victorian era: acres of polished oak paneling and floors, hidden conversation nooks, and homey, overstuffed furniture. Mohonk has endured the last century with timeless grace, and today visitors will find many things unchanged. The resort is still dedicated to preserving the natural world, and the gardens have won awards for their beauty. Mohonk sits next to a trout-stocked lake that becomes the focus of special winter carnival weekends. There is a stone tower atop the mountain that offers a six-state view on sunny days. Hikers, birders, horseback riders, and cross-country skiers will find Mohonk unequaled. Day visitors are welcome, but it takes more than a day to even sample all of the surprises at Mohonk; plan at least a long weekend if possible.

Old Dutch Church (914-338-6759), 272 Wall Street in the uptown area of Kingston. Hours vary; visitors must call ahead for tours. Free. Organized in 1659, the Reformed Protestant Dutch Church of Kingston has served the people of the area continuously since. The present building was built in 1852; its bluestone exterior is in the Renaissance Revival style, and the windows were made in the Tiffany studios. Local tradition once held that the bell was cast from silver and copper items donated by the congregation and that one of the steeples (from an earlier church that stood on the site) may have been haunted by a goblin. Inside you will see several bronze statues as well as artifacts from the 1600s onward. Take time to walk through the churchyard and view the fine examples of early gravestone art (Governor Clinton's gravesite is located here). In spring thousands of yellow and red tulips planted in honor of the Netherlands line the church walks.

Opus 40 and **The Quarryman's Museum** (914-246-3400). Follow Route 212 west from Saugerties; Opus 40 is located on Fite Road, off Glasco Turnpike. Open May through October; Saturday and weekdays except Tuesday 10–4; Sunday, noon–5. Admission fee. In 1938 artist Harvey

Fite's bluestone quarry outside Saugerties was merely the source of material for his sculpture. But as work on the individual pieces progressed, Fite realized that the terraces and steps he had created as a backdrop for the sculpture had themselves become the focus of his work. Naming the site Opus 40 because he believed it would take 40 years to complete, Fite set about creating a vast environmental work that would eventually contain 6 acres of steps, levels, fountains, pools, and paths. Each of the hundreds of thousands of bluestone pieces was hand cut and fitted, and the 9-ton central monolith was lifted into place with a boom and winches. Today, Opus 40 is open to the public as an environmental sculpture and concert site. Fite, who had studied theology and law and worked as an actor and teacher, also built a museum to house his collection of quarrymen's tools and artifacts. The museum offers a rare glimpse into a lost way of life.

Senate House (914-338-2786), 312 Fair Street, Kingston. Open April through December; Wednesday through Saturday 10–5, Sunday 1–5. Free. When the New York State government was forced to leave New York City during the Revolution, it sought safety upstate. The house in which the men met was built in the 17th century by a Dutch settler, Wessel Ten Broeck, and was partially burned by the British in 1777. After numerous additions and changes to the building, the house has been restored to reflect its part in history. Visitors can see several rooms, including the kitchen with its kitchenware and huge fireplace, and the meeting room where the state constitution was hammered out. There

Visitors to the Senate House in Kingston, the state's first capital, can tour this room where New York's first Senate met on September 9, 1777.

is a special tour of the lovely rose garden in June, when the flowers are in full bloom. A second building on the site, the Loughran House, was added in 1927, and it houses a museum with historic displays and changing exhibits that reflect the story of Kingston. One room is given over to the works of John Vanderlyn, a Kingston native who was considered one of the finest painters of 19th-century America. This site offers special events including concerts, slide shows, and lectures throughout the year; a Dutch Christmas is also celebrated.

SCENIC DRIVES

Ulster County has hundreds of miles of well-maintained roads, coupled with some of the most spectacular scenery in the Hudson Valley. It doesn't matter if you travel in autumn, with all the riotous color, or in winter, with its icy beauty—Ulster will always surprise.

For a drive that offers history as well as scenery, start at Kingston (Exit 19 on the NYS Thruway) and go south along Route 209. This is one of the oldest roads in America—the Old Mine Road, which was a trading route between Upstate New York and Pennsylvania in the 17th century. As you pass by Hurley, Marbletown, and Stone Ridge, you will see acres of fields planted with sweet corn, the area's largest agricultural crop. The architectural styles of the homes range from Dutch stone to late Victorian, and you'll see many farm stands in summer and autumn. At Route 213, head east through High Falls, along the old Delaware and Hudson Canal. Stop in at the High Falls Co-op if you like natural foods, or just continue down the road that follows the canal. At Route 32 you can head south into New Paltz and explore the old stone houses or head north back to Kingston.

For a second scenic route from Kingston, take Route 9W south along the Hudson River. At West Park, you may want to follow the signs to Slabsides, once the writing retreat of naturalist John Burroughs; it's on your right, down across the railroad tracks (park at the bottom of the hill and walk up). Back on Route 9W, continue south and take Route 299 west through New Paltz, then follow Route 44/55 for some fine overlook sites. At Route 209, head back north past old Dutch farms and stone houses to Kingston.

From Kingston, you can also follow Route 28 to Route 28A around the Ashokan Reservoir, a special treat in autumn. Follow the signs to the pump station and walk around the fountain or have a picnic—it is an uncrowded, still undiscovered area.

TO DO

ADVENTURE

Adventurous visitors can do more than take a walk or dine out; they can participate in some sports that are unusual and challenging. Mountain climbing rope-descent technique, otherwise known as rappeling, is taught at **The Sundance Academy** (914-688-5640), Route 214, Phoenicia. The instructors have taught groups of everyone from beginners to experienced climbers, and a class-and-lodgings package is available. When you make it down the 60-foot tower, you get a certificate.

Hang gliders and ultralights are featured at **Mountain Wings Hang Gliding Center** (914-647-3377), 150 Canal Street, Ellenville; and at **Thermal Up, Inc.** (914-647-8021), 10 Cragsmoor Road, Cragsmoor.

Those who want to learn rock climbing (a special sport in the Shawangunks region) should contact Jon Ross at **High Angle Adventures** (914-658-9811), New Paltz, which has full-day instruction with some of the best climbers in the East; and Jim Munson at **Mountain Skills** (914-687-9643), Stone Ridge, where instruction and guided climbs can be arranged.

BOAT CRUISES

The Hudson runs the length of Ulster County, and visitors can select from several companies that cruise the river. Even if you don't know port from starboard, there are tours that take all the work but none of the fun out of a river trip. One warning: It can be very breezy and cool out on the river; bring a hat and scarf and sweater unless the day is blazing hot.

Great Hudson Sailing Center (914-338-7313), Rondout Landing, Kingston, is open from mid-May through October and offers day and sunset sailings with wine and cheese.

The *Rip Van Winkle* (914-255-6515; 255-6618 for credit card orders only), at Rondout Landing, Kingston offers cruises on a roomy ship that features plenty of seating, rest rooms, and a snack bar. Because the river tends to be less choppy than the ocean, the ride is smooth and pleasant. Cruise season is May through October, weather permitting, and music is provided on some trips. Day cruises to West Point and back depart daily. A recent addition is the new ferry service. The *Indy 7*, a 40-foot ferryboat, leaves from the Rondout Landing on Saturday and Sunday (daily in July and August) every hour 12:30 PM–3:30 PM. Visitors can disembark at Rhinecliff and visit the Rondout Lighthouse. Call for information and prices.

Hudson Rondout Cruises (914-338-6280), Rondout Landing, Kingston, is the perfect choice if you are in the mood for a short trip. The boat sails to the Kingston Lighthouse, where passengers disembark for a tour, then continues south to the Esopus Meadows Lighthouse. Cruises run daily June through October, with special events like dinner and brunch sailings. Visitors can also take the *Sea Explorer* from the Rondout Landing (914-679-8205) daily June through August, weekends April, May, September, and October. Short local tours and sunset tours are the specialty of this company and include narration and lighthouse tours.

North River Cruises (914-679-8205), Rondout Landing, Kingston, is run by Captain John Cutten. His boat, the *Teal*, fitted with rich wood and brass, takes you back to a time of genteel river travel but offers all the modern amenities. Available for private charters and corporate parties.

FARM STANDS AND PICK-YOUR-OWN FARMS

Some Ulster County farms are still owned by the families that founded them; still others have been cultivating the same site for centuries. The harvest season here stretches from early-summer strawberries to late-fall pumpkins and even some holiday greenery. Some farm stands offer freshly baked pies and cakes, while others have recipes for you to take home, along with food and other regional goodies. Pick-your-own farms and stands let you do the work as well as giving you the choice of what you want in the basket. Most of these stands provide containers, but if you bring your own, the price is usually lower. However you decide to gather in the harvest, the following is just a sampling of places to try.

The two **Gill Corn Farms** (914-331-8225), Hurley Mountain Road or Route 209, both outside Kingston, are open May through November. Both farms are in sweet corn country, and that's what they specialize in, although a wide variety of other fruits and vegetables are offered, including several pick-your-own crops.

Davenport Farms Market (914-687-7446), Route 209, Stone Ridge, open April through November, has an extensive selection of local produce, including raspberries, grapes, corn, apples, pumpkins, and melons.

Barthels Farm Market (914-647-6941), farther south on Route 209, in Ellenville, is open May through November. You can pick your own strawberries and select fruits and vegetables from the stand.

Three Brothers Egg Farm (914-338-6689), down the road, offers a different type of local "harvest." Eggs, honey, maple syrup, and organically raised free-range chickens are available.

The final stop on Route 9W is in Port Ewen at **The Apple Bin,** the Nemeth Orchards shop, where many varieties of local corn, fruit, and apples are offered; they also stock an excellent selection of baked goods. Open April through December.

Alyce & Roger's Fruit Stand (914-688-5615), Route 28, Mount Tremper. A dazzling array of local produce is found here, and there are lots of jack-o'-lanterns come October.

Some local fruit farms that specialize in pick-your-own fruits include: **Mr. Apples** (914-687-9498), Route 213, High Falls, with several varieties of apples and cider; **Moriello's Apple Hill Farm** (914-255-0917), Route 32, New Paltz; **Minard Farms,** (914-883-5755), off Ohioville Road, Clintondale, with apples, cider, picnic areas, and a hay ride; **Clarke Westervelt Fruit Farm** (914-795-2270), 182 Clarke's Lane, Milton, with apples; and **Wright's Farm** (914-255-5300), Route 208, Gardiner.

A few larger farm markets that are worth stopping at: **Adam's Fairacre Farm**

(914-336-6300), on Route 9W in Lake Katrine; **Hepworth Farms** (914-795-2141), on Route 9W in Milton; and **Wallkill View Farm** (914-255-8050), on Route 299 in New Paltz. The produce and baked goods here are first rate.

FISHING

Ulster County offers fishing enthusiasts a chance to try their luck in scores of streams, a reservoir, and the great Hudson River. The waters are well stocked with a variety of fish—trout, bass, pike, pickerel, and perch are some of the more popular catches. Fishing areas are well marked, and New York State licenses are required, as are reservoir permits. Call the Department of Environmental Conservation (914-255-5453), New Paltz, for information.

Some of the better-known fishing streams in Ulster County include Esopus Creek (access points along Route 28, west of Kingston), Rondout Creek (access point on Route 209, south of Kingston), Plattekill Creek (access near Route 32 in Saugerties), and the Sawkill (access along Route 375 in Woodstock). Most of the main access points are indicated by brown-and-yellow state signs; many also have parking areas. If you are uncertain about the stream, ask; otherwise, you may find yourself on the receiving end of a heavy fine. Holders of reservoir permits will want to try the Ashokan Reservoir (Route 28A, west of Kingston), with 40 miles of shoreline and trout, walleye, and bass lurking beneath the surface. The Kingston City Reservoir requires a city permit for fishing, but it is worth the extra effort.

Many sports shops offer fishing licenses, gear, repairs, and expert information. Try **Folkerts Brothers** (914-688-9936), Main Street, Phoenicia, which offers a fly-fishing school from mid-April through mid-October, or **Sportsman's Corner** (914-657-6700), Route 28, Boiceville (it has a serve-yourself bait machine!).

GOLF

Ulster County golf courses can be dramatic, relaxing, and colorful, by turns, and the areas that offer golf cater to a wide range of skills and interests. Hotel courses are usually open to the public, but it is recommended that you call ahead, since they schedule special events and competitions.

In Ellenville, **The Fallsview Hotel** (914-647-4960), Route 209; **The Nevele** (914-647-7315), Route 209; and the **Shawangunk Country Club** (914-647-6090), Leurnkill Road, all have championship golfing.

Mohonk Mountain House (914-255-1000), New Paltz, maintains lovely greens and fairways high above the valley (see *Historic Sites*).

New Paltz Golf Course (914-255-8282), 215 Huguenot Street, New Paltz.

Kingston is home to **Green Acres Golf Course** (914-331-7807), Harwich Street; **Jeto's Miniature Golf and Driving Range** (914-331-2334), Sawkill Road; and the **Twaalfskill Golf Club** (914-331-6266), 282 West O'Reilly Street. The latter has restrictions on use for nonmembers.

HIKING

Ulster County has some of the best hiking in the Hudson Valley, with views that go on for miles and trails that range from an easy walk to a hard day's climb. The following suggestions for afternoon or day hikes provide magnificent vistas, but it is recommended that you use maps, available locally, in order to make your hike as safe as possible.

Belleayre Mountain (914-254-5600), in Highmount, has a marked cross-country ski trail that provides a nice walk in the woods, and a hike to the summit will reveal a sweep of mountains below.

Frost Valley YMCA and Conference Center, Route 47 from Route 28 in Big Indian, has hundreds of acres to explore.

For a variety of walks in the woods on nicely graded trails, don't overlook **Mohonk Mountain House,** Mountain Rest Road, New Paltz; and **Minnewaska State Park** (914-255-0752) Route 44/55, New Paltz. Both are day use only and charge a fee. The Shawangunk trails found at both sites are excellent, although somewhat crowded on summer weekends. Mohonk has 128 miles of paths and carriage roads to hike, and there are some first-rate spots for rock climbing as well (see *Adventure*).

Overlook Mountain, in Woodstock, is a moderate walk up a graded roadbed. From Tinker Street at the village green, take Rock City Road to Meads Mountain Road, which leads to the trailhead, just across from the Tibetan monastery. The summit takes about an hour to reach, depending on how fast you travel the 2-mile ascent. You will pass the ruins of the Overlook Mountain House on the way up, and there are a lookout tower and picnic tables at the top; the view of the valley and river is incomparable.

Vernooy Kill Falls in Kerhonkson can be reached by taking Route 209 to Lower Cherrytown Road, then bearing right and continuing 5 miles to Upper Cherrytown Road. In another 3 miles you'll see the parking lot on the right and the trailhead on the left. The trail is 3.6 miles up and back.

With lots of back roads to explore, walkers might enjoy a trek along Route 212 in Woodstock. Start in the center of town and travel west toward Bearsville or along parts of Route 209 near Stone Ridge (park and begin in town). Hurley, Route 209 south of Kingston, also has pretty streets and byways, with many historic homes along the way.

TUBING

Very popular in the area, tubing isn't so much a sport as it is a leisurely pursuit. It doesn't take any special skills and can be done by just about anyone. All you do is rent a huge, black inner tube, put it in the water, and hop on for rides that last anywhere from 1 to 3 hours. Maneuvering can be done with the hands, and proper tubing attire consists of shorts and T-shirts, or bathing suits, and old sneakers. A life jacket is recommended for those who are not strong swimmers. Although most of the waters are not very deep, they are cold and the currents can be swift. The tubing season runs from the first warm weather until the last—somewhere between late May and early September. You will have to leave a security deposit for the tubes, and rental does not include extras like life jackets or "tube seats," which keep you from bumping along the rocky bottom; some sites will also arrange to transport you back after the trip. Tubes and gear, including helmets, may be rented at **Four Seasons Sports Shop** (914-688-7633), Main Street, Phoenicia; **Town Tinker Tube Rental** (914-688-7633), the granddaddy of tubing services, with their well-stocked headquarters at Bridge Street, Phoenicia; and **Rubber Ducky Tube Rental** (914-688-7877), just off Route 28, at the Hayloft Restaurant, Shandaken. The **Railhead Tube Company** (914-688-7400), Route 28, Mt. Pleasant, lets you take a train ride upriver, then tube back.

CROSS-COUNTRY SKIING

Ulster is a good place for cross-country enthusiasts. When valleys, meadows, and fields receive a cover of snow, new trails are broken and old ones rediscovered. **Belleayre Mountain** (see *Downhill Skiing*) has several marked, ungroomed trails that cover 4 miles. They follow the old Ulster and Delaware Turnpike and even pass an old family cemetery. Lessons are available (call 914-254-5600 to schedule), and rentals are offered just across the road from the trails. There is no fee and no charge for parking or use of the lodge. Expert "skinny skiers" can purchase lift tickets and use the mountains.

Frost Valley YMCA. Take Route 28 in Oliverea to Route 47 and go 15 miles. Twenty miles of groomed trails wind in and out of lovely forests and alongside streams. The trails are color coded, and there is a warming hut. A small use fee is charged; call for lesson and rental information.

Mohonk Mountain House (914-255-1000), in New Paltz, has 35 miles of carriage-road trails opening onto views of distant mountain ridges, glens, and valleys. Trails are color-coded and mapped, and there is a use fee. Rentals and refreshment sites available; call before you go.

Lake Minnewaska, Route 44/55 near New Paltz, has 150 miles of cross-country trails for everyone, from novices to advanced skiers.

Williams Lake Hotel (914-658-3101), Rosendale, has excellent cross-country skiing for the beginner and for skiers with young children. Great lake views.

DOWNHILL SKIING

Downhill skiing in Ulster County offers the best of all worlds: Country surroundings and challenging slopes are convenient to cities like Albany and New York. The largest downhill ski area in Ulster is **Belleayre Mountain** (914-254-5600); follow Route 28 west from Kingston to Highmount, at the western edge of the county. Open daily Thanksgiving through March, 9–4. Owned by New York State, Belleayre has a top elevation of 3365 feet and full snowmaking capabilities and is the only ski area in the state that has a natural division: The upper mountain is for intermediate and expert skiers; the lower mountain is for beginners and intermediates. There is plenty of free parking, and a courtesy shuttle runs all day. At the upper mountain, 16 trails are serviced by snowmaking equipment, triple and double chair lifts, and a T-bar. Runs range from intermediate to extreme expert. For those who want even more of a challenge, there is a complete racing program, including clinics, competitions, and coin-operated starting gates. The ski school at Belleayre is outstanding, with patient, capable instructors who can teach the youngest beginner or help advanced experts polish their skills. Snowboards are allowed on certain trails (rentals, sales, and instruction are available), and there are special events all season. The Upper Lodge is a huge, welcoming log building with a fieldstone fireplace, bar, ski shop, nursery, cafeteria, lounge area, and outside deck; the Lower Lodge has a cafeteria and ski shop. Both offer rental equipment, rest rooms, and locker areas. Belleayre has great children's programs (including the SkiWee program), and a fully equipped nursery; call for reservations before you go. They also sponsor inexpensive learn-to-ski days, ski clubs, special events, and other activities throughout the season, and they are very family- and service-oriented.

GREEN SPACE

Ice Caves Mountain and **Sam's Point** (914-647-7989), Route 52, Ellenville. Open daily April to November. Admission fee. It is suggested that visitors wear comfortable shoes and bring a sweater. These are Registered Natural Landmarks—areas that have been set aside as exceptional examples of American natural history. The park and lookout point are circled by a road that offers wide views of Ulster and the surrounding counties, but it's at Sam's Point that you will want your camera. Formed by glaciers, the point is a little less than half a mile above sea level and offers a flat viewing area from which you can see five states on a clear day. There are safety walls, but you'll feel suspended over the valley below; if you don't like heights, don't stop here. Sam's Point supposedly got its name from a trapper who, fleeing a Native American war party, jumped over the edge and landed safely in some trees. Nature trails lead to **Cupid's Rock, Moss Pool,** and the **Fabulous Snow Springs.** The trails are well marked and equipped with handrails, and tours are self-guided with signs and brochures. A walk will take you past chasms and tunnels, around incredible balanced rocks, and into lit caves with remarkable mineral formations. Explore at your own pace and enjoy the natural surroundings.

Kingston Point Beach and **Hudson River Landing Park** (914-679-5297). Take Broadway to the end, make a left, and follow East Strand (which becomes North Street) 1 mile to the park. The beach is open year-round, dawn to dusk. Park hours vary with special events, and admission is charged. Kingston Point Beach offers a nice view of the river; there is swimming in summer and a small playground, and visitors can watch sailboards and sailboats at play. The Hudson River Landing Park, a privately owned site on the river, hosts special events such as flea markets and country fairs year-round.

The Mohonk Preserve (914-255-0919 or 255-1000), Mountain Rest Road, New Paltz. Open daily year-round dawn to dusk. Admission fee. This 5600-acre nature preserve is owned and operated by a private nonprofit environmental organization. It surrounds 2000 acres owned by the Mohonk Mountain House resort. From the visitors center, 26 miles of hiking trails and 19 miles of wider carriage roads stretch out in all directions. Maps are available. The trails are ideal for cross-country skiing and walking. From the tower at Sky Top, the highest point along the trails (1500 feet above sea level), you can see six states on a clear day (NY, NJ, PA, CT, MA, and VT). Sky Top is about 2.5 miles from the visitors center. The tower was built in 1920 as a memorial to Albert Smiley, one of the founders of Mohonk Mountain House, which opened in 1870. The preserve offers some of the most scenic views in the Hudson Valley.

Minnewaska State Park (914-255-0752), Route 44/55 (PO Box 893), New Paltz. Open daily from 9 AM until dusk most of the year. Hours are adjusted seasonally and are posted each day at the entrance. Located on the dramatic Shawangunk Mountain Ridge, this park offers spectacular mountain views, waterfalls, and meadows. Lake Minnewaska itself is surrounded by a network of woodland trails and carriageways that are excellent for hiking, horseback riding, and cross-country skiing. The paved carriageways are excellent for biking. You can take a leisurely 2-mile walk around the lake, which is a nice way to get oriented in this large park. Swimming is permitted at the sandy beach area, and there is a lifeguard on duty. Another good place to swim in the park is Lake Awosting, approximately a 3-mile walk from the entrance. Minnewaska is a day-use area only; no camping is permitted. There are several fine places to picnic and some of these have raised portable grills. Those who visit in November and December should be aware that hunting is permitted in certain outlying areas of the park.

Shale Hill Farm and Herb Garden (914-246-6982), 6856 Hommelville Road, Saugerties, just off Route 32. Gardens open spring and summer, shop open year-round; call for hours. This farm is a perfect stop for flower fanciers and herb lovers—the extensive gardens bloom with color and fragrance, and the owner, Patricia Reppert, is an expert in herb lore and use. The shop carries herbal products, plants, gifts, and antiques, and special workshops are offered on weekends (wreath making, cooking, and the like). A nice spot to stop and select some additions to your garden.

LODGING

Many of the bed & breakfasts in Ulster County are tucked away down private roads or are off the beaten path and in private homes. They are sometimes difficult to contact as well, since they do not always have separate listings in local telephone directories. The most up-to-date listings may be obtained by calling the Ulster County Public Information

Office, 1-800-DIAL UCO, or by writing to them at PO Box 1800 TG, Kingston 12401.

The Alpine Inn (914-254-5026), Alpine Road, Oliverea 12410. ($$) A pristine mountain lodge nestled on a hillside near the base of one of the tallest peaks in the Catskills, this inn will appeal to those who enjoy exploring the outdoors. Complete with an Olympic-sized pool. Breakfast, lunch, and dinner are served. Twenty-two rooms with private baths and air-conditioning. Children are welcome. Open year-round.

Baker's Bed and Breakfast (914-687-9795), RD #2, Stone Ridge 12484. ($$) Surrounded by mountains, fields, and woods, this 1780 stone farmhouse is furnished with antiques, and there is a greenhouse with a hot tub. Breakfast is served in the solarium and includes home-baked goodies. The suite with sitting room has a private bath; five other rooms share two bathrooms. Children permitted on weekdays only. Open year-round.

Bed by the Stream (914-246-2979), 7531 George Sickle Road, Saugerties 12477. ($$) This peaceful lodging is located on 5 acres of streamside property and offers an in-ground pool and creek swimming. Marked hiking trails are available nearby, and Hunter Mountain and Ski Windham are only a short drive away (see *Downhill Skiing* in "Greene County"). Bed by the Stream offers three bedrooms: two with a private entrance and shared bath, one with a private bath, in the house overlooking Blue Mountain. Country breakfast is served; children are welcome.

Birchcreek Inn (914-254-5222), Birchcreek Road, Pine Hill 12465. ($$) This inn is located in a remote but wonderful spot, with a sign indicating its location just off Route 28. A 100-year-old estate on 23 private acres, it combines the rustic and the refined for an informal yet elegant ambience. Every guest room has a private bath. Check out the Champagne Room for a special occasion: It's huge, as is its luxurious bathroom.

Cafe Tamayo Bed and Breakfast (914-246-9371), 89 Partition Street, Saugerties 12477. ($$) The official name of this establishment is Upstairs at Cafe Tamayo, Bed and Gourmet Breakfast, and that about says it all. Located above the Cafe Tamayo, an outstanding dining spot (see *Dining Out*), the bed & breakfast features private baths and a gourmet breakfast prepared by chef/owner James Tamayo. The café is a short walk from the antiques shops and boutiques of the village and a short drive from Woodstock, Kingston, and the main ski areas.

Captain Schoonmaker's Bed and Breakfast (914-687-7946), Route 213, High Falls 12440. ($$$) A fine spot for antiques lovers, this 18th-century house will make you feel as if you were stepping back into an earlier time. Schoonmaker's has been featured in many publications, and the hostess serves a seven-course breakfast that should hold you until dinner. Eight rooms share six bathrooms. Children not permitted. Open year-round.

Copper Hood Inn and Spa (914-688-9962), Route 28, Shandaken 12480. ($$) Tucked away alongside a well-known fishing stream, the Copper Hood is really an intimate, full-service spa. Along with fine dining, the inn offers one of the few indoor heated pools in the region; Jacuzzi, massage, and herbal wraps; hiking trails; and, of course, fishing. All rooms with private baths. Children are welcome. Open year-round.

Deerfield (914-687-9807), RD #1, The Vly, Stone Ridge 12484. ($$) Once a boardinghouse, this turn-of-the-century building has been renovated for modern overnight guests. The rooms are airy and light, and there is a nice mix of antiques and country throughout the inn. There are more than 30 acres to explore, and antiques shops and points of interest are within a short drive. Guests can enjoy an in-ground pool, private baths, a Steinway piano, and a large gourmet breakfast.

The Guesthouse at Holy Cross Monastery (914-384-6660), Route 9W, PO Box 99, West Park 12493. ($$) This monastery has spectacular views of the Hudson River and provides a rather unique bed & breakfast experience. The per-person fee of $60 per night includes a room and three meals served in a large dining room with the monks. On some weekends special educational programs are offered; you can write or call for a schedule of events. Open year-round.

Haus Elissa (914-657-6277), Route 28A, West Shokan 12494. ($$) This bed & breakfast is run by a mother/daughter team, Helen and Gretchen Behl, and it is the only German-style lodging of its type in the region. Three cozy guest rooms, two with shared bath, the other with a private bathroom, reflect the Continental and American influences with prints and needlework, and even a resident cat named Rip Van Winkle. The Behls are well known for their home-baked German specialties, and breakfast is served on the porch in summer. They also have a vintage movie collection, as well as a wide selection of local books and maps. Only a few minutes away, guests can discover hiking trails, fishing, swimming, and shopping. Children over 12 welcome. Open year-round.

The Inn at Stone Ridge (914-687-0736), Route 209, Stone Ridge 12484. ($$) For a romantic getaway, this gem should be at the top of your list. It's beautiful year-round but particularly so in spring, when the flowers around the stone swimming pool bloom. The former Hasbrouck House is an 18th-century stone mansion set on 40 acres and gardens. Listed on the National Register of Historic Places, the inn is open all year; a first-rate restaurant, Milliways, is found on its first floor (see *Dining Out*). There is a lovely gift shop, **Creations,** on the premises, which is open 2–9 PM daily.

Jingle Bell Farm (914-255-6588), 1 Forest Glen Road, New Paltz 12561. ($$) This 210-year-old stone house is furnished with fine country antiques and offers visitors more than 25 acres to explore. In summer take a dip in the landscaped pool. The farm, complete with sheep and horses, is a short drive from skiing, fishing, and shopping. An elegant retreat serving a full breakfast; four rooms. Children not permitted.

Locktender's Cottage (914-687-7700), Route 213, High Falls 12440. ($$$) The Locktender's Cottage is a romantic getaway situated alongside the

Delaware and Hudson Canal in the center of picturesque High Falls. The Victorian cottage once served as a lodging for the "canawlers," the sturdy men who manned the barges; today, it is owned by John Novi, chef and proprietor of the DePuy Canal House, right across the road (see *Dining Out*). The deluxe top-floor suite has a kitchenette, Jacuzzi bath, and air-conditioning; the bedrooms on the lower floor have air-conditioning and private baths. Four-star dinners are served at the Canal House, and the cottage is within minutes of many local activities. Open year-round.

Mohonk Mountain House (914-255-1000), Mohonk Lake, New Paltz 12561. ($$–$$$) This National Historic Landmark is a mountaintop Victorian castle that stands in the heart of 22,000 unspoiled acres. Dazzling views are everywhere, and serene Mohonk Lake adds to the dramatic setting. Although the hotel offers a museum, a stable, modern sports facilities, and many outdoor activities, the place is still very much the way it was more than a century ago (it is still managed by the same family). Midweek packages are available, and special-events weekends are held throughout the year (see *Historic Sites*). Activities are offered for children ages 2–13. Of the 293 rooms, 140 have working fireplaces and 200 have balconies; all but a few have private bathrooms, and those that don't are available at reduced rates. Rates include three meals a day. Men must wear jackets for the evening meal. Open year-round.

Mt. Tremper Inn (914-688-5329), Route 212 and Wittenberg Road, Mount Tremper 12457. ($$) A 23-room house, this inn was built in 1850 and has always served as a guest house. One of the largest bed & breakfasts in the Catskills, the inn has a Victorian parlor with bluestone fireplace, a game room, library, and porch. Hearty breakfasts feature homemade breads and other baked goods. One suite and one room with private baths; 10 rooms share five bathrooms (all rooms have sinks). Children not permitted. Open year-round.

Mountain Meadows Bed and Breakfast (914-255-6144), 542 Albany Post Road, New Paltz 12561. ($$) This lovely country home nestled in the foothills of the Catskills is a fine place for people who enjoy a casual atmosphere, lounging by the pool, relaxing by the fireplace, or playing a game of pool in the recreation room. The spacious landscaped grounds offer croquet, badminton, and horseshoes. All rooms have private bathrooms, central air-conditioning, and a king- or queen-sized bed. Located only 4.5 miles from NYS Thruway Exit 18. Open year-round.

Nana's (914-255-5678), 54 Old Forge Road, New Paltz 12561. ($$) Located on 20 acres of woodland and meadows, this charming country home is a perfect retreat for nature lovers. Deer, raccoons, foxes, and birds all pay visits, and guests will enjoy walking the grounds. The owner offers a full breakfast, and easy—optional—exercise sessions each morning. One room with private bath. Children are welcome. Open year-round.

Mohonk Mountain House parlor

The Nevele Hotel (914-647-6000 or 1-800-647-6000), Route 209, Ellen-
ville 12428. ($$$) This beautifully maintained, full-service resort has
been in business since 1901. The facilities are first-rate and include a
par-70 golf course, an Olympic-sized ice rink (open October through
April), an indoor and outdoor pool complex and fitness center, tennis
courts, and riding trails. During the winter months there are cross-coun-
try ski trails and downhill slopes with snowmaking. There are always
scheduled activities for children, and from late June through Labor Day
there is a day camp program for kids 3–10.

Nieuw County Lloft (914-255-6533), 41 Allhusen Road, New Paltz 12561.
($$) This cozy, 18th-century Dutch stone house has six fireplaces,
beamed ceilings, and wide-plank floors. Three bedrooms (one with fire-
place) are dressed up with period furniture and quilts, and the country
breakfast is a hearty way to begin a day. Locally produced wines are
offered in the evening. Walkers will enjoy the on-site nature trails; many
outdoor activities are located a few minutes' drive from the inn. Three
rooms share a bathroom. Children not permitted. Open daily July and
August; September through June weekends and holidays.

Onteora, The Mountain House (914-657-6233), Pine Point Road,
Boiceville 12412, has the most spectacular mountain views of any B&B
in the Catskills. Located 1 mile off Route 28, it was the estate of Richard
Hellman, the mayonnaise mogul. There are four bedrooms, all with ca-
thedral ceilings; only one has a private bath. Breakfasts are individually
made to order, with orders taken the evening before. Open year-round.

Pine Hill Arms (914-254-9811), Main Street, Pine Hill 12465. ($$) First opened in 1882, the Pine Hill Arms now caters to skiers. The cozy bar is where everyone meets after the lifts close and where hot spiced wine and great snacks are served. There is also an outstanding greenhouse dining room (see *Dining Out*). All 30 rooms have private baths. Children are welcome. Open year-round.

Rocking Horse Ranch (914-691-2927; 1-800-437-2624 outside New York State), 600 Route 44/55, Highland 12528. ($$$) This family-owned and -operated ranch resort has offered a variety of vacation packages for over 20 years. A stay includes two sumptuous meals, and horseback riding on acres of trails. During the summer months there are waterskiing and boating on the lake. The ranch has heated indoor and outdoor pools, saunas, a gym, a petting zoo, and daily organized activities for the kids. Open year-round.

Rondout Bed and Breakfast (914-331-2369), 88 West Chester Street, Kingston 12401. ($$) This late-19th-century house is located close to Kingston's restaurants, museums, and river landing, and guests will enjoy the personal attention as well as the location's convenience. Hearty breakfasts may include waffles and homemade maple syrup, and evening refreshments are served by the fireplace. Well-behaved children welcome. Four rooms; two with private bathrooms. Open year-round.

Rose Hill (914-687-0600), Rose Hill Road, Stone Ridge 12484. ($$$) Elaborate gourmet breakfasts are the special attraction at this 18th-century Colonial, which is furnished with antiques, wood stoves, and a fireplace. Guests can walk the surrounding acres, or hike, bike, and ski nearby. Open year-round.

Shandaken Inn (914-688-5100), Route 28, Shandaken 12480. ($$$) With only 12 rooms, this inn is a cozy mountain retreat. It is open weekends only, and the rate includes breakfast and an excellent French country dinner.

Twin Gables: A Guest House (914-679-9479; or 914-679-5638), 73 Tinker Street, Woodstock 12498. ($$) The architecture and furnishings of the 1930s create a relaxed, easy ambience at this guest house; its service and hospitality have earned it a reputation for comfort and affordability. There are nine guest rooms, and a living room and refrigerator are available to visitors. Twin Gables is only a short walk from restaurants, shopping, galleries, and entertainment. The New York bus line stops right in front, so it's a great spot for those traveling to Woodstock without a car. Some rooms are air-conditioned; both private and shared baths are available. Children are welcome at the owner's discretion. Open year-round.

Ujjala's Bed and Breakfast (914-255-6360), 2 Forest Glen Road, New Paltz 12561. ($$) Innkeeper Ujjala Schwartz has renovated this charming Victorian frame cottage surrounded by apple, pear, and quince trees on 3.5 acres. The house is bright and cheery, with skylights and lots of plants, and a full breakfast with homemade whole grain breads, fruit, and vegetarian specialties is included. Three rooms share one bath; one private room with fireplace and bath. Children are welcome. Open year-round.

Val D'Isere Inn (914-254-4646), Route 28, Big Indian 12410. ($$$) In addition to their restaurant of the same name (see *Dining Out*), Marguerite and Serge Bertrand operate this inn, which has lovely mountain views. Bus travelers can disembark just outside the inn's doors, so it is an excellent choice for people who want to get away but don't have a car. Fishing, hiking, and skiing are nearby. Continental breakfast is served, and the restaurant offers fine French country dinners. Six rooms share two bathrooms. Children are welcome. Open year-round.

Woodstock Country Inn (914-679-9380), Woodstock 12498; call for directions. ($$) This quiet, elegant inn is located in the countryside outside of Woodstock, yet it's near enough that a short drive will bring you to all the cultural action the village is famous for. The inn, which belongs to an artist, has been restored and filled with antiques and has charming nooks to relax or dream in. Private and shared baths are available. Special midseason rates. Open year-round.

Woodstock Inn on the Millstream (914-679-8211), 38 Tannery Brook Road, Woodstock 12498. ($$) This is almost a motel—efficiency units are available—but it has special charms most motels never dream of. Set right on the local brook, the inn gives you the option of enjoying breakfast waterside or in the sun room. There is a porch for rocking, and a short walk brings you to the village green. Children are welcome. Open year-round.

WHERE TO EAT

DINING OUT

Armadillo (914-339-1550), 97 Abeel Street, Kingston. ($) Open daily except Monday, for lunch and dinner. Tex-Mex Southwest cuisine from an enormous menu includes great ribs, fajitas, and chicken specialties. A nice touch: You can draw on the paper tablecloths.

Bear Cafe (914-679-5555), Route 212, Woodstock. ($$) Open daily except Tuesday for dinner at 5. This is a French American bistro that serves a range of entrées, from grilled chicken to steak sandwiches and pasta dishes. There is a nice view of the Sawkill Stream from the dining area.

Benson's (914-255-9783), Route 208 and Route 44/55, Gardiner. ($$) Open daily for dinner at 5. Blessed with a panoramic view of the Shawangunk Mountains, the building that houses this restaurant dates back to the early 1860s, when it was used by farmers for cattle auctions. Since 1974 it has been an elegant restaurant owned by the Benson family. It specializes in fine Continental cuisine. We strongly recommend the duck.

Blue Mountain Bistro (914-679-8519), Routes 212 and 375 at the Woodstock Golf Club, Woodstock. ($$) Open daily for lunch 11:30–3; dinner 5–9, Friday and Saturday 5–10. This cozy spot overlooking the golf course is a terrific place to stop for lunch after shopping in town. The Mediterranean cuisine includes imaginative lunch items like the pita bread with herbed chicken, mozzarella, sun-dried tomatoes, and mushrooms served with a green salad. Two of the popular dinner entrées are the salmon in parchment paper and the 7-hour leg of lamb with red wine, garlic, and fresh rosemary. Enjoy streamside dining on the deck during the summer and fireside dining in winter. The freshest local produce is used whenever possible, and the chef has his own salad and herb garden in the summer.

The Butterfly (914-339-2184), 33–35 Crown Street, Kingston. ($$) Open Monday through Saturday for lunch (11:30–2:30) and dinner (5–10). Located in the historic Stockade District, this fine establishment serves Continental and American cuisine, with such specials as poached salmon in champagne sauce and devastating Mississippi Mud Pie.

Cafe Tamayo (914-246-9371), 89 Partition Street, Saugerties. ($$) Open for dinner Wednesday through Sunday 5–10; Sunday brunch 11:30–3. A popular bistro, housed in a renovated 1864 landmark building, Cafe Tamayo serves home-style American and international cuisine and features such specialties as country pâté with spicy red cabbage, garlic, and green chili, braised duck legs with mole sauce; and cassoulet. Children are welcome.

Christy's (914-679-5300), 85 Mill Hill Road, Woodstock. ($$) Open Tuesday through Saturday 5–11. This restaurant is located in an authentic English gatehouse with a two-sided fireplace, beamed ceilings, and cozy taproom. Fine artwork by local talent often decorates the walls. House specialties include baked smoked chicken with honey and mustard glaze, and roast duck. The hearty portions and reasonable prices attract a dedicated following. Children can select from a special menu.

DePuy Canal House (914-687-7700 or 687-7777), Route 213, High Falls. ($$) Open Thursday through Sunday for dinner at 5; Sunday brunch 11:30–2. If you want a spectacular meal on a special occasion, then make certain you dine at this establishment, which is housed in an 18th-century stone house that was once a tavern (see *Lodging*). Try the rabbit pâté with pignola, and the chocolate date truffle in Sabra mole for dessert. Dinner is prix fixe. Three courses, $25; four courses, $33; seven courses, $46; plus a la carte menu every night except Saturday.

Emiliani Ristorante (914-246-6169), 147 Ulster Avenue, Saugerties. ($$) Open daily for dinner from 5. Some of the finest northern Italian cuisine you'll find anywhere is served in this informal yet elegant establishment. The pastas are made on the premises, and all dishes are made to order.

Jake & Pepper's (914-338-2600), 614 Broadway, Kingston. ($$) Open for lunch weekdays except Tuesday 11:30–4; open for dinner daily 5–10:30.

Located across the street from UPAC (the Ulster Performing Arts Center). An upscale, traditional steakhouse where they butcher and dry-age their own beef. There's a raw bar with oysters, clams, king crab legs, and fresh Maine lobsters. Elegant atmosphere with a 40-foot oak-and-mahogany bar.

Jake Moon Restaurant and Cafe (914-254-5953), Route 28, Big Indian. ($$) Open Thursday, Friday, and Monday from 4:30; Saturday and Sunday from noon; extended summer hours. An exceptionally scenic dining spot nestled in the mountains. The decor includes large banners showing the four phases of the moon rising over the Catskills. The menu features local ingredients and recipes from local cooks, such as the blue corn and garlic pancakes with smoked local trout. There is also Catskill Mountain foie gras with white port and spinach. The outside dining deck is enchanting in warm weather, with masses of flowers and striped awnings. In winter, light-decked trees can be seen.

Little Bear Chinese Restaurant (914-679-8899), Route 212, Woodstock. ($$) Open daily for lunch and dinner, noon–10:30. Sit along the Sawkill Stream and enjoy fine Chinese cuisine prepared by Chef Kuo from Hunan, China. There is a dim sum brunch Sunday, noon–4, and Tuesday night is sushi night.

Locust Tree Inn (914-255-7888), 215 Huguenot Street, New Paltz. ($$) Open Tuesday through Friday 11:30 AM–2:30 PM and 5:50–10 PM; Saturday 5:30–10 PM; Sunday 11 AM–2 PM and 3–8 PM. Located in an 18th-century stone house, this casual country restaurant has a fireplace in every dining room. The specialties are duck, coquilles Saint-Jacques, and fresh fish.

Marcel's (914-384-6700), Route 9W, West Park. ($$) Open daily for dinner 5–10. This is a romantic and cozy spot, with a fireplace, dimmed lights, and fine French food. Try the rack of lamb, pasta with seafood, and chicken Provençal. Not recommended for children.

Mariner's Harbor (914-691-6011), 46 River Road, Highland. ($$) Open daily March 1 to late November for dinner at 4. Enjoy a seafood dinner with a view of the Hudson. There are daily fish specials like farm-raised catfish, grilled tuna, stuffed flounder, and Long Island bluefish; exceptional shellfish dishes, such as lobster tails, scallops, and clams; and excellent homemade desserts. Outdoor seating in summer.

Milliways (914-687-0736), Route 209, Stone Ridge. ($$) Open Wednesday through Sunday for dinner from 5. Enjoy fine American regional cuisine in this stone house that dates back to the 18th century (see *Lodging*). The owner, Dan Hauspurg, travels America in search of the right foods to serve here. He changes the menu every two weeks to include items from the Pacific Rim, Mississippi Delta, and Hudson Valley. Entrées range from $12.95 to $21.95. Our favorite is the Chesapeake crabcakes.

Mountain Gate Restaurant (914-254-6000), McKinley Hollow Road,

New World Home Cooking, a first-rate restaurant with multinational cuisine

Oliverea; also 4 Deming Street, Woodstock. ($$) Open daily for dinner. A fine selection of Indian dishes is served here, including vegetarian dishes and traditional tandoori chicken.

New World Home Cooking (914-679-2600), 424 Zena Road, Woodstock. ($$) Open daily for dinner 5–11; Lunch, Monday through Friday 11:30–2:30. Located at the Woodstock Tennis Club. The house specialties are Jamaican jerk chicken, Thai mussel stew, and black sesame seared salmon. Eating here is like taking a tour of America's finest and funkiest restaurants. The emphasis is on peasant flavors, and the colorful, casual ambience reflects the many cultures represented on New World's menu.

Northern Spy Cafe (914-687-7298), Route 213, High Falls. ($$) Open daily except Tuesday; lunch 11:30–3, dinner 4:30–10, Sunday brunch 9–3. "International soul food" is the way the chef, a Culinary Institute graduate, describes the imaginative fare in his informal eatery. He takes pleasure in adding interesting touches to traditional favorites from around the world. One popular entrée is the Moroccan-style chicken with ginger and cilantro. Desserts include a Northern Spy pie named for the apples from the orchard in back of the restaurant. You can enjoy dinner at the bar or on the terrace in warm weather.

Pine Hill Arms (914-254-9811), Main Street, Pine Hill. ($$) Open daily for dinner 5–11; open for lunch Saturday and for brunch Sunday, noon–4; open daily noon–4 in July and August. The best steak fries in the region aren't the only reason to dine here—this old stagecoach stop also serves great grilled chicken, fish, and steaks in the greenhouse dining room. The spot is cozy, and the desserts are out of this world (sample the cream cheese brownie with chocolate sauce and ice cream or the chocolate mousse pie).

Portobello (914-338-3000), Corner of Fair and John Streets, Kingston. ($$). Open for lunch Monday through Friday 11–3; for dinner Monday through Saturday 5–10; closed Sunday. Portobello specializes in northern Italian cuisine. The freshly made pastas are first-rate, and so are the salads.

Reginato Ristorante (914-336-6968), Leggs Mill Road, Lake Katrine. ($$) Open for lunch Monday through Friday 11:30–2:30; dinner Monday through Saturday 5–10, Sunday 1–10. Enjoy homemade northern Italian specialties in a relaxed atmosphere.

Reservoir Inn (914-331-9806), Route 1 and Dike Road, West Hurley. ($$) Lunch Tuesday through Saturday 11:30–2; dinner Tuesday through Sunday 5–11. Consistently good family fare at reasonable prices is offered in a cozy atmosphere. Italian specialties include pizza and pasta as well as early-bird specials on weekdays before 6 PM.

Riccardella's Restaurant (914-688-7800), Main Street, Phoenicia. ($$) Open Wednesday through Saturday 4:30–10, Sunday 2–10. This Italian restaurant offers diners fine food in an informal atmosphere.

Schneller's (914-331-9800), 61 John Street, Kingston. ($) Open daily for lunch; dinner Thursday through Sunday at 6. Dine on authentic German cuisine in the historic uptown area of Kingston. The menu features schnitzel, goulash, sauerbraten, and fresh fish. Dessert specialties include excellent homemade strudels, tortes, and cheesecake. The upstairs dining room has a European flavor, and the outdoor garden café is a breezy stop on a summer's day. Enjoy the gourmet cheese, game, and meat market downstairs—a perfect place to plan a picnic. Children welcome.

Ship Lantern Inn (914-795-5400), Route 9W, Milton. ($$) Open for lunch Tuesday through Friday, noon–2; dinner Tuesday through Saturday 5–10, Sunday 1–8. This charming old restaurant has nautical decor and serves Continental cuisine. The food and service are consistently excellent. House specialties include fresh fish, mignonette of beef Bordelaise, and saltimbocca Romana. Children are welcome.

The Thymes (914-338-0434), 11 Main Street, Kingston. ($$) Open daily except Monday for lunch 11:30–3; dinner at 5. Modern American cuisine with a new twist. The menu features veal, fresh fish, and game, and an emphasis is placed on local ingredients. The setting is a charming uptown building, and the food is superb.

Val D'Isere (914-254-4646), Route 28, Big Indian. ($$) Open daily except Tuesday, at 5. Specialties at this casual French restaurant owned by a former chef to the French president have included excellent pâtés, baby rack of lamb, and chicken with maple sauce. For dessert, the chocolate mousse with hazelnuts is a treat. Children are welcome.

The Would Bar & Grill (914-691-2516), 120 North Road, Highland. ($$)
Open for lunch Monday through Friday 11:30–2; dinner daily 5–10. A
former gin mill once known as the Applewood Bar, this informal restau-
rant is becoming renowned for its high-quality creative cooking. There
is a mix of international and New American cuisine with several unique
touches. The Oriental chicken salad with roasted almonds and Chinese
noodles is popular for lunch. The dinner menu includes grilled lamb
chops on roasted walnut-mint pesto with Mediterranean vegetable
compote. The pastry chef bakes focaccia and pesto bread as well as
great desserts—try the flaky apple pie spiced with cinnamon or the rasp-
berry-chocolate brûlée.

EATING OUT

Bluestone Country Foods (914-679-5656), 54C Tinker Street, Wood-
stock. ($) Open daily 11–7. Tasty vegetarian dishes, fresh pasta, and
naturally sweetened desserts are the highlights here. Children welcome.

Bread Alone Bakery (914-657-3328), Route 28, Boiceville; also located
on Tinker Street, Woodstock. ($) Do not miss this bakery, renowned for
its fantastic bread—Norwegian farm, mixed grain, Swiss peasant, Finn-
ish sour rye, and others—all baked in a wood-fired oven. Stop in at their
pastry section, have a cup of tea or coffee, and satisfy your craving for
something sweet and rich.

Brio's (914-688-5370), Main Street, Phoenicia. ($) Open daily 7 AM–10 PM.
This luncheonette is a good place to stop for a basic sandwich or snack.
Kids love the spaghetti and meatballs.

Chez Joey (914-255-7313), 52 Main Street, New Paltz. ($) Open daily ex-
cept Monday, 11–10. This restaurant serves hearty Italian pizza, pasta,
deli specialties, excellent calzones. A giant hero, up to 10 feet long, is
sold by the foot. Good for kids.

Country Deli (914-687-7157), Route 209, Stone Ridge. ($) Open daily 7
AM–8 PM; Sunday until 5. The vegetarian fare here is first-rate, from the
brown rice burgers and tofu salad to the carrot apple raisin salad. The
chicken, macaroni, and potato salads are delicious as well. Save room
for the chocolate cupcakes with mocha buttercream icing.

Cynfres (914-336-5088), Lohmaier Lane, Lake Katrine. ($) This bakery
boasts some of the finest cakes in the region. They also serve lunch
weekdays 11:30–2:30.

Deising's Bakery & Coffee Shop (914-338-7503), 111 North Front
Street, Kingston. ($) Open daily at 7 for breakfast and lunch. The best
place for baked goods in the city of Kingston, Deising's has excellent
pastries, breads, and other baked goods (try their cream napoleons).
The coffee shop offers large, overstuffed sandwiches, fresh, rich
quiches, and hearty soups and salads, all made fresh daily.

The Egg's Nest (914-687-7255), Route 213, High Falls. ($) Open daily 11
AM–2 AM. Located in a former parsonage, this cozy restaurant with its
funky decor has homemade soups, great sandwiches, and a special
crispy-crusted praeseau. Children welcome.

La Florentina (914-339-2455), 604 Ulster Avenue, Kingston. ($) Excellent pizza and other baked specialties. A traditional wood-fired oven is used. Even the cheeses are homemade, and there are outstanding dishes such as pizza with veal and broccoli (the dough is yeast-free). Great Italian and Sicilian desserts include cannoli, ices, and layer cake. Children welcome.

Gateway Diner (914-339-2455), Washington Avenue, Kingston. ($) The standard diner fare is fresh and well prepared. Murals adorn the walls, and the diner, open 24 hours, is convenient to Exit 19 on the NYS Thruway.

Golden Duck Chinese Restaurant (914-331-3221), 11 Broadway, Kingston. ($) Located near the waterfront in the Rondout section of Kingston, this restaurant serves lunch and dinner daily 11:30–9:30. The luncheon special is a real bargain.

Gypsy Wolf Cantina (914-679-9563), Route 212, Woodstock. ($) Open daily for dinner from 5. This is an authentic Mexican cantina with colorful decor and a festive atmosphere. The chips and salsa are first-rate, and the Gypsy Wolf Platter includes a little of everything to put in your tortillas.

Jane's Homemade Ice Cream (914-338-8315), 305 Wall Street, Kingston. ($) Open Monday through Friday 9–6, Saturday 10–5; closed Sunday. Homemade ice cream is the specialty, along with cakes, cookies, and scones. Breakfast and lunch are served, and there is a variety of soups, salads, sandwiches, and vegetarian specialties.

Joyous Kitchen Café (914-331-2111), 307 Wall Street, Kingston. ($) Open Monday through Saturday 10–5. The menu features some of the best gourmet vegetarian fare anywhere, and the prices are exceedingly reasonable. This is a must stop—try the JK rollers, whole wheat flatbread rolled with meat or vegetarian fillings like artichoke and sun-dried tomatoes. The honey-mustard roast turkey with sweet horseradish dressing is excellent. Save room for fabulous desserts and coffee.

Kathmandu Café (914) 679-5417), 54C Tinker Street, Woodstock. Open daily except Tuesday, noon–7 PM until midnight Friday and Saturday. Authentic Tibetan cuisine served in a "gallery of sacred arts" or, in summer, on a streamside patio. Enjoy a hot cup of India chai and choose from a tempting selection of savory desserts.

Main Course (914-255-2600), 232 Main Street, New Paltz. ($) Open daily except Monday for lunch and dinner 11:30 AM–10 PM. Unusual spa cuisine and contemporary American dishes including grilled fish and homemade pasta are the offerings here. Casual and relaxing.

Maria's Bazar (914-679-5434), Tinker Street, Woodstock. ($) Open daily 8:30–7. Maria is well known for her home-cooked Italian specialties. Excellent salads, fresh pastas, homemade soups, and outstanding pastries are here; vegetarians will find many selections. Children are welcome.

Phoenicia Wok (914-688-2194), Main Street, Phoenicia. ($) Open daily noon–10. Tasty, basic Chinese cuisine at reasonable prices.

Plaza Diner (914-255-1030), New Paltz Plaza, New Paltz. ($) Serving patrons for over 20 years, the diner is open 24 hours daily. For breakfast, the French toast and pancakes can't be beat. The service is fast and the food reliable.

Pyramid Café (914-679-5295), 17 Tinker Street, Woodstock. Open daily 9 AM–6 PM. American favorites, as well as an Egyptian menu with excellent falafel and hummus. Breakfast served until 4 PM.

Raccoon Saloon (914-236-7872), Main Street, Marlboro. ($) Lunch served daily 11:30–2:30; dinner Tuesday through Sunday 5–9. Some of the best burgers in the region, along with excellent fries, chicken, soups, and salads. A casual stop for lunch or dinner.

Rasher's Café (914-679-5449), 13 Tinker Street, Woodstock. ($) Open Monday through Thursday 7–5; Friday through Sunday 7AM–9PM. This bistro-style breakfast and lunch spot is well known in Woodstock for its homemade soups, salads, sandwiches, and desserts. If you visit during the summer, make sure you try the incredibly refreshing strawberry mint lemonade.

Sweet Sue's (914-688-7852), Main Street, Phoenicia. ($) Open daily at 7 AM. This is a great breakfast and lunch place, with more than a dozen types of pancakes (including fruited oatmeal) and French toast (including walnut-crunch). Everything from muffins to soups and all desserts is homemade here. A casual, truly outstanding café. Nice for children.

Winchell's Pizza (914-657-3352), Reservoir Road and Route 28, Shokan. ($) Open daily 11:30–9:30. Unusually tempting pizzas with a thick crust and creamy homemade ice cream for dessert. Great salad bar.

ENTERTAINMENT

ARTS

Maverick Concerts (914-679-2007 or 679-6482), Maverick Road just off Route 375, Woodstock. Open July and August; call for concert schedules. Admission fee. Founded in 1916 by author Hervey White, the Maverick Concerts were to be a blend of the best that chamber music and the natural world had to offer. White wanted to encourage other "maverick" artists, and attracted some of the best string and wind players to the glass-and-wood concert hall. The small building seats only 400, but many people enjoy hearing the concerts from the surrounding hillside, a setting that was White's idea of perfection. The concerts are known as the oldest chamber series in the country, and they are still attracting the best chamber groups in the world, among them the Tokyo, Mendelssohn, and Manhattan String Quartets and the Dorian Wind Quintet.

River Arts Repertory at Byrdcliffe Theatre (914-679-2100). From Woodstock, take Rock City Road to Glasco Turnpike; go approximately 1 mile; Byrdcliffe Road is on the right. Performance schedules vary.

Admission fee. Built in the early 20th century in reaction to the artistically poor industrial revolution, this cluster of buildings has remained a refuge for visiting artists. The theater hosts a variety of performances each summer and is home to River Arts Repertory, which offers original and experimental plays with professional casts that include some big names. Some performances are held at the **Bearsville Theater,** 2 miles west of the town of Woodstock.

SELECTIVE SHOPPING

IN WOODSTOCK
The **Kleinert Arts Center and Crafts Shop** is housed in an 18th-century building in the middle of town. The center is a showcase for the visual and performing arts, with gallery shows and concerts presented throughout the year. Fine photography can be viewed at **The Catskill Center for Photography,** and changing exhibits appear at the **Cox Gallery** and **Paradox Gallery** on Mill Hill Road. There are shops for rare books (**Blue Mountain Books**), pens and fine paper (**Letters and Lace**), New Age publications (**Mirabai Books**), batik (**Laughing Bear Boutique**), and beads (**Beyond Beadery**). **The Rare Bear** stocks antique and new teddy bears, **Anatolia** has Turkish kilims, and **The Gilded Carriage** carries a wide selection of kitchenware, pottery from around the world, and children's toys. Stop in at **Bazar and Bluestone Country Foods** for a snack or the makings of a gourmet picnic. Don't miss any of the side streets either, where tiny shops are tucked away in corners.

ANTIQUES
Ever since the 17th century, people in Ulster have been accumulating things, which now turn up as valuable antiques. But even if you don't collect rare furniture, you can enjoy hunting down that special collectible vase or a colorful quilt. Auctions are listed in the local newspapers, and yard sales bloom each weekend like dandelions. There are many antiques shops throughout the county, but the following centers offer several dealers under one roof and give browsers a wide selection. And since no listing of a center's stock is ever comprehensive, visitors will never know what treasures they may find.

The Country Store Antique Center (914-255-1123), Route 44/55, Gardiner, has furniture and country collectibles.

Towpath House Antiques (914-687-0615), High Falls, is on the towpath of the old Delaware and Hudson Canal. Open year-round.

Catskill Mountain Antique Center (914-331-0880), Route 28, Kingston, has all types of furniture, collectibles, and textiles. Open year-round.

Saugerties Antiques Center and Annex (914-246-3227) is located in the downtown Partition Street antiques district. Open daily year-round.

Skillypot Antique Company (914-338-6779), 41 Broadway, Kingston, is a co-op of 25 dealers who offer lamps, furniture, glassware, and collectibles. Open year-round.

Kingston is also the base for **Festival Promotions** (914-331-8852 or 338-7113), which sponsors several excellent large antiques shows at the Kingston Armory; call for schedules.

Winchell's Corners Antiques (914-657-2177), Route 28, Shokan, has everything from postcards to jewelry. Open year-round.

BOOKSTORES

The Bookmart (914-679-4646), 40 Mill Hill Road, Woodstock. This well-stocked, full-line bookstore has a great selection of fiction, nonfiction, regional books, and tapes. It is across the street from The Joyous Lake nightclub.

Esoterica (914-255-5777), 81 Main Street, New Paltz, is a first-rate New Age book- and gift shop.

Ariel Booksellers (914-255-8041), 3 Plattekill Avenue, New Paltz, is a 20-year-old full-line bookstore specializing in local books, carefully chosen remainders, and books for SUNY classes.

The Painted Word (914-256-0825), 36 Main Street, New Paltz. New and used books with an emphasis on works of interest to gays and lesbians. Café.

Barner Books (914-255-2636), 69 Main Street, New Paltz, has a large selection of used books and of first editions.

SPECIAL EVENTS

Music and the Mountain Sky Summer Music Festival (914-254-5600), Belleayre Ski Center, Route 28, Highmount. Call for ticket information. Tickets are now required for all concerts. This new music festival has been attracting outstanding performers to its mountain setting. The likes of the Brooklyn Philharmonic, Pete Seeger, Ruth Laredo, the West Point Military Band, and Glimmerglass Opera alumnae have entertained thousands, and the festival keeps growing. There are seats under a tent and lawn for the weather-wary, and the evening concerts offer a cooling summer's night of entertainment.

Belleayre Mountain Fall Festival and Concerts (914-254-5600). Highmount is just off Route 28, about 40 miles west of Kingston; watch for signs to the upper lodge. Open 10–5. Free (there is a charge for the ski lift). Held Saturday and Sunday of Columbus Day weekend, this festival attracts thousands of leaf-peeping visitors. The fun goes on all day and includes bands, crafts, entertainment, German food and beer, chicken barbecues, and ski equipment sales. The festival is well run, and the site has magnificent views of the mountains. Wear appropriate clothing and get there early; it is held rain or shine.

Woodstock/New Paltz Art and Crafts Fair (914-679-8087), Ulster County Fairgrounds, off Libertyville Road; follow Route 299 to turn-off and signs. Shows are held Memorial Day and Labor Day weekends, Saturday through Monday 10–5. Admission fee. This huge arts fair offers more than just booths of crafts; some of the region's finest artists are on hand each year to exhibit their works. Working craftspeople demonstrate their skills, which have included quilting, scrimshaw, weaving, etching, and broom making. There is even a children's center with things to do and exhibits of young artists' works. Furniture and architectural crafts, craft supplies, entertainment, food, and health care products are all on display and or sale, and there are plenty of snack stands. There are tents on site, but dress appropriately for the weather—it can get very hot, both inside and out.

Amazing Threads (914-336-5322), 2010 Ulster Avenue, Lake Katrine. This shop sponsors workshops in the vanishing needle and fiber arts, year round. It is also a must-see for lovers of wool and fiber. Call for special class schedules.

Mum Festival (914-246-2809), Seamon Park, Route 9W, south of Saugerties. Open dawn to dusk. Park is free; admission fee to festivals. For the entire month of October, Seamon Park is one big chrysanthemum celebration. Thousands of mums bloom throughout this 17-acre park, and the display of yellow, lavender, and rust flowers in shaped beds is breathtaking. Weekend festivals offer music, entertainment, and food, and there is a parade on opening day.

Hudson Valley Garlic Festival (914-246-6982), Cantine Field, Saugerties, late September. Free. Visitors won't have to use a map to find this festival; the nutty fragrance of garlic attracts tens of thousands to the one-day affair, where garlic-flavored foods, from pizza to ice cream, await the connoisseur. Crafts vendors and entertainment enliven the day, and there are lots of garlic vendors and culinary information on hand as well. An unusual and really fun day, regardless of how much garlic means to you.

Michael's Candy Corner (914-338-6782), Pine Grove Avenue, Kingston, open year-round, is one of the few shops that manufacture candy canes. Tours are limited to the holiday season when groups are welcome, but you can stop in anytime and purchase an unusual hand-made confection.

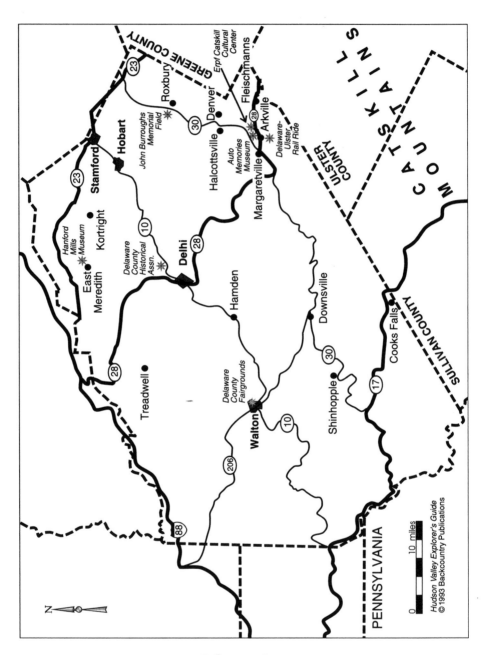

Delaware County

Delaware County

One of the largest counties in New York (about the size of Rhode Island), Delaware County is a region of rolling meadows, curious cows, and tiny towns that look as if they were plucked from a 19th-century picture book. More than 64,000 acres are state-owned and have been proclaimed "forever wild." This foresight has resulted in an area that is a paradise for anglers, hunters, hikers, bikers, and walkers, and those who just enjoy rural charm and an old-fashioned way of life coupled with modern convenience and an easy drive.

Much of the charm of Delaware County comes from the strong influence of the 19th century, which turns up in local architecture and community get-togethers. Towns throughout the county are filled with homes and commercial buildings of Federal, Queen Anne, Gothic Revival, and other styles; drive along the back roads and you'll find dairy farms and mountain views nearly unchanged for a century and more. From the winter pancake breakfasts to the holiday open houses, from county fairs to summer auctions, the region brings back a sense of community celebration that has been lost in much of modern life.

GUIDANCE
Delaware County Chamber of Commerce (1-800-642-4443 or 607-746-2281), 97 Main Street, Delhi 13753.

GETTING THERE
Delaware County is most easily reached by taking the NYS Thruway, Exit 19 at Kingston, to Route 28 West (Pine Hill sign), and following Route 28 into the county. Route 30 intersects with Route 28 in Margaretville.

MEDICAL EMERGENCY
Margaretville Memorial Hospital (914-586-2631), Route 28, Margaretville.

TO SEE

Delaware County Historical Association (607-746-3849), Route 10, two miles north of Delhi. Open May through October; hours vary. Admission fee. A fascinating site composed of historic buildings that have been donated, purchased, or just rescued from neglect, where visitors can get a taste of life in rural America during the 19th century. The main building houses a library and exhibit hall, where changing displays of farm tools, household goods, folk art, and crafts are offered each season. There are additional interpretive exhibits that focus on different aspects of farm life in several of the other buildings. The Gideon Frisbee House, a 1797 example of Federal-style architecture, once served as a tavern, county meeting room, post office, and private home. The interior has been restored to reflect the changes in life from pioneer days to the period just before World War I. Decorative arts and furniture collections include Belter chairs, woven rugs, souvenir glassware, and a chair that tradition held was used at the Constitutional Convention. The Frisbee barn houses a collection of farm implements and a permanent exhibit entitled "It's a Fine Growing Time," which guides the visitor through the joys and hard work of a farmer's year. Other buildings include the gunsmith's shop, the schoolhouse (still in use for educational programs), a tollhouse (where there is a gift shop), a farm lane, and even a small family cemetery. Special events include a house tour, Victorian fashion show, Tavern Day, and a farm festival.

Hanford Mills Museum (607-278-5744). Follow Route 28 to the intersection of Routes 10 and 12 in East Meredith; follow the signs. Open May through October, with some special events off-season; hours vary. Admission fee. Once the industrial center of the surrounding farm country, today the mill has been restored to its clanking and chugging past. Flour, lumber, wooden goods like butter tubs and porch posts, and electricity (courtesy of nearby Kortright Creek) were all produced at Hanford Mills, one of the few remaining industrial mills of the last century that are still in use. Visitors will see lathes, jigsaws, and other machines used to produce woodenware, along with the pulleys and belts that were once the staples of manufacturing. Inside the mill itself, a series of catwalks and walkways winds through the workrooms, where museum interpreters are still hard at work; downstairs the enormous metal reconstruction of the original wooden waterwheel is turned by the millpond waters. Throughout the site, water-generated electricity powers lightbulbs and other machines, a reminder of the time when light didn't come with the simple flick of a switch. Also on the site is the Gray Barn, in which there are agricultural and farm equipment displays, a shingle mill, the millpond, and the mill store, where local crafts are sold. Hanford Mills hosts several special events each year, including a children's fair, fly-fishing clinics at the millpond, Independence Day complete with ice cream and speeches, Draft Horse Day, and Ice Harvest Day (when the ice is stored for the summer ice cream social).

HISTORIC SITES

Delaware and Ulster Railride (914-586-DURR), Route 28, Arkville. Open late May through October; schedules vary. Entrance to the site and depot is free, but admission is charged for the ride. The Catskill

Mountains were once a daily stop for tourist and milk trains from New York City, but when the service stopped in the 1960s, many believed the toot of a train whistle was gone forever from the valleys. The Railride has resurrected some of the favorite trains that rattled along the tracks, and there is no better way to sample the fun of old-time travel than to hop aboard any of the vintage cars. Try the Doodlebug, also known as the Red Heifer, one of the few self-propelled trains still at work. Or take some photos of the farms and homes, wave at the cows, and enjoy the open-air observation car. The conductor may tell a tale or two about train history, and special events, held throughout the summer, include a costumed train robbery complete with horses, a Teddy Bear Train, a Fiddler's Picnic, Rail Fan Appreciation Day, and more. All the tours begin at the restored Arkville Depot, and there is a gift shop, snack caboose, rest rooms, and wheelchair access on site.

John Burroughs Memorial Field. Take Route 30 north through Roxbury and follow signs. Open year-round, weather permitting. Free. Although this is not an "active" site, the former writing studio and grave of nature writer John Burroughs is worth the stop. A friend of Teddy Roosevelt, Henry Ford, and Thomas Edison, Burroughs is a respected American nature writer, whose many essays spoke of Delaware County, the Catskills, and the Hudson Valley. Today his writing nook, Woodchuck Lodge, is maintained at Memorial Field. The area also contains Boyhood Rock (where Burroughs spent many hours observing the natural world) and the Burroughs grave site. This is a quiet spot, with a breathtaking view of the Catskills, a lovely place to sit and enjoy the same scene that inspired a great author.

FOR FAMILIES

Church Street Station (914-586-2425), Church Street, Arkville (watch for signs from Route 28). Open daily, late May through September, depending on the weather. Admission fee. A delightful mini–amusement park, this site offers kids of all ages a batting area and a miniature golf course full of items of local interest, including a covered bridge, a railroad station, and a giant pig! A nice stop on a hot summer's evening.

SCENIC DRIVES

Delaware County offers the driver many lovely views and well-maintained main roads, but as in any other rural area, some of the back roads can be tricky in bad weather. Dirt roads are charming, but all but the toughest truck can become bogged down in mud or snow along them. Deer and other wildlife are also a problem, especially at night, so be aware and don't rush. Unless you know exactly where you are going, you may want to stay on the paved roads.

If you want to see dairy farms, cornfields, the county seat, and the Pepacton Reservoir, start in Margaretville and follow Route 28 to Delhi (the town square made the cover of the *Saturday Evening Post*). Then take Route 10 south to Walton, Route 206 east to Downsville, and Route

30 back to Margaretville. The roads are well marked, and you will pass two covered bridges along the way, one near Hamden, the other outside of Downsville. (They are thought to have been built in order to make it easier for horses to cross over the streams.) This drive also takes you past farm stands (some let you choose your produce and put your money in a box), including Octagon Farms near Walton, where an eight-sided house has been made into a bed & breakfast (see *Lodging*). Legend says that the ghost of a young woman killed in a carriage accident roams the road at night. If you have the time, you can detour through Delhi and follow the signs west to Franklin on the Franklin Turnpike, a winding road that offers beautiful vistas in summer.

A second county drive follows part of the old turnpike, which was a major stagecoach route through the area. From Margaretville, follow Route 28 east to Andes and then to Delhi, then take Route 10 north to Stamford, make a right onto Route 23 and drive to Grand Gorge, and, finally, turn right onto Route 30 and head south back to Margaretville. If you have a chance, stop in Stamford and look at some of the grand homes that made this village a popular turn-of-the-century resort area and gave it the name Queen of the Catskills.

If you wish to drive up Mount Utsayantha, follow Route 23 east to Mountain Avenue; the twisty road is accessible in spring, summer, and fall, and the views are beautiful. Call the Department of Environmental Conservation (607-652-7364) for more information about this drive or hike. The headwaters of the Delaware River East Branch rise alongside Route 30 between Grand Gorge and Roxbury, and the road back to Margaretville passes through farm country.

TO DO

AUCTIONS

If it seems that everything is auctioned off in Delaware County, don't be surprised—it is. Cows, puppies, cabbages, eggs, Shaker chairs, Irish pewter, even antique coffins have all shown up in the hands of auctioneers. Auction lovers don't need to plan ahead; just pick up a copy of the local newspaper and look for a sale. Some auctions are weekly institutions, attended by locals and weekenders alike; other auctions are specialty sales for real estate or farm equipment; still others are one-time-only house sales, where the contents of a home can include some surprises.

Country auctions are fun, but there are some tips. Get there early: You have to examine the goods before the sale and sign up for a card or paddle. Bring a chair for outdoor auctions, a hat or umbrella depending on the weather. Most auctions advertise that they accept "cash or good checks"; in the latter case, this can be tricky if you are from out of state or not known to the auctioneer; call ahead for information. Don't buy anything you can't carry, unless you plan to make shipping arrangements. And finally, know what you are bidding on: Don't buy the overstuffed armchair because you thought you were getting the Tiffany lamp.

Every Saturday night at 7, year-round, **Roberts' Auction** (914-254-4490), Main Street, Fleischmanns (park in the lot or along the street), sells everything from fine antiques to a better grade of junk. Auctioneer Eddie Roberts keeps the sale moving, and you'll never be bored. The crowd is a good, often lively mix of local people and visitors; there are rest rooms and a snack bar. Get there early, since some seats are reserved and the others go fast.

McIntosh Auction Service (607-832-4829), Old Creamery, Route 28 north to Route 6, Bovina (watch for signs for Bovina Center), has Saturday auctions at 6:30 PM year-round. There is plenty of parking here, both behind the barn and in the field, not far from the cows, and the Creamery is heated in winter and has a rest room and snack bar. Seats go fast, and auctioneers Chuck McIntosh and Bob Burgin keep everyone happy with quick sales and good humor. Everything from furniture to blackberries to fine antiques is sold here, and the setting is country at its best. They also do many on-site auctions throughout the summer.

Although **Lettis Auction Service** (607-432-3935) is based in Otsego County, Jim Lettis does well-organized, fast-moving house auctions throughout Delaware County.

Robinson Brothers Auction Barn (607-865-5253), Route 10, Hamden, holds auctions filled with country finds, antiques, and just plain stuff on Thursday nights at 7.

CANOEING

The best canoeing in Delaware County is along the western border near Pennsylvania, but canoeing, like all other water sports, should not be attempted unless you are familiar with the rivers. Both the Delaware and Susquehanna can be treacherous, especially in spring or after a heavy rain. Your best bet is to use one of the canoe outfitters, who will provide you with the right equipment, maps, and even a shuttle service.

Al's Sport Store (607-363-7135), Shinhopple, is a clearinghouse for canoe and fishing information.

Also in Shinhopple is **Peaceful Valley Campsite** (607-363-2211), which offers limited outfitting services.

DeNys Canoe Sales (607-467-2303), Deposit, also rents canoes for day trips.

FARM STANDS

When the harvest begins in early summer with strawberries and flowers, the farm stands begin to blossom along the roadsides as well. In Delaware County there are many farm stands where you can pick out the produce, bag it, and leave the money for the owner. Other stands are a bit more formal, but they all stock the best of local fruits, vegetables, maple syrup, and honey. Days and hours of operation vary widely with the season and the stock, and some crops, including strawberries, seem to disappear after only a few days, so the best way to find local produce is to watch for roadside stands or stop and ask at the nearest town.

The first **farmers market** in Delaware County is held every Saturday from the week before Memorial Day to Columbus Day, starting at 9 AM. (The location may change from year to year; call 914-586-4655 for information.) Free admission. Vendors offer everything from fresh trout and field-raised exotic mushrooms to fine crafts like jewelry and pottery. You'll also find the freshest corn, baked goods, flowers, and other produce. Selections change with the seasons, and there is plenty of food on hand to sample for breakfast and lunch.

Mac's Farm Stand is located on Route 28 near Delhi, just before the turn into the town. The stand stocks a wide variety of produce throughout the summer and into apple season.

Octagon Farm Market, Route 10, Hamden, sells its own fruits and vegetables, along with lots of other local offerings, and has a large selection of apples and excellent cider in the fall.

Hamden German Butcher (607-746-MEAT), just down the road, is a rare find for the person who loves homemade sausages and smoked meats. You'll find one of the finest selections of local farm-raised meat and poultry in Upstate New York.

If you drive farther into Delaware County, you might want to stop at **Johnsons Farm Market** (607-563-1061), on West Main Street in Sidney, and the **Meadowbrook Farm** (607-829-6000), on Main Street in Franklin.

Honey lovers may want to check out **Herklotz Apiaries** (607-829-8687), Merrickville Road, Franklin (open year-round), for their selection of sweets, candles, and other honey-related items. **Crescent Valley Apiaries,** New Kingston Road, Bovina (watch for signs), also stocks honey from its hives, as does **Ballard Honey,** Main Street, Roxbury.

Because the tree-tapping season is so changeable, maple syrup lovers should call the **Delaware County Chamber of Commerce** (607-746-2281) for up-to-date information on farms that offer saphouse tours.

FISHING

Delaware County is crisscrossed by the East and West Branches of the Delaware River, and the Susquehanna and Beaverkill Rivers, and served by the Cannonsville, Pepacton, and Schoharie Reservoirs, making fishing a popular sport in this region. New York State fishing licenses are required, although they are easy to purchase in most towns; check with the town clerk or at the village offices. For reservoir fishing, special permits are required—call the **Environmental Protection Agency** offices at 607-363-7501 for information on permits and maps. Stream fishing areas open to the public are indicated by brown-and-yellow wooden signs along the streams and rivers; most areas offer off-road

parking as well. Detailed maps are available where you purchase your fishing license or at town offices; riverfront property may be posted or off-limits as part of the New York City water supply, so the maps should be consulted. Further information on specific fishing areas can be obtained by calling 1-800-642-4443 (outside New York State); or 1-800-356-5615 (in New York State).

GOLF

Golf enthusiasts will appreciate the courses in the Delaware County area, where the lush greens of summer and the blazing trees of autumn provide everyone, duffer and hacker alike, a lovely setting in which to play. Greens fees vary depending on the season and the length of the membership, so call for specific information.

Hanah Country Inn and Golf Resort (914-586-2100), Route 30,

Margaretville, has an 18-hole course, practice greens, and a driving range. There is also a golf school on the premises.

Shepherd Hills Golf Course (607-326-7121), Golf Course Road, Roxbury, has a hilly 18-hole course with beautiful views of the countryside.

State University of New York (607-746-4281), off Route 28 near Delhi (follow signs), has a course that is used as a training area for students in the turf management program. It's a small gem and rarely overcrowded.

Stamford Golf Club (607-652-7398). Take Route 10 to Taylor Road in Stamford. Complete facilities, 18 holes, and a driving range.

Those who just want to practice their techniques should head to the **Meadows Driving Range** (914-586-4104), Route 28, Margaretville. A golf school is held on the site throughout the summer as well.

HIKING AND BIKING

A large part of Delaware County is part of the "forever wild" park system in New York State, and as such has not been developed with easy-to-use trails or tourist-related sites. Many of the existing hiking trails are for experienced hikers only, and some require overnight stays in simple trail huts; those who would like detailed, safe trail information should contact the New York Department of Conservation at Bear Spring Mountain (607-865-6161). Marked bike trails are also scarce in Delaware County, although many of the roads listed under *Scenic Drives* can be navigated safely by bicycle. In fact, just about any road should lead to lovely vistas and scenic overlooks, but bike rentals are hard to come by.

LODGING

Bed & breakfasts provide a special way to see Delaware County, and most are moderately priced and offer package rates as well. Call before you go, since many are booked for holiday weekends and special events. For information call 1-800-DEL-INNS.

Aching Acres (607-865-8569), Freer Hollow Road, Box 201R, Walton 13856. ($$) A lovely country home where guests can enjoy the farm country, which seems so far from city life. Named for the work involved in clearing the land, Aching Acres has beautiful gardens and vistas of mountains and valleys and is a short drive from many local attractions, including museums, swimming holes, and antiques centers. Two guest rooms share a bath. Children are welcome; no smoking allowed.

Bella Vista Ridge (607-746-2553), Route 10, Hamden 13782. ($) An Italianate home set above the surrounding farmland looking across to the mountains. Guests can visit their gift shop or walk into town. Nearby are fishing, hiking, swimming, and places of historic interest. Six rooms share three bathrooms. Full breakfast. Open year-round.

Carriage House (607-326-7992), Main Street, Halcottsville 12438. ($) This 100-year-old Victorian house still has many of its original furnishings; it is run by the builder's granddaughter, whose homemade breakfast breads and muffins are local favorites. Sherry and herbal tea are offered to guests in the afternoon. The house is set in a tiny hamlet that lies along the Delaware River, and there are many places to stroll the country lanes. Four rooms share two bathrooms. Children welcome. Open year-round.

Churchside (607-832-4231), Main Street, Bovina Center 13740. ($) This Greek Revival farmhouse has been owned by the same family since the mid 19th century. Antiques fill the rooms, and a full breakfast greets guests each morning. The house is located in a charming village that was once a dairy center; a popular Saturday night auction is just up the block at the Old Creamery (see *To Do—Auctions*). Two rooms and two bathrooms. No smoking or pets allowed. Open year-round, by reservation only.

Creekside Acres (607-746-3309), Elk Creek Road, RD #2, Box 241, Delhi 13753. ($$) Children will enjoy the Belgian draft horses and other farm animals, and fishing enthusiasts will discover a trout stream right on the premises of this working farm. There are more than 270 acres to cross-country ski, hike, and explore. A hearty country breakfast starts out the day for guests. Three rooms and two bathrooms. Open year-round.

Hanah Country Inn (914-586-2100), Route 30, Margaretville 12455. ($$$) A full-service resort, the inn has a championship 18-hole golf course (see *To Do—Golf*), health club, tennis courts, swimming pool, fishing stream, and restaurant. Golfers should note that there is a nationally recognized school held at the inn every summer. All rooms have private baths. Children welcome. Open year-round.

Heritage House (607-326-4781), Bridge Street, Roxbury 12474. ($$) A beautifully restored Victorian home, complete with antiques and a flower-filled porch for lazing away summer days. Visitors can stroll the charming village paths and parks and will find dozens of seasonal activities, like skiing, fishing, and antiquing only minutes away. Open year-round.

Highland Fling Inn (914-254-5650), Main Street, Fleischmanns 12430. ($) The owners are Scottish and German, and their charming inn consists of two Victorian homes and six summer cottages. The full breakfast features European specialties. Tennis courts and a pool are within walking distance. Three rooms share one bath; nine have private bathrooms. Children welcome. Open year-round.

Lake Wawaka Guest House (607-326-4694), Old River Road, Halcottsville 12438. ($$) Located on the meandering East Branch of the Delaware River, this quiet, spacious farmhouse is close to a wide variety of recreational activities. Full breakfast is served. Six rooms share two full bathrooms. No children under 10 allowed. Open year-round.

Margaretville Mountain Inn (914-586-3933), Mountain Road, Margaretville 12455. ($$) This restored 11-bedroom Victorian home was built as a boardinghouse and functioned as a working farm. It offers a spectacular view of the New Kingston Valley from the old-fashioned veranda. It's just a short drive from town. A full breakfast is served in an elegant dining room, outdoors in the summer. Five rooms, three with private bathrooms. There are limited facilities available for children and pets; call ahead for information. Nonsmoking environment. Open year-round.

Octagon Bed and Breakfast (607-865-7416), Route 10, Walton, 13856. ($) This bed & breakfast is in a historic octagonal house built in 1855; it is also opposite the farm stand run by the owners. The farmer's breakfast served here is hearty and may include pancakes and sausage or eggs and waffles. Four rooms share 1½ baths. Children welcome. Open year-round.

Open Studios Bed & Breakfast (914-676-3538), Gladstone Hollow Road, Andes 13731. ($$) Artists who are looking to get away from it all will appreciate this charming inn. The owners are artists as well and offer guests lovely rooms in an 1816 farmhouse, along with the use of a separate studio at no extra charge. Gourmet breakfasts are included in the price and are served on the veranda in summer. The setting is really lovely, and it is a short drive to the country town of Andes. Private bathrooms available. Open year-round.

River Run (914-254-4884), Main Street, Fleischmanns 12480. ($$) This restored 20-room house has seven guest rooms with either private or shared baths. The yard slopes down to the river, and guests can walk into town (there's a great country auction only minutes away every Saturday night). The unusual aspect of this inn is that they welcome both children *and* pets (just give them some notice about the four-footed family members). Breakfast is hearty and healthy, and the inn has lots of antiques, stained glass, and old-fashioned comfort to offer visitors.

Roundup Ranch (607-363-7300), Wilson Hollow Road, Downsville 13755. ($$$) A stay at this 2000-acre ranch is a great way for a family to enjoy a vacation. A wide range of activities is available, including horseback riding, golf, fishing, tennis, and swimming, as well as hay rides, square dancing, and rodeos. Three meals served daily. Forty rooms; seven share bathrooms. Open year-round.

Silver Maples (607-746-3516), DeLancey 13752; call for directions. ($$) A pretty location any time of year, but you may want to schedule a visit in very early spring, when the farm is busy with maple syrup production. Of course, breakfast features the local sweetener, and guests can take country walks, fish, swim, or shop nearby. Private baths available. Open year-round.

WHERE TO EAT

DINING OUT

The Hidden Inn (607-583-9259), Main Street, South Kortright. ($$) Open daily for dinner, Monday through Saturday 5–9; Sunday, noon–7. French and Continental cuisines are combined here, and a wide variety of fine entrées including veal, lamb, seafood, and beef is offered. The house specialty is prime rib, but the boneless duck with Grand Marnier glaze is also quite popular with diners. Enjoy the atmosphere of a French country inn in this charming establishment.

The Old Schoolhouse Inn (607-363-7814), Upper Main Street, Downsville. ($$) Open daily except Monday, for lunch 11:30–2:30, for dinner 5–9. Brunch is served Sunday 11:30–2:30. This restaurant is housed in a renovated schoolhouse that dates back to 1903. In a Victorian-style dining room, hearty portions of standard American favorites are the mainstay. The French lobster, prime rib, and seafood medley are the most popular entrées, and the homemade desserts are first-rate. Thanks to a local taxidermist, a grizzly bear, buffalo, and bison decorate the bar!

EATING OUT

Casual is the word for Delaware County restaurants, where moderate prices are the rule at dinner. Hours and days of operation vary with the seasons, so it is smart to call ahead before you go. In general, reservations are not needed, except for holiday weekends.

Binnekill Square (914-586-4884), Binnekill Square, Main Street, Margaretville. ($$) Open daily at 11:30 for lunch and dinner; Sunday brunch at noon. A casual, relaxing restaurant, Binnekill Square has windows and a dining deck overlooking a small stream. The food has a Swiss touch, and the veal dishes are particularly good. Venison is served in season, and there are excellent daily specials. Everything is cooked to order. Children are welcome.

Buswell's Restaurant & Sweet Shop (914-586-3009), Granary Lane, off Bridge Street, Margaretville. ($) This is a real local place, in the best sense of the word. Open daily for breakfast, lunch, and early dinners, there are excellent specialties like fruit pancakes and home-baked goods on hand for the sweets lover. Kids are always welcome, and the informal atmosphere is homey and relaxed.

Café Etcetera (914-586-2555), Main Street, Margaretville. ($) A nice selection of baked goods from local kitchens and a variety of light lunches and snacks make this a restful stop after shopping.

The Cheese Barrel (914-586-4666), Main Street, Margaretville. ($) Open daily 9–5. An excellent selection of snacks and cheese is found in this tiny shop, and the dishes are great for takeout and picnics. The homemade soups are satisfying, and there is a dining area.

ENTERTAINMENT

ARTS

Roxbury Arts Group (RAG) (607-326-7908), just off Vega Mountain Road, Roxbury. Event schedules vary; call for hours and admission fees. While not a historic or recreational site, RAG is an active sponsor of special events throughout the year in its own community center and arts building. RAG's two-day outdoor art show in July, held along charming tree-shaded Main Street in Roxbury, offers the best works from artists across the Catskills; the Country Fair, held in a small riverside park on Labor Day weekend, offers folk music, dancing, and food from dozens of vendors. Throughout the summer, RAG also hosts performances by children's theater groups, string quartets, folksingers, concert soloists, dancers, and artists. Art and theater workshops are held at their home site in Roxbury, and special events (including square dances and gallery shows) are also hosted by RAG.

West Kortright Centre (607-278-5454, or write Box 100, East Meredith 13757). Take Route 28 to East Meredith, then follow signs to the center, which is in West Kortright; or follow signs from Route 10, two miles north of Delhi near Elk Creek Road. Open July through September; performance schedules vary. Admission fee. Nestled in a hidden valley, the West Kortright Centre is housed in a charming white clapboard 1850s church that was rescued from neglect by dedicated volunteers. Stained-glass windows and kerosene chandeliers glow in the twilight. The center offers unique performances throughout the summer, with concerts and special events for every taste, from bluegrass to zydeco, performance art to dance. Concerts are held both outdoors, in the green fields, and inside, where guests are seated in unique rounded pews; the lawn is often dotted with preconcert picnickers. The intimate setting makes all events a delight, and you may just bump into the evening's featured performer as he or she warms up in the churchyard.

SELECTIVE SHOPPING

Delaware County has several unique crafts and specialty shops, although you can find good shopping in just about every village. Arkville is home to a lively flea market on Route 28 every Saturday and Sunday from spring through autumn, weather permitting. It begins at 9 AM. **Rocko!** (914-586-3978) at the Crossroads Building on Route 28 has a wide selection of fine jewelry, minerals, and geologic collectibles (including a dinosaur egg!). And parents will adore **G. W!ll!kers** (914-586-1976) off Route 28 (watch for signs). Open Monday through Saturday 10–5, this is a factory outlet store featuring colorful, durable children's clothing.

Bear Hugs & Busy Hands (914-676-3266), Route 28, Andes, stocks collectible teddy bears, limited-edition figurines, and other fine gift and toy items. Down the block, **Paisley's Country Gallery** (914-676-3533) has an amazing collection of baskets from all over the world. Blown glass is created at **Sweetwater Glass Studios and Gallery** (914-676-4622), Fall Clove Road, Andes, with ornaments, goblets, and glasses the specialties.

Delside Acres Studios (607-746-3285), Back River Road, Dehli, displays the paintings, carvings, and prints of award-winning wildlife artist Ward E. Herrmann. **Parker House Gifts** (607-746-3141), Main Street, is a cornucopia of fine jewelry, gifts, and tableware.

Purple Mountain Press (914-254-4062), Main Street, Fleischmanns, publishes and stocks a large number of books about the Catskills and New York regional history, though they are not open to the public; call for their catalog. For an unusual gift, try **Carl Pickhardt, Boatbuilder** (607-326-4071 or 914-586-3101), where the old art of handcrafting quality wooden canoes, boats, and sailboats lives on. Call for directions to the Halcottsville shop.

On Main Street in Margaretville, **Discoveries** (914-586-3990) carries an eclectic selection of antiques and fine jewelry, while the **Department Store** (914-586-4214) has "Catskill Offerings," a lovely section devoted to the artists and crafters of the Catskill region. There are also separate shops that sell fine antiques and quirky collectibles. **BodyWorx** (914-586-3101) offers guests a full-service massage center in a relaxing mountain setting, with therapeutic, sports, and Swedish massages available. In Binnekill Square on Margaretville's Main Street, several shops are filled with unusual and fine goods, and you can enjoy music on the square throughout the summer. At **Coyote Junction** (914-586-3088) the American Southwest meets Catskills country. Furniture, clothing, fine arts, and crafts range from the unusual—custom lodgepole furniture and blacksmith-created lamps—to the colorful—western shirts and children's wear. At the **Mill Shoppe** (914-586-2099) pick up a fine sweater for a child or an adult from some of the best labels, at a bargain price. The **Village Homemaker** (914-586-3620), with its selection of hundreds of fabrics and calico gift items, is a quilter's delight and is located in a beautifully restored landmark building.

SPECIAL EVENTS

Since Delaware County is still a rural area, the special events here tend to take place during the "better weather" months, from early spring until autumn. For specific dates and times, unless otherwise noted, contact the **Delaware County Chamber of Commerce** (607-746-2281).

In June, the **Arkville Fair** is held on Route 28, complete with parade, marching bands, entertainment, crafts, and food.

The week of July Fourth ushers in the **Firemen's Field Days** at the village park in Margaretville, where a carnival, rides, entertainment, games of skill (and chance), and food concessions keep everyone busy. At the Andes Presbyterian Church, Route 28, Andes, the **Strawberry Festival** is celebrated each July Fourth weekend.

July also brings the **Lumberjack Festival** (607-278-5744), Riverside Park, Deposit, which includes fireworks, an art show, raft races on the Delaware River, a walking tour of historic homes, and lots of food, along with demonstrations of lumberjack skills. The **Peaceful Valley Bluegrass Festival** (607-467-2673), Downsville, features some of the best in traditional music. Dozens of bands perform all weekend, and there are square dances and food concessions. Held on a 500-acre farm, the festival is great for families. There are camping facilities; performances are given in a tent in bad weather. The **Round Barn Festival** (914-586-3326), Halcottsville, is sponsored by the Erpf Cultural Institute, which also holds gallery shows and concerts year-round.

In August, the charming village of Franklin hosts **Old Franklin Day** on Main Street, with sales, open houses, displays, and special events. Call the Delaware Chamber of Commerce for dates and times.

The Delaware County Fair (607-746-2281), at the fairgrounds off Route 10 in Walton (follow signs), usually runs the second week of August. Open daily 9 AM–10 PM. Admission fee. Part of the agricultural and social life of Delaware County for more than a century, this is one of the last of the truly agricultural county fairs in New York State. Each year, hundreds of 4-H members gather to show off their prize goods, including sheep, pigs, cows, horses, and rabbits. The finest local produce is displayed and sold, and the handiwork building bursts with the colors of hundreds of quilts, afghans, and doilies. The celebration begins on Main Street with a parade, and visitors will enjoy the show of the best livestock and the latest farm equipment and agricultural news, demonstrations, and other "country stuff." Sample some milk punch served by the Delaware Dairy Princess and her court; try your hand at games of skill and chance; let the kids have fun on the carousel and Ferris wheel (a delight at night). You probably won't bid on the livestock, but you will enjoy the demolition derby with its action and noise, the tractor pulls, the horse shows, and the popular animal dress-up days. Don't worry about going hungry here: The pancake and pie tents, the sausage sandwiches, and the antique popcorn wagon—itself on the National Historic Register—will take care of the greatest appetite.

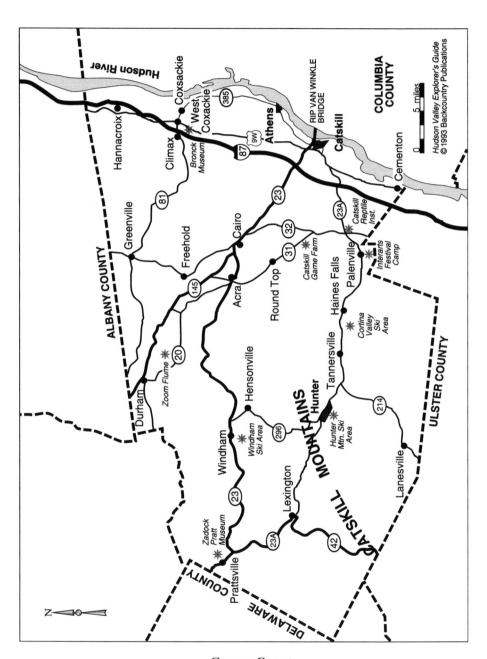

Greene County

Greene County

Greene County offers the perfect outdoor experience any time of year. In winter dramatic, snow-filled gorges yield to delicate, misty water-falls, and skiers are very likely to run across bear tracks as they fly down the slopes at Hunter, Ski Windham, and Cortina Valley, which provide some of the best downhill skiing in the East. In spring bright wildflowers cling to wind-scraped rocks, and visitors to the county can watch the Spring Rush, a running, biking, and canoeing competition. Each June there is a tour of homes in Palenville, one of the county's historic towns. Summer celebrates its warmth with the gifts of icy brooks for tired feet and a flood of cultural festivals. This is a fine time of year to visit North and South Lakes and Kaaterskill Falls. Fall is a season to wonder at the colors that transform the hills and towns into paint pots full of orange and red—the magic that drew Rip Van Winkle to Catskill still enchants visitors today. Other ghosts haunt Greene County as well; in Leeds, if you walk along a dark country road, you might run into the spirit of the servant girl who was dragged to her death by her master and his horse. You'll find both an Irish Cultural and Sports Center and a Butterfly Museum in the same town—East Durham. There are also hiking trails, museums, country auctions, breathtaking waterfalls, waterfront villages, festivals, and fine restaurants to enjoy.

GUIDANCE
Greene County Promotion Department (518-943-3223), Box 527, Catskill 12414.

GETTING THERE
Greene County is off Exit 21 of the NYS Thruway. Routes 23 and 23A run east-west across the county; Route 32 runs north-south. Almost all sites here can be accessed from these roads.

MEDICAL EMERGENCY
Columbia Greene Medical Center (518-943-2000), 159 Jefferson Heights, Catskill.

TO SEE

Bronck Museum (518-731-6490 or 731-8862), off Route 9W on Pieter Bronck Road in Coxsackie. Open the last Sunday in June through the

Sunday before Labor Day; call for hours. Admission fee. Once home to nine generations of the Bronck family (who also gave their name to the Bronx), the museum's collection traces the history of the Upper Hudson Valley. Visitors should begin with the original structure, a 1663 stone house that contains an Indian lookout loft—from a time when settlers were not welcome. The house was remodeled in the late 18th century, when a wing was added along with fine paneling and fireplaces. Displays include an impressive exhibit of local textiles, looms, and spinning wheels that chronicle the production of Bronck cloth and clothing. An earlier addition, the 1738 Brick House, was connected to the stone house through hyphen-hall. This part of the family home is now used to display, among other things, a fine collection of paintings by 18th- and 19th-century artists, including Ammi Phillips, John Frederick Kensett, Frederic Church, and Thomas Cole. Outside is a kitchen, a charming, tiny house itself, set apart from the main house in the style of plantations. The displays here consist of furniture and kitchen tools. Farm buffs will enjoy the three barns that are found at the complex, each representing a different era. The Dutch barn, with its huge beams; the center pole–supported, 13-sided Liberty Barn; and the Victorian house barn each offer the visitor a look at the tolls, carriages, and wagons of the day. A walk through the family and slave cemeteries will bring you even closer to the people who made the Bronck complex a working and living farm. The Bronck Museum also sponsors a Greene County house tour each June, when a different area of the county offers a look into many fascinating historic homes.

Thomas Cole House (518-943-6533), 218 Spring Street, Catskill (off Route 385). Open June through Labor Day; call for hours. Admission fee. Once called Cedar Grove, the Thomas Cole House was purchased for preservation by a group of New York City art dealers and is now open to the public. As the popularity of the Hudson River School faded in the beginning of the 20th century, Cole's fame declined as well, and family members occupied the house, which fell into disrepair. Today the home needs lots of attention, and there are no original Cole works of art on site. Still, art buffs may want to view the slides, photographs, and engravings that trace the history of Cole's genius.

Zadock Pratt Museum and **Pratt's Rocks** (518-299-3395), Route 23, Prattsville. Open Memorial Day through Columbus Day, Wednesday through Sunday 1–5. Admission fee. Born in 1790, genius businessman Zadock Pratt started out as a harness maker and soon went into the tanning business. He became such a prominent community leader that the town of Prattsville was named in his honor. His tanning facilities were among the largest in the state, and he built many of Prattsville's homes for his workers. In later years, Pratt served in both the state and federal governments. Today, Pratt's home is a museum that shows what life in New York was like in the 1850s. Exhibits focus on the tanning industry and the story of Greene County, with rooms displaying period furniture and decorative arts. In a separate gallery the work of local artists is shown and special events like the holiday decorating show and crafts workshops are held. Just outside of Prattsville are Pratt's Rocks, a memorial Pratt had carved by an itinerant stonemason. The huge stone reliefs show Pratt's son, a favorite horse, and Pratt himself. There is a small picnic area.

FOR FAMILIES

Catskill Game Farm (518-678-9595), Game Farm Road, off Route 32, Catskill. Open daily May through October. Admission fee. One of the oldest game farms in the country, the Catskill Game Farm is also the most popular in the East. With more than 2000 animals such as lions, tigers, and bears to see and enjoy, a visit here should take up several hours. Special shows may include pigs, elephants, or monkeys, and the petting zoo is still one of the most popular places for children. There is a small train that transports visitors from one section of the zoo to another (at an additional charge), and an amusement park and picnic and play areas. It's best not to leave young children alone in the petting area, since they may feel overwhelmed by all the friendly deer.

Clyde Peeling's Reptiland (518-678-3557), Route 32, Catskill. Open daily 10–6 Memorial Day through Labor Day; weekends through Columbus Day. Admission fee. If snakes and reptiles interest you, visit this intriguing display. You'll find 60 types of rare snakes and reptiles, from the yellow spitting cobra and Eastern diamondback rattler to a 15-foot-long African rock python. There are local snakes to wonder at as well as exotic creatures right out of a Rudyard Kipling story, and all are housed in habitats that duplicate the animals' natural environment. Tour guides are available with lots of reptile rap, and guests are encouraged to take photographs. Reptile shows are held throughout the day. Even people who are frightened of snakes leave the institute with a better under-standing of these remarkable creatures.

Zoom Flume (518-239-4559), just off Route 145, Shady Glen Road, 2 miles north of East Durham. Opens late June, weather permitting; open daily June through Labor Day. Call for hours. Admission fee. Billed as an "aquamusement park," this playground is set in the Shady Glen canyon, a natural formation of steep walls and running water. The Raging River Ride and the Zoom Flume let you slosh and slide your way down the canyon; there's also a pool, a game area, and the Mountain Coaster, a sort of small coaster that zips down the hillside. The Soak-A-Buddy section is great for splashing a friend or two. There are also nature trails, scenic overlooks and waterfalls, and a restaurant with an observation deck for drying out.

SCENIC DRIVES

Mountains, deep gorges, valleys, and waterfalls can all be seen during a leisurely drive through Greene County, and a tour can take all day or only a few hours, depending on the number of stops you want to make.

Some of the roads are narrow and winding, though, so use the designated parking areas to take in scenic views. And be careful to check driving conditions if you take a ride in winter or early spring.

Some lovely parts of the county can be seen by taking Route 42 north over the Deep Notch, which is cool even on the hottest days. At Route 23A, head east through Hunter, Haines Falls, and Palenville. Along the road you will see Hunter Mountain, breathtaking waterfalls, winding streams, and the Amphitheatre, a natural, bowl-shaped rock formation. Follow Route 23 into Catskill, where you can pick up the NYS Thruway at Exit 21.

Another tour starts at the junction of Routes 23A and 23C; follow 23C east to Jewett. The large and elegant homes lining the roads and tucked into the hills were part of Onteora Park, a "cottage" colony where many wealthy families summered during the last century. The junction of Routes 25 and 23C shelters the Old Stone Church, in which there are some lovely murals. (The church is closed in winter.) At County Route 17, head south to Route 23A, where you can pick up the scenic drive above, into Catskill.

To see some exceptional churches, begin on Route 23A in Jewett Center. Here you will see the St. John the Baptist Ukrainian Church and the Grazhda, which were constructed in the traditional style using large beams and wooden pins instead of nails. The interior of the church is decorated with wood carvings and panels, and the education building has displays relating to Ukrainian history. There are concerts and arts shows held in the Grazhda (call 518-263-3862 for information). Continue on Route 23A to Haines Falls, where you'll find the grotto of Our Lady of the Mountain. This shrine was constructed in the 1920s and recalls the miracle at Lourdes. The grotto is open to the public. Continue on 23A to Palenville, where the Gloria Dei Episcopal Church is open for tours on Saturday. Then take Route 23A to Route 32 north into Cairo, then Route 24 to South Cairo. There you will find the Mahayana Buddhist Temple (518-622-3691), a retreat complete with Chinese temple, dragon decorations, and fine artwork. The walkways are open to the public year-round. From South Cairo, you can take Route 23B east to the NYS Thruway.

TO DO

AIRPLANE TOURS

With its rolling meadows and steep mountain heights, Greene County is a wonderful place to see through the window of an airplane. Recreational flights add some excitement to a vacation, and a call to the following airports will put you in touch with pilots.

Freehold Airport (518-634-7626), in Freehold, is a full-service airport that offers pleasure flights and a glider school.

Maben's Airport (518-299-8585), Route 23A, Prattsville, will arrange flights, lessons, and even parachuting for the more adventurous.

At **Cairo Airport** (518-622-9736), Bross Street, Cairo, you can arrange scenic flights or use their campgrounds and enjoy the special fly-in events for pilots.

BIKING

Enthusiasts looking for an interesting way to spend a summer or autumn day may want to make tracks to **Mountain High Bike & Ski Company** (518-263-4223), Hunter Mountain, Route 23A, Hunter, where you can ride the trails by yourself or take the ski lift up the mountain and follow a guide down a trail suited to your abilities. There are complete rental facilities on the site, and organized tours are offered throughout the season. **Ski Windham** (518-734-4300), Route 23, Windham, also has bike rentals, marked trails, and lessons for the beginner or expert mountain biker.

FARM STANDS AND PICK-YOUR-OWN FARMS

Greene County is filled with farm stands: big ones, little ones, and specialty stands that carry everything from maple syrup to mushrooms. At **Osborn Mushroom Farm** (518-731-8730), Route 9W, Coxsackie, you can buy fresh mushrooms and learn about cooking them properly. Open year-round.

Bennett's Berry Patch (518-756-9472), Independence Lane, Hannacroix, is open June and July and has strawberries only.

Story Farms (518-678-9716), Route 32, Catskill, allows you to pick your own strawberries, peas, and tomatoes, but they also offer a lot of other local produce. Open year-round.

Apples for the picking are the specialty at **Henry Boehm's** (518-731-6196), County Road 26, Climax, open September through February, and at **Sunset Orchards** (518-731-8846), Route 81, Climax. **Duncan's Farmstand and Cider Mill,** (518-622-8400), Route 23B, Cairo, open daily except Wednesday through the summer, has local goodies and produce to take home to dinner.

At the **Kaatskill Cider Mill** (518-678-5529), Route 32, Catskill, apples, cider, maple syrup, and honey make this one sweet stop for regional-food lovers. Open year-round.

A great combination can be found at **Traphagen's** (518-263-4150), Route 23A, Hunter, where pick-your-own strawberries are offered along with gourmet, flavored honeys. Open year-round.

Black Horse Farms (518-943-9324), Route 9W, Athens, is open June through December and stocks everything from herbs to apples, all locally grown.

Maple Glen Farm (518-589-5319), Scribner Hollow Road, East Jewett, offers tours of its maple syrup production area. The farm is open all year for sales. In early spring, don't pass up a stop here.

Corn lovers should stop at **God's Bountiful Acres** (518-966-8765), Route

32, Greenville, where the ears are yours for the choosing.

Blossom Farm (518-966-5722) is located on Johnny Cake Lane in Greenville and offers visitors the chance to pick and cut flowers and wildflowers from more than 30 acres. There are farm animals and special events throughout the season, including a hayride and pumpkin festival.

FISHING

Fishing in Greene County can mean a lazy day spent pondside or an exciting, nerve-ripping hour fighting a sturgeon in the Hudson. There are more than 58 streams that shelter wild trout here, as well as lakes, ponds, and, of course, the Hudson River. A state fishing license is required in Greene County, and town permits are also needed for the Potuck Reservoir in Catskill and the Medway Reservoir in Coxsackie. Permits and licenses can be obtained at many of the bait and tackle and sports shops across the county, as well as in town clerk's offices and the county clerk's office in Catskill. Seasons and limits vary with the species of fish; check with the **Department of Environmental Conservation** (914-256-3000) for specifics. In Greene County, public fishing areas are marked by yellow signs, and parking spaces are available, although they're sometimes limited. If you want to catch one of the more than 150 species of fish that are found in the Hudson River—shad, perch, herring, and sturgeon among them—you may want to use the public boat ramps that can be found in Athens, Coxsackie, and Catskill. Route 23A will take you past Rip Van Winkle Lake in Tannersville, Schoharie Creek, and the Schoharie Reservoir, all of which are great fishing areas. Route 145 leads to Lower Catskill Creek, Upper Catskill Creek, and Ten Mile Creek, while Route 296 provides access to the Batavia Kill boat launch and the East Kill Trout Preserve. BASSmaster invitational fishing tournaments have been held in Greene County; information may be obtained by calling the **Greene County Promotion Department** (518-943-3223).

GOLF

The greens of Greene County require widely varying levels of skill, but no one who picks up a club will leave the region disappointed. Many resorts have their own private courses (see *Lodging*), but the following establishments are open to the public. It is suggested that you call before you go to determine hours and availability.

Nine-hole golf courses in Greene County include: **Blackhead Mountain Country Club** (518-622-3157), Round Top; **Rainbow Golf Club and Motel** (518-966-5343), Route 26, Greenville, which also offers vacation apartments just off the course, as does the **Sunny Hill Golf Club Resort** (518-634-7698), Greenville; the lovely **Rip Van Winkle Country Club** (518-678-9779), Route 23A, Palenville; and the gracious **Windham Country Club** (518-734-9910), South Street, Windham.

HIKING

Greene County provides some of the best hiking and views in the Catskill region. You don't have to be a seasoned hiker to enjoy a day walking on the clearly marked trails, and the magnificent views have inspired Thomas Cole and other Hudson River painters.

Although the **Escarpment Trail** runs from Kaaterskill Creek on Route 23A to East Windham on Route 23 (24 miles in all), there are several short hikes along the path to Kaaterskill High Peak, North Point, and Mary's Glen. The trails in the North Lake area are renowned for their waterfalls and fantastic views of the entire Hudson Valley. **Kaaterskill Falls** and the **Catskill Mountain House** are particularly noteworthy sites. The easy-to-find entry point for these trails is at the junction of Route 23A and Kaaterskill Creek on the north side of the highway. These hikes are usually very popular on summer weekends, so you might want to go during the week to avoid the crowds. North Lake and good campgrounds are nearby for those who want to take a swim or stay overnight.

For more experienced and adventurous hikers, there is the **Devil's Path,** named for its steepness and relative isolation. The path passes over much rugged terrain, particularly Indian Head Mountain, and includes Hunter Mountain Trail and the West Kill Mountain Range Trail. To reach the trailhead, turn south off Route 23A at the only light in Tannersville. Go 1⅓ miles until the road intersects with Bloomer Road. Turn left, and after about ½ mile bear left onto Platte Clove Mountain Road. Stay on this road for 1 mile to Prediger Road, then go ¼ mile farther to find the trail. Each single mountain on the Devil's Path can be hiked in a day or less.

At 4040 feet, **Hunter Mountain** is the second highest peak in the Catskills and is best hiked on the trail that starts on Spruceton Road. To get there, take Route 42 north from Lexington and go 4 miles to Spruceton Road. The trailhead and trail are well defined.

Another pleasant day hike takes you to Diamond Notch and West Kill Falls. Located 5 miles north of Phoenicia, near Route 214, it is also easy to find. From Route 214, take Diamond Notch Road about 1 mile to a bridge, cross it, and park. The hike is about 4½ miles and should take 4 hours or less.

Highland Flings (1-800-HLF-6665), PO Box 1034, Kingston 12401, specializes in guided hiking and walking tours through the Catskill Forest Preserve and Hudson River Valley. They will arrange the hikes, accommodations, and food; the guides themselves are charming and exhaustively versed in local history and hiking.

CROSS-COUNTRY SKIING

Greene County is home to some of the best cross-country ski areas in the state. Well over 1000 acres of groomed and ungroomed trails snake their way through the county's forests and fields, and many of the areas are patrolled by Nordic Ski Patrol members.

Hyer Meadows (518-589-5361), Route 23C, Tannersville (watch for signs), has 35 km of groomed trails that are marked according to difficulty. Full facilities are available, including rentals, lessons, tours, a cafeteria, and baby-sitting. Night tours are available with special reservations.

White Birches Ski Area (518-734-3266), Nauvoo Road, Windham, has 17 miles of groomed, patrolled, and marked trails for everyone from novices to experts; they also sponsor races throughout the season.

Winter Clove Inn Nordic Skiing Area (518-622-3267), Winter Clove Road, Round Top, is located on the grounds of a country inn, but the facilities, including 400 acres, are open to the public and rentals are available; the same applies to the **Villaggio Resort** (518-589-5000), Haines Falls, with 14 km of trails.

DOWNHILL SKIING

Skiers from beginner to expert will enjoy excellent snow conditions, modern facilities, and some of the best skiing and most spectacular views anywhere in Greene County, which lies right in the New York snow belt, where sudden storms can dump several inches of powder in an hour. Ski season here lasts at least 6 months and slopes are open daily, weather permitting. In addition to their specialty offerings, the following slopes have rentals, baby-sitting and child care services, dining facilities, picnic areas, and ski shops.

Hunter Mountain (518-263-4223), Route 23A, Hunter. Their reputation as the snowmaking capital of the East is well deserved. The three different mountains—Hunter One, Hunter West, and Hunter Mountain—offer skiers of all skill levels a chance to test themselves on nearly 50 different trails. Runs at Hunter can extend more than 2 miles, with vertical drops of 1600 feet, and there are some extremely difficult areas for the expert. Double, triple, and even quadruple chair lifts cut some

Ski Fest is celebrated at Ski Windham during President's Holiday Week in February.

of the lines down to size, but this is such a popular area that you should be prepared for crowds on holidays and weekends. Hunter offers ski lessons for all levels and a wide variety of amateur and professional races during the season, including ones for chefs, firemen, snowboarders, and nurses. Hunter also offers 100 percent snowmaking capability, so the season sometimes begins as early as early November and last into May. You will find complete facilities here, including babysitting, cafeterias, a lodge, a ski shop, and even a ski museum and art gallery. There is plenty of parking.

Ski Windham (518-734-4300), Route 23, Windham, has 27 trails and vertical elevations of 1500 feet at the base and 3050 feet at the summit. Trail difficulty ranges from easy to expert, and the longest trail is more than 2 miles long. Windham has won awards for its courtesy services, and it offers valet parking, business meeting rooms with computers, and excellent dining facilities, along with a senior skier development program and lessons in racing, freestyle skiing, and snowboarding. They are also well known for their work with disabled skiers. Mountain bike lovers may wish to inquire about the autumn special events at Windham, when bike rentals are offered and trails are open for the hearty adventurer (see *Biking*).

Cortina Valley (518-589-6500), Route 23A, Haines Falls, has a base elevation of 2000 feet, the highest in the Catskills, and 90 percent snowmaking capability. The 11 slopes and four lifts serve skiers of all skill levels, and the site also offers night skiing and a guest lodge.

GREEN SPACE
North and South Lakes (518-589-5058 or 518-943-4030). Take New York Route 23A to County Route 18 (O'Hara Road), Haines Falls. Open daily late May through early December, from 9 AM until dusk. Admission, with an extra charge for campsites. This recreational area offers breathtaking scenery and a multitude of activities. Visitors can swim in a mountain lake with a clean, sandy beach. Boat rentals and fishing are also available. It is only a short hike from the lakes to Kaaterskill Falls, one of the highest falls on the East Coast. The falls were a popular subject for Hudson River School artists. The area also has a multiuse campground with hookups for recreational vehicles; it is advisable to make reservations early in the season, since this is a popular site and it gets busy on summer weekends. An ideal spot for a family outing.

LODGING

Greene County is an extremely popular resort area, and there are hundreds of B&B inns, motels, and campgrounds. Some of the establishments cater to lovers of Irish, Italian, or Scandinavian life; others offer a full range of camping facilities on lakes and rivers. The following listing is only a sampling of what can be discovered throughout the county.

Albergo Allegria Bed and Breakfast (518-734-5560 or 734-4499), Route 296, Windham 12496. ($$$) Step up on the wickered porch here and feel the grace and beauty of days gone by. The Victorian theme is continued throughout this bed & breakfast with antique furnishings and period wallpaper and decorations. A continental breakfast of fresh fruit, home-baked muffins, croissants, and local honey and jams is served daily. In summer, enjoy breakfast on the porch. The main lounge, with its overstuffed couches and fireplace, and the library are especially warm and inviting. Four suites and 12 rooms, all with private baths; a Jacuzzi is available. The inn also schedules cooking seminars throughout the year.

Country Suite Bed and Breakfast (518-734-4079), Route 23, Windham 12496. ($$) This restored farmhouse is only minutes from skiing, shopping, and festivals, and guests will enjoy the country furnishings and antiques. There are rooms with and without private baths. Reservations suggested. Open year-round.

Eggery Inn (518-589-5363), County Road 16, Tannersville 12485. ($$) Nestled amid the majestic ridges of the Catskill Mountains at an altitude of 2200 feet, this rustic inn offers sweeping views. The wood-burning Franklin stove and antique player piano make for a cozy atmosphere, and the dining room has a handcrafted oak bar and an abundance of plants. During the hearty breakfast, enjoy an unobstructed view of Hunter Mountain. Dinner is served on Saturday nights December through mid-March and July through October. Eleven rooms have private baths; two share a bathroom. Open year-round, except April.

Golden Harvest (518-634-2305), 37 Golden Hill Road, East Durham 12423. ($$) A nice family place, the inn has a separate, two-bedroom apartment for guests, complete with VCR and screened-in porch. The Golden Harvest is located on the site of a former orchard, and the extensive grounds include a duck pond; volleyball, croquet and horseshoe courts; and reading benches. There are also picnic and barbecue facilities, and a full breakfast is served in the main dining room. Open year-round.

Greenville Arms (518-966-5219), South Street, Greenville 12083. ($$$) Special care is taken to provide a quiet retreat for guests at this gem of a Victorian home built by William Vanderbilt in 1889. Each room is decorated with antiques, and the 7 acres of lush lawns and gardens are a riot of color each spring and summer. Old-fashioned country cooking is the specialty at breakfast, and dinner is by advance reservation. Twenty rooms offer a variety of options, including private and shared baths and private porches. Children welcome; open year-round.

Kaaterskill Creek Bed and Breakfast (518-678-9052), Malden Avenue, Palenville 12463. ($) Cozy rooms, a fireplace, and a front porch make this country inn a delight. The view is of the creek and the distant mountains, and guests can enjoy nearby swimming, hiking, skiing, and more.

A full breakfast is served in an enclosed gazebo. Three rooms share a bath. Open year-round.

Leeds Country Inn (518-943-2099), Route 23B, Leeds 12451. ($$) Although this is a motel, the inn itself is located in a Victorian manor house. Rooms have private baths, air-conditioning, and television, and a continental breakfast is served in the dining room. Children welcome; open May through October.

Palenville House (518-678-5649), Route 32A, Palenville 12463. ($$) This charming, turn-of-the-century Queen Anne offers rooms with private and shared baths and a full breakfast. One suite has a Jacuzzi. Children are welcome. Open year-round.

Redcoat's Return (518-589-6379), Dale Lane, Elka Park 12427. ($$$) The picturesque locale of this 1850s farmhouse will delight outdoors lovers. There is fishing in nearby Schoharie Creek and skiing at nearby Hunter Mountain. The owners are British, and they cook a first-class breakfast; the inn features a fine restaurant (see *Dining Out*). Closed November, and April to mid-May.

River Hill (518-756-3313), Box 253, New Baltimore 12124. ($$) Away from it all, but not too far away, this restored historic home has spacious grounds, and there are spectacular Hudson River views from its rooms. Guests are welcome to enjoy the downstairs, which includes a living room with fireplace and grand piano. Breakfast is served on the terrace or in front of the fireplace in the dining room. Open year-round.

Scribner Hollow Lodge (518-263-4211), Route 23A, Hunter 12442. ($$$) For people who enjoy a full-service lodge; the main building offers private rooms, and town houses can also be rented. Every room is different, and the lodge has a sauna, a whirlpool, and an unusual grotto swimming pool. Open year-round.

Stewart House (518-945-1357), 2 North Water Street, Athens 12015. ($$) A restored Victorian hotel that dates back to 1883, with panoramic views of the Hudson River. Athens is a charming town with a lighthouse (you can see it from room 8). Enjoy a full country breakfast while watching the boats pass by. Five rooms with private baths. Open year-round. Excellent restaurant downstairs.

The Windham Arms (518-734-3000), Route 23, Windham 12496. ($$) Take the NYS Thruway to Exit 21 to Route 23 West; it's 25 miles to the motel. Only ½ mile from Ski Windham, this establishment combines a country setting with comfortable rooms and spectacular mountain views. It is ideal for families, with a dining room, coffee shop, tennis court, indoor recreation center, and outdoor pool on the premises. It combines the convenience of a motel with the warmth of a country inn. All 55 rooms have TV, telephone, and private bath. Open year-round.

Winter Clove Inn (518-622-3267), Winter Clove Road, Round Top 12473. ($$$) Located on 400 acres adjoining the Catskill Mountain Preserve, this inn opened in 1830 and is still run by the same family. There are swimming pools, a tennis court, a golf course, cross-country skiing, and even hay rides and a bowling alley. All baked goods are homemade, and many of the recipes have been passed down by the family for generations. Children are welcome. All meals are included in rates unless special arrangements are made in advance. Fifty-one rooms with private baths. Open year-round.

WHERE TO EAT

DINING OUT

Antonio's (518-589-5197), Elka Park. ($$) Open daily for dinner most of the year, but hours vary with the season. During the summer there is one seating at 6:30, and the menu is limited. This cozy spot offers Italian American favorites of all kinds. Dinners all include salad. The inn is located along a scenic road. Call for reservations.

Brandywine (518-734-3838), Route 23, Windham. ($$) Open daily except Monday for lunch and dinner at noon. An excellent informal dining spot, the Italian specialties here are superb. Try the rich fettuccine Alfredo, the shrimp Brandywine, or the chicken Scarpariello. Desserts include fantastic cheesecake. There is a bright greenhouse room for dining and cozy booths in the main area. Children are welcome.

Chalet Fondue (518-734-4650), South Street, Windham. ($$) Open weekdays except Tuesday, at 4; Saturday at 4; Sunday and holidays at 2. Swiss, Austrian, and German dishes are the specialties here and include veal entrées and a full line of fondues. Children are welcome.

Chateau Belleview (518-589-5525), Route 23A, Tannersville. ($$) Open daily except Tuesday, at 5. Fine Continental cuisine and spectacular mountain views are found here, along with candlelight and fine service. Not recommended for children.

La Conca D'Oro (518-943-3549), 440 Main Street, Catskill. ($$) Open weekdays except Tuesday, for lunch 11:30–2:30 and dinner 5–10; open Saturday 3–10 and Sunday 2–10. The name means "the golden bay," and this unpretentious Italian restaurant serves fine food at exceedingly reasonable prices. The veal entrées, chicken dishes, and homemade mozzarella are house specialties. For dessert, there are excellent cannoli. Children are welcome.

La Griglia (518-734-4499), Route 296, Windham. ($$$) Open daily except Monday, at 4:30 PM. Bakery is open for coffee and treats at 8 AM—the selection of fine cakes, pastries, cookies, and breads is incredible and worth the trip. Rated one of New York's best restaurants, this elegant inn serves excellent northern Italian dishes. House specialties include osso buco Milanese, roast duck with fig and honey sauce, and pasta. Desserts are prepared by the restaurant's bakery and include chocolate specialties to die for. Children welcome. Reservations suggested.

Redcoat's Return (518-598-6379 or 598-9858), Dale Lane, Elka Park. ($$) Open daily for dinner at 6; closed Tuesday and Wednesday in winter. A taste of England in the Hudson Valley, this inn serves up British dishes including steak and kidney pie, trifle, and prime rib. The surroundings are old-world elegant, and dinner is served in a cozy library-like dining room with book-lined walls. Children welcome.

La Rive (518-943-4888), Old Kings Road, Catskill (call for directions). ($$$) Open May through November, Tuesday through Saturday at 6, Sunday at 2. Located in a farmhouse off a winding dirt road. No detail has been overlooked. The hors d'oeuvres plate includes samples of 13 different dishes. Not recommended for children. Reservations recommended.

Stewart House Restaurant and Bistro (518-945-1357), 2 North Water Street, Athens. ($$) Open for dinner Tuesday through Saturday 5–10; brunch Sunday 11:30–2, dinner 3–10. The bistro serves a limited menu later in the evening as well. New American cooking is featured here, with an emphasis on the freshest seasonal ingredients. The chef uses herbs from his garden along the Hudson River during the warm-weather months. The wood-grilled swordfish is a specialty. All baking is done on the premises, so make sure to sample some of the wonderful pies and desserts, like chocolate torte with raspberry filling.

Vesuvio (518-734-3663), Goshen Road, Hensonville. ($$) Open daily at 4:30. The warm atmosphere and provincial charm make this Italian restaurant a popular stop. Candlelight makes dining elegant, and the specialties include veal and fish, along with outstanding desserts like tortoni and spumoni. Children are welcome.

EATING OUT

Beaver Lodge (518-945-2790), Route 9W, Athens. ($) Open daily 7 AM–8 PM. In this unpretentious eatery, all the food is home-cooked. There are terrific burgers and 38 different desserts made on the premises.

Bell's Coffee Shop (518-943-4070), 387 Main Street, Catskill. ($) Open daily 8–3. This is an old-fashioned luncheonette with large portions and low prices. The home-cooked turkey sandwich is a favorite among local residents.

Jimmy O'Connor's Windham Mountain Inn (518-734-4270), South Street, Windham. ($) Open daily at 8 AM. A nice stop for an Irish coffee and a hearty sandwich or a rib-sticking breakfast.

Last Chance Antiques and Cheese Cafe (518-589-6424), Main Street, Tannersville. ($) Open daily at 10 AM. A retail gourmet store, antiques shop, and café all in one. Cheeses, chocolates, quiche, homemade soups, and huge sandwiches make this a great take-out stop.

Maggie's Krooked Cafe (518-589-6101), Main Street, Tannersville. ($) Open daily at 7 AM. Hearty food is the specialty here, from breakfast to dinner. Try a market omelet, homemade pancakes, or fried shrimp in beer batter.

Mike's Catskill Point (518-943-5352), 7 Main Street, Catskill. ($) Open Tuesday through Sunday 4–10:30. Located on the Hudson River, this is a great spot for outdoor dining in the warm-weather months. The pizza, hamburgers, and turkey and roast beef sandwiches are popular selections.

Point Lookout Inn (518-734-3381), Route 23, Windham. ($) Open daily at 7 AM on weekends; 3 PM on weekdays. Eat here on a clear day and you can see five states from your dining booth. The food is hearty, and big sandwiches are the standouts. A nice lunch stop.

ENTERTAINMENT

Hunter Festivals (518-263-3800), Hunter Mountain, Route 23A, Hunter. Dates vary. Admission fee varies with festival; there is a small parking charge. Although Hunter is known as one of the top skiing mountains in the United States, it is also the site of more than 10 music and dance festivals. The shows are colorful and filled with ethnic diversity; the foods sold at stands range from pizza to Belgian waffles, bangers and potatoes to fried bread and pumpkin soup. There are festivals celebrating Italy, Poland, the German Alps, country music and Americana, as well as Ukrainian, Celtic, and Native American culture. All offer crafts demonstrations and daylong entertainment; performers have included Tony Bennett, the Oak Ridge Boys, and the Chieftains. During the festivals, the Hunter Sky Ride is in service (additional fee), and the Skiing Hall of Fame (free) offers an interesting look at the men, women, and equipment that helped create American skiing.

Interarts Festival (518-678-3332). Take Route 9W to Route 23A; take 23A west into Palenville (watch for signs). The season runs July through September. Admission fee. This theater festival, workshop series, and summer arts colony is rooted in the 19th-century tradition of arts colonies. It all started when the Bond Street Theater Company of New York City stopped in Palenville during a summer tour. The directors discovered a children's camp they felt would serve as the perfect retreat for traditional, ethnic, and folk performers; the camp was leased for the next season, and the Interarts group soon began to work with the town in developing an active, popular theater organization. Through workshops and classes, the townspeople—both adults and children—join in each year as performers and behind-the-scenes workers. Shows have featured circus arts, Taipei magicians, and modern dance and jazz groups. Special children's shows are offered each Saturday morning, and most of the productions are imaginatively staged and fun to watch. Arrangements to stay at the Interarts camp for a weekend can be made.

SELECTIVE SHOPPING

ANTIQUES
Greene County offers the antiques lover everything from the funky to the fabulous, with a wide range of shops, auctions, and flea markets. Al-

Hunter Mountain's International Celtic Festival

though many establishments are open all year, their hours tend to be limited in the off-season, so call before you go.

American Gothic Antiques (518-263-4836), Route 23A, Hunter, stocks a wonderful array of antique lamps and accessories.

Stone House Gallery (518-989-6755), in Lexington, is for art deco lovers: jewelry, folk art, and Early American furniture in an eclectic mix.

Another stop for people in search of fine jewelry, paintings, and lamps is the

Tiffany House Gallery (914-622-3566), Route 23, Acra.

Two unusual shops cater to the collector who knows his or her wants: **Mudge's Gun Shop** (518-734-3517), Route 296, Hensonville, has antique guns, and the **Old Piano Roll Store** (518-622-3160), Route 23, Acra, has antique player pianos and rolls.

Athens Antiques Center (518-945-1240), Flats Road, Athens, has early glassware, primitives, and furniture.

Kathleen Seibel Antiques (518-943-2256), 40 North Jefferson Avenue, Catskill, offers rare painted furniture.

Prattsville Exchange (518-299-3389), Route 23, Prattsville, sells decorative arts of the 20th century.

Open Gates Antiques (518-943-3806), Route 23A, Catskill, has stained glass, furniture, clocks, and lamps from two centuries.

And if all that shopping makes you hungry, stop in at the **Last Chance Antiques and Cheese Cafe** (518-589-6424), Main Street, Tannersville, where you can have a gourmet snack and then buy the furniture out from under the other diners (see *Eating Out*).

A trip to Preston Hollow will bring you to several antiques stops. **The Antiques Center of Preston Hollow** (518-239-4251), Route 145, stocks the wares of more than two dozen dealers. **Green Acres** (518-239-4891), just along Route 145, is a well-stocked multidealer shop. **The Green Barn** (518-239-4109) on Fox Creek Road also represents the finds of several antiques lovers.

Auctions are also popular throughout the county and they attract buyers from all over the state. If you go to one, be sure to inspect all merchandise before you buy, because it's usually "buyer beware." Look for auction listings in the local newspaper, and check to see if the auction also charges a buyer's premium.

A solid collection of antiques can be found at the following auction houses: **Savoia & Fromm Auction Gallery** (518-622-8000), Route 23, Cairo; **Durham Auction Barn** (518-239-8475), Route 145, Durham; **Lincoln Auction Service** (518-943-2704), Route 9W, West Coxsackie; and **Tannersville Auction and Sales** (518-589-5554), Main Street, Tannersville.

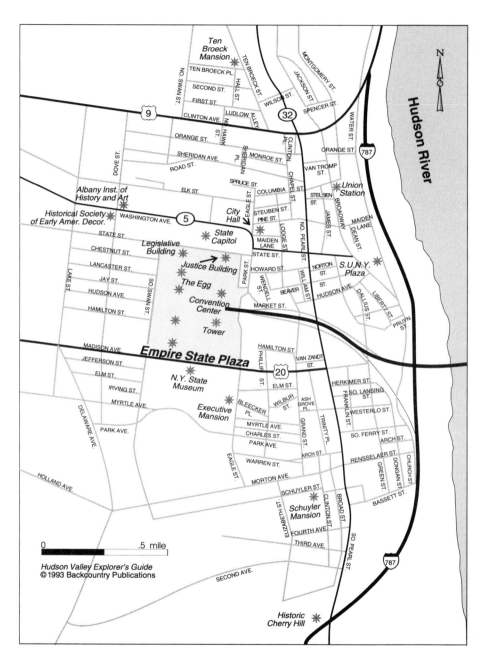

City of Albany

City of Albany

Long before Albany received its city charter, granted July 22, 1686, by Governor Thomas Duggan, the settlement was an important river stop and trading center. After Henry Hudson visited the region in 1609, Albany's fertile valleys and abundant game attracted Dutch settlers. Albany was to become a city of tremendous contrast—stagecoaches and steamboats, muddy roads and medical colleges, farmers and politicians. But through a combination of pride, pluck, and foresight, Albany has made the best of it all. A visit to the city today can focus on many things—history, politics, art, architecture—and can be made at any time of year. Spring brings the blossoming of thousands of tulips, pools of color that reflect Albany's Dutch origins. The Pinksterfest, a weekend celebration in May, welcomes the warm weather in the Dutch tradition, and the city parks come alive with fairs and shows. In summer, the great Empire State Plaza becomes a unique combination of outdoor park, art gallery, and seat of government, and autumn turns out to be a perfect time to explore the city on foot and discover the tiny side streets that still remain from three centuries ago. Winter ushers in Victorian greenery displays, snow festivals, and the lighting of the state Christmas tree. Whatever the season, be prepared to discover an area where the past and future work together.

GUIDANCE
Albany County Convention and Visitors Bureau (518-434-1217), 52 South Pearl Street, Albany 12207.

GETTING THERE
Albany is located off Exits 23 and 24 of I-87 (Quickway); watch for signs.

MEDICAL EMERGENCY
Albany Medical Center (518-445-3131), 43 New Scotland Avenue.

TO SEE

The Albany Institute of History and Art (518-463-4478), 125 Washington Avenue. Donation suggested. Open year-round; call for hours. Founded in 1791, this exceptional museum is one of the oldest in the United States, and it is still providing visitors with a chance to see varied, changing exhibits that focus on the Hudson Valley's cultural history. The building itself is a graceful collection of individual galleries and sweeping staircases, and there is even a small display area in the entrance hall. The institute's collections include fine European porcelain and glass; Dutch furniture, paintings and decorative arts from the early settlement period in Albany; pewter and silver produced by local smiths in the 18th century; and breathtaking examples of the Hudson River School of painting. The Dutch Room offers an interesting look into early Albany family life. Be sure to see the Egyptian Room on the lower level, where several mummies are on display along with some of their prized belongings. Changing exhibits are featured throughout the year, and special events include noontime art talks, the Explorers Club for children, a lecture and slide series, an antiquarian book show, and the colorful holiday Festival of Trees. The Luncheon Gallery is a nice place for a snack, and it is run by museum volunteers. The gift shop stocks many books about New York State history.

Albany Urban Cultural Park Visitors Center (518-434-5132), 25 Quackenbush Square. Open daily 10–4. Free. This site offers guests interactive displays that highlight history and culture in the capital city and provide an overview of the region. The same building is also home to the Henry Hudson Planetarium (518-434-5132), which has star shows on Saturdays and special school break programs during the year.

New York State Museum (518-474-5877), Empire State Plaza. To reach the plaza take Exit 23 off the NYS Thruway. Pick up I-87 and get off at the Empire Plaza exit. Open year-round (except Thanksgiving, Christmas, and New Year's Day) 10–5. Free. Today it anchors one end of the Empire State Plaza, but the museum has been a part of the state's history since 1836, making it one of the oldest state museums in the country. It is not, however, a dusty old repository with outdated displays of rocks and unidentified bones. This museum is alive with multimedia presentations that allow you to experience everything from a thunderstorm to a Lower East Side pushcart alley of the 1920s. The permanent exhibits include "Adirondack Wilderness," which explores the natural history of that region; "New York Metropolis," which focuses on New York City and the surrounding counties (here you'll find an Ellington-era A train and a set from *Sesame Street*); "Gems of New York State" and "Birds of New York," two dazzling exhibits that emphasize New York's wealth in these areas; and "Fire Fighting," a look at the brassy way in which fires were once fought. Changing exhibits may feature folk art or contemporary art, and shows are given in the museum's theater. Special events are scheduled all year, so visitors may get to enjoy a Victorian holiday, or a children's sleepover in the museum, or even a visit with an American artist.

HISTORIC HOMES

Historic Cherry Hill (518-434-4791), 523½ South Pearl Street. Open February through December; call for hours. Admission fee. Built in

1787 by Philip Van Rensselaer in order to replace what was called the Old Mansion, this Georgian house was the centerpiece of a 900-acre farm. Cherry Hill remained in the family for five generations, until 1963, and provides the visitor with a rare picture of the growth and care of a home over 176 years. The farm has, of course, disappeared under Albany streets, and the view across the road is of oil tanks instead of orchards, but the house itself still offers a sense of grace and elegance. A visit begins in the basement orientation center, where a wall chart untangles the complicated knot of marriages and relationships that kept Cherry Hill in the family. Upstairs, many of the 31 rooms have not been restored to match one particular period but contain the designs, belongings, and personal touches of their inhabitants. The collections found there are irreplaceable as a record of America's social history. There are more than 150 chairs, more than 30 tables, and thousands of decorative objects, which include 18th-century paintings, 19th-century oriental export ware, and even 20th-century clothing. Although the house was modernized over the years, things such as heating ducts and plumbing are carefully hidden away. Cherry Hill is a special place, chock-full of New York history and spirit. A holiday tour is offered in December and often features rarely exhibited toys from the museum's collection.

Schuyler Mansion (518-434-0834), 32 Catherine Street. Open April through December; Wednesday through Saturday 10–5; Sunday 1–5. Free. Once home to Philip Schuyler, a general in the Revolutionary War, the Schuyler Mansion was completed in 1764 on a rolling plot of land known as the Dutch Church Pasture. Schuyler was an important figure during the war, and many well-known statesmen, including Washington, Franklin, and the defeated English general John Burgoyne, visited the mansion over the years. During the war, Schuyler's daughter married Alexander Hamilton here, and a kidnap attempt was later made against her by the Tories; a gash on the wooden banister is said to have been made by a kidnapper's tomahawk. The house did not remain in the family after Schuyler's death but passed through a succession of owners before being purchased by New York State in 1912. Although there have been numerous changes to the exterior of the house over the years, including the removal of all the outbuildings, visitors today can still see many examples of 18th-century furniture, glassware, pottery, and art, as well as Schuyler family possessions. An herb garden has been added to replace the original plantings.

Ten Broeck Mansion (518-436-9826), 9 Ten Broeck Place. Open March through December; Wednesday through Friday 2–4, Saturday and Sunday 1–4. Closed holidays. Donation suggested. Home of the Albany County Historical Association, this Federal mansion was built in 1798 for General Abraham Ten Broeck, who was a member of the Continental Congress and fought in the nearby battle of Saratoga. Once called Arbor Hill, the house now offers a look at the lifestyle of Albany's upper class during the last two centuries. Exhibits include period furniture and decorative items, and the house also contains a wine cellar, which when rediscovered during renovations was found to have a valuable collection of very aged wines!

HISTORIC SITES

Capitol Building (518-474-2418), located at the State Street end of the Empire State Plaza. Open daily except major holidays year-round, 9–4. Free. Tours leave from the guide center inside the capitol. This fairy-tale building, with its red towers and hundreds of arched windows, is one of the few state capitols in the country that isn't topped by a dome. Construction, completed in 1899, took more than 30 years and cost the then-unheard-of sum of $25 million. This is where the state Senate and assembly meet, and where you'll find the governor's offices once used by Charles Evans, Theodore Roosevelt, Nelson Rockefeller, and Franklin D. Roosevelt. Throughout the building are thousands of fine stone carvings, a tradition that can be traced back to the great churches of the Middle Ages. Many were caricatures of famous politicians and writers; others were of the families and relatives of the artisans; still others were self-portraits of the stone carvers themselves. But the most compelling carvings are the ones that form the Million Dollar Staircase, which took years to complete and is the best known of all the capitol's embellishments. Another unusual architectural feature is the Senate fireplaces: The huge chimneys did not draw well, so their original function was abandoned in favor of using them as private "discussion nooks." And if you enjoy military history, don't miss the small military museum here; it traces the history of the state militia and National Guard. Flower lovers should make a special point of visiting the Capitol Park in spring, when thousands of tulips blaze into red and yellow bloom.

WALKING TOURS

There is so much to see in this historic city that a walk down just about any street will give you a glimpse into Albany's colorful past. The following are not specific tours but suggestions for starting points on an Albany exploration.

An example of a 19th-century row house community, the Pastures Historic District is bounded roughly by Morton and Second Avenues and Elizabeth and Pearl Streets. Here you will also find the Schuyler Mansion (see *Historic Homes*) as well as many impressive private homes. The Mansion Historic District, bounded by Eagle, Dongan, Hamilton, and Ferry Streets, is a kaleidoscope of building styles, Italianate, Federal, and Greek Revival being only a few. Although the area became run-down earlier in this century, people have been redis-covering the richness of the district, and there is a sense of renewal here. The Center Square–Hudson Park Historic District, bounded by South Swan Street, Madison Avenue, South Lake Street, and Spring

The state capitol at Albany

Street, is the largest historic district. Its centerpiece is Washington Park, a 90-acre area that once served as parade grounds and cemetery. Throughout the park you will find statues, lovely flower beds, and a lake. The district itself has scores of restored houses and commercial buildings.

If you don't want to walk, take the trolley from the **Albany City Trolley Company** (518-465-3632), 25 Quackenbush Square. There is a downtown trolley loop, and guided tours are available. Or if a carriage ride appeals to you, the **Albany Carriage Service** (518-465-5973), 1000 Delaware Avenue, will arrange for a trip around town or park. The more adventurous may wish to ascend a rock wall or climb ice, and two companies will accommodate them: **Albany's Indoor Rock Gym** (518-459-ROCK), 4C Vatrano Road, has an indoor caving and climbing system and outdoor tours; **Ascents of Adventure** (518-459-4966), 147 Cherry Avenue, Delmar, offers adventures in the open air year-round.

GREEN SPACE

Nelson A. Rockefeller Empire State Plaza (518-474-5877). The Plaza is located off Exit 23 of I-87 and is bounded by Swan, Madison, State, and Eagle Streets. Open daily year-round. Free. Popularly called the Plaza, this is really a government complex that includes office buildings, a convention center, a performing arts center known as the Egg, a concourse, and the state museum (see *To See*). Built at a cost of more than $2 billion and finished in 1978, the Plaza has fulfilled then Governor Rockefeller's dream of a government center that would draw visitors and allow them to feel in touch with their state government. Tours of the Plaza are offered several times a day, but you may enjoy walking it yourself. The esplanade area is wonderful to explore, with tranquil reflecting pools, plantings, and modern sculpture by artist David Smith, and even a play area known as the Children's Place. An environmental sculpture called *The Labyrinth* offers benches to the weary. The New York State Vietnam Memorial salutes the people who served in that war. Lining the interior halls of the concourse are fine examples of modern art on permanent display—the largest publicly owned and displayed art collection in the country, and it is all the work of New York artists. More than 92 sculptures, tapestries, paintings, and constructions are displayed, among them works by artists such as Calder, Nevelson, Frankenthaler, and Noguchi. Special art tours are offered (call for hours) or stop at any of the tourist booths and ask for the tour brochure. For an above-the-clouds view of the entire mall, take the elevator to the 42nd floor of the Corning Tower. The observation deck, open 9–4, is free, and you can see the Catskills, the Adirondacks, and the Berkshires. Outside near the wide stairway to the New York State Museum, concerts and special events are held throughout the summer, among them an Independence Day celebration, a Tulip Festival, and the Empire State Plaza Farmers Market. Children who like to walk will enjoy the activities on the mall.

LODGING

Note: All listings are in Albany unless otherwise indicated.

Albany Marriott Hotel (518-458-8444 or 1-800-443-8952), 189 Wolf Road 12205. ($$$) This hotel is near four major shopping malls, a 5-minute drive from the airport, and less than 20 minutes from downtown Albany. Each room in this luxury hotel is equipped with a color television, HBO, and other modern amenities. There are indoor and outdoor pools, a sauna, a whirlpool, and exercise rooms. A continental breakfast is served and there are restaurants on the site. Open year-round.

The Desmond (518-869-8100 or 1-800-448-3500), 660 Albany Shaker Road 12211. ($$$) The best features of an inn and a hotel are combined at The Desmond, with its period furniture, paintings, and handsome wood paneling, and courtyards that bloom with flowers and plants all year. All rooms have custom-made furniture, and guests can use two heated pools, a health club, saunas, exercise rooms, and a billiard room. Open year-round.

Mansion Hill Inn (518-465-2038), 115 Philip Street 12202. ($$) This bed & breakfast is within walking distance of the state capitol and the downtown business district. This inn won a preservation award, and each suite includes a living room, study, kitchen, large bedroom, and deck. Choose from a wide variety of dishes on the breakfast menu. Three suites with private bathrooms. Children welcome. Open year-round.

Omni Albany (518-462-6611 or 1-800-THE OMNI), Ten Eyck Plaza. ($$$) Located in the heart of the downtown area, near the Capitol Complex and Empire State Plaza, this luxury hotel has 386 newly decorated guest rooms and 18 suites. There is an exercise room, indoor heated pool, and whirlpool. Complimentary airport transportation and free parking are provided; a gift shop, auto rental facilities, and an airline office are on site. The hotel's restaurant, Fitzgerald's, has an excellent and reasonably priced lunch buffet Monday through Friday 11:30–2.

State Street Mansion Bed & Breakfast (518-462-6780), 281 State Street, 12210. ($$) This B&B is located in the center of the city's historic Center Square district. It is only one block away from the Capitol and Empire State Plaza. Cultural activities, entertainment, and dining are readily accessible. The brownstone dates back to 1889 and has been in business as a guest house for 80 years. There are 12 rooms; 5 have private baths and 7 share four baths. A continental breakfast is served. Parking is available and is included in the charge for the room.

WHERE TO EAT

DINING OUT

Albany has a wealth of restaurants to choose from, and they offer cuisines from nouvelle to Indonesian. The following were selected for their unusually good food or interesting surroundings; they provide only a hint of the culinary treasures in the capital city.

L'Auberge (518-465-1111), 351 Broadway. ($$) Open for lunch Monday through Friday, noon–2:30; dinner Monday through Saturday 6–10. Fine French cuisine, including duck with pear sauce and a rich rack of lamb with garlic and rosemary. Even if the food weren't as excellent as it is, the building with its towers and curves would be intriguing.

Caffe Italia (518-482-9433), 662 Central Avenue. ($$$) Open for lunch Monday through Friday at 11:30; dinner Monday through Saturday 5–11. This family-run Italian restaurant is a popular spot with members of the state legislature (there is even a dish or two named after lawmakers). Everything is prepared to order, and the veal and pasta specialties are worth the trip. Reservations required. Not recommended for children.

Jack's Oyster House (518-465-8854), 42 State Street. ($$) Open daily for lunch and dinner 11:30–10. This is Albany's oldest restaurant, and for 75 years it has been run by the same family. The steak and seafood are traditions, and the specialties are consistently good. Children are welcome. Reservations suggested.

Ogden's (418-463-6605), Lodge and Howard Streets. ($$) Open for lunch Monday through Friday from 11:30; for dinner Monday through Satur-

Lower Kaaterskill Falls

day from 5:30. Closed Sunday. Enjoy Continental and New American cuisine with such specialties as aged Angus beef with Roquefort sauce and grilled Norwegian salmon with ginger tamari beurre blanc. Salads and sandwiches predominate at lunchtime. The black bean soup has been on the menu for 17 years, and Ogden's is well known for this Cuban-style dish throughout Albany. All breads and desserts are made on the premises and every dish is prepared to order. An elegant yet casual spot located in a restored turn-of-the-century building with food that is consistently excellent. This is one of the best establishments in the capital.

Pasta Express (518-438-2012), 492 Yates Street. ($$) Open for dinner Monday through Saturday 6–10:30. A mahogany bar and pressed-tin ceilings and walls set the tone here. All types of pasta dishes are available and the pasta is made fresh daily.

La Serre Restaurant (518-463-6056), 14 Green Street. ($$$) Open daily except Sunday for lunch 11:30–2; dinner from 6. This elegant Continental restaurant is housed in a historic building complete with bright awnings and window boxes full of flowers. The service is superb, and specialties include an award-winning onion soup, bouillabaisse Marseillaise, loin of veal with béarnaise sauce, and steak au poivre. Sumptuous desserts are made fresh daily. Children are welcome. Reservations recommended.

The Shipyard (518-438-4428), 95 Everett Road. ($$) Open Monday through Friday at 11:30 for lunch; open daily for dinner from 5:30. This lovely restaurant is not only pretty to look at, it also has excellent

Continental and regional American food. Specialties include grilled chicken, lamb, and seafood; everything is fresh and made to order.

Sitar (518-456-6670), 1929 Central Avenue. ($$) Open Tuesday through Sunday for lunch (11:30–2:30) and dinner (5–10). Indian specialties prepared to your taste, among them tandoori and curry dishes and chicken and vegetarian entrées.

Yono's (518-436-7747), 289 Hamilton Street, Robinson Square. ($$) Open Monday through Saturday for dinner at 5. The taste of Indonesian cuisine is found here along with Continental specialties. Chicken, vegetarian dishes, and excellent steaks are on the menu. In summer, the garden patio is open for dining. Reservations suggested.

EATING OUT

Arita's (518-482-1080), 192 North Allen Street. ($) Open Wednesday through Friday for lunch, noon–2; Wednesday through Sunday for dinner 5–10. At this informal Japanese restaurant you can watch the chef prepare your meal on the hibachi table or enjoy the fare from the sushi bar.

Carmela's Cafe (518-869-3636), 1893 Central Avenue. ($) Open daily 11 AM–midnight, this café serves solid Italian fare, including pasta, seafood, pizza, and, on Sundays, an all-you-can-eat special with soup and salad.

Coco's (518-456-0197), 1470 Western Avenue. ($$) Open daily for lunch and dinner (11–10). A casual, offbeat place where the soups and breads are hearty and a large carousel horse stands atop the salad bar. Fun and funky for lunch.

El Loco Cafe (518-436-1855), 465 Madison Avenue. ($) Open Tuesday through Saturday for lunch and dinner 11:30–10. This lively café specializes in Tex-Mex fare and is located in a restored 19th-century building. El Loco is well known for its chili (the heat is up to you) and its large selection of Mexican beer. Even after all the chili and beer you can down, the desserts are still tempting.

Justin's (518-436-7008), 301 Lark Street. ($) Open for lunch Monday through Friday 11:30–2:30; dinner Monday through Saturday from 5; late-night menu available until 1 AM. Located in Albany's answer to Greenwich Village, part of this restaurant dates back to the 1700s, and there has been a tavern or inn on this site ever since. All soups are made fresh daily, and the crab, mussel, and tomato-dill bisques are excellent. There are daily specials and a café menu with gourmet sandwiches. Jazz is featured on some evenings. Not appropriate for children. Reservations suggested.

Mamoun's Falafel (518-434-3901), 206 Washington Avenue. ($) Open daily 11–10. In addition to the vegetarian fare at this Middle Eastern restaurant, there are a variety of chicken and lamb dishes. Try the shish kebob—it's a house specialty.

Quintessence (518-434-8186), 11 New Scotland Avenue. ($) Open daily for breakfast, lunch, and dinner 8 AM–4 AM. This art deco diner bustles with good food and special theme nights, including Italian, seafood, German, and international. A large menu with something for every taste. Children welcome.

ENTERTAINMENT

ART GALLERIES
Many fine publicly and privately owned galleries are scattered throughout the city. At the **Nelson A. Rockefeller Empire State Plaza** (see *Green Space*), free tours are given to enhance the appreciation of the great treasures found throughout the plaza.

University Art Gallery (518-422-4035), 1400 Washington Avenue, Fine Arts Buildings, State University at Albany, focuses on contemporary art with a variety of changing exhibits, some drawn from the gallery's own holdings, others from the works of both established artists and university students. The gallery's hours change during the year, so call before you go.

Harmanus Bleecker Center (518-465-2044), 19 Dove Street, has changing displays of the works of regional artists. The center is associated with the Albany Institute of History and Art, so classes and special events are held as well.

Rice Gallery (518-463-4478), at the Albany Institute of History and Art, 125 Washington Avenue (see *To See*), has several different shows each year, including juried exhibits of works by regional artists.

Picotte Gallery (518-454-5185), 324 State Street, a small gallery at the College of Saint Rose, offers works by contemporary artists.

If you enjoy marine art, then stop at the **Albany Art Gallery** (518-482-5374), Stuyvesant Plaza, Western Avenue, which carries art from the last century as well as the present.

McLean Gallery (518-465-8959), 231 Lark Street, exhibits antique and new paintings.

SELECTIVE SHOPPING

BOOKSTORES
Albany has many first-rate bookstores; this is only a selection.

The Book House (518-489-4761), Stuyvesant Plaza, is an independent, full-line bookshop with an extensive selection of maps and guides—local and otherwise. Attached is The Little Book House for children.

Hodge Podge Books (518-434-0238), 272 Lark Street, is a remarkable children's store—small and crammed with books—where reading is emphasized.

Haven't Got a Clue (518-464-1135), 1823 Western Avenue, staffed by knowledgeable mystery buffs, sells new and used mysteries and books on tape.

New York State Museum Shop (518-449-1401), Cultural Education Center (next to the New York State Library). A must stop for tourists, with lots of crafts, books, jewelry, and local stuff. And, of course, the museum exhibits!

Dove & Hudson Old Books (518-432-4518), 296 Hudson Avenue, and **North River Book Shop** (518-463-3082), 386 Delaware Avenue, offer extensive selections of carefully chosen used books with an emphasis on literary and scholarly works.

SPECIAL EVENTS

Tulip Festival, Pinksterfest, and **Kinderkermis.** These festivals are usually held over a long weekend in May and include outdoor crafts and food fairs, entertainment, the crowning of the Tulip Queen, and a dance. The celebrations are colorful and peopled with costumed performers. For information on the exact dates, call the Albany County Convention and Visitors Bureau (518-434-1217).

Other festivals held throughout the year include ethnic and art celebrations, the New York State Chocolate Festival, and the fabulous First Night, which offers citywide New Year's Eve entertainment; call the visitors bureau for information.

An unusual way to spend a morning is to take a trip out to the sugarbush and watch maple sap boiled down into rich, sweet maple syrup. Two sugarhouses allow visitors during the season, which usually runs from March into April: **Bassler's Sugarhouse** (518-872-2023), 2180 Becker Road, Berne, and **Sugarbush Farm** (518-872-1456), 1755 Township Road, Knox.

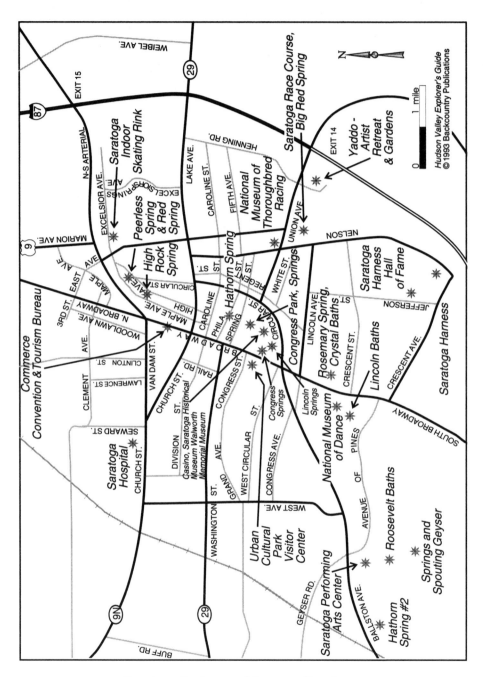

Saratoga Springs and Surrounding Areas

Saratoga Springs and Surrounding Area

It is nearly impossible to describe Saratoga Springs—elegant, gracious, exciting, mysterious, and eccentric are only a few of the words that come to mind. Since the 18th century, when medicinal springs were discovered in the region, Saratoga Springs has played host to visitors from around the world. There are modern spas in which to relax and plenty of outdoor activities to stretch the muscles. Classical music and dance enthusiasts can enjoy a picnic dinner while great orchestral selections and dances are performed under the stars. Lovers of Victorian architecture can merely stroll down a side street or two, where they will spot grand old mansions and exquisite gardens (some planted right in the middle of the road!). With all of this, Saratoga Springs also offers the best thoroughbred horse racing in the world. Each August, this quiet place pulses with the color, crowds, and excitement of the famed Saratoga Race Course, where the best jockeys and horses vie for enormous winnings and fame. In addition, there are horse auctions, polo matches, and art exhibits, and the public is invited to just about everything. You can spend a month in Saratoga Springs and still not experience all it has to offer. The only thing you must not do is miss it.

GUIDANCE
Greater Saratoga Chamber of Commerce (518-584-3255), 494 Broadway, Saratoga Springs 12866.

GETTING THERE
Saratoga Springs is located north of Albany on I-87 (Adirondack Northway), Exits 13N and 15.

MEDICAL EMERGENCY
Saratoga Hospital (518-587-3222), 211 Church Street, Saratoga Springs.

TO SEE

Canfield Casino and **Congress Park** (518-584-6920), Congress Park, Broadway, and Circular Street. The park is open daily year-round; the casino is open year-round, but hours vary widely during the winter and racing season, so call ahead. Admission charged for the casino. Part of the daily life of Saratoga Springs a century ago was "taking the waters," and Congress Park was a popular watering hole. The wealthy who came to Saratoga Springs each summer to escape the plagues and stink of the industrial cities would stay at the area's fine hotels and stroll along the park's pathways to various fountains (see *Springs*). Today the park has lovely plantings, places to sit and ponder the past, and some interesting decorative offerings. Daniel Chester French's statue *The Spirit of Life* greets visitors near the entrance (he also created the seated president's statue in the Lincoln Memorial), and two huge, lovely urns called "Day" and "Night" bloom with flowers each summer. Tucked in the back of the park is a small reflecting pool with the most popular of the park's denizens: a pair of Triton figurines who shoot out streams of water and are nicknamed "Spit" and "Spat." Enjoy walking among the columns in the Italian Gardens. Also located in the park is the Canfield Casino, once one of the most famous gambling establishments in the country, today home to a museum and art gallery. Upstairs, the Saratoga Historical Society maintains a lovely series of rooms that offer vignettes of life in Saratoga Springs during the Gilded Age of the late 19th century, when Lillian Russell, Diamond Jim Brady, and a host of others sparkled each night over the gaming tables. Downstairs in the museum's art gallery there are changing exhibits of works by local and regional artists. The museum also hosts several crafts shows each summer and fall (call for dates).

National Museum of Dance (518-584-2225), South Broadway. Open May through October; call for hours. Admission fee. This is the only museum in the country dedicated to preserving the history and art of dance in America, and it does a superb job. Changing exhibits feature costumes, artwork, personalities, and choreography of American dance. Videos help to place various dances in their historic settings, and it is one of the few places where dance enthusiasts may get up close to the costumes and accessories of their favorite dance "characters." Younger dance lovers may want to try and get tickets for the behind-the-scenes tours that are sometimes offered during the ballet season, but you must call ahead and make reservations long in advance.

National Museum of Thoroughbred Racing (518-584-0400), Union Avenue. Open year-round; hours vary widely, especially during racing season, so call ahead. Admission fee. This museum has only recently been updated into one of the most modern sport exhibits in the world, and it is a must-see for anyone who ever enjoyed the sight of a racehorse leaving the starting gate. The film *Race America* is an introduction to the racetrack, and throughout the various galleries video and audio exhibits let visitors experience the sounds and sights of racing. Silks, fine paintings, furniture, and historic items all tell the story of the thoroughbred in America, and the museum covers nearly 300 years of history. Even if you've never placed a bet in your life, the gift shop here will turn you into a horse fan immediately. Harness racing fans will want to visit the Saratoga Harness Racing Museum and Hall of Fame (518-587-4210), 352 Jefferson Street, which is located at the Saratoga Harness Raceway and offers memorabilia and artwork depicting the history of harness racing (free).

HISTORIC SITES

Saratoga National Historic Park (518-664-9821), State Route 32, Stillwater. Open daily year-round 9–5. The Philip Schuyler House is open daily Memorial Day to Labor Day; closed Thanksgiving, Christmas, and New Year's. Admission fee. The Battle of Saratoga turned the tide of the American Revolution, and history buffs will enjoy spending several hours here. The British hoped to cut New York into sections with a three-pronged attack and destroy communications among the areas. At Saratoga, the supposedly untrained, undisciplined American troops won the field, and history was changed. Your tour should begin at the battlefield visitors center, where dioramas, maps, and explanatory exhibits show how the battle was fought and won. Weapons, uniforms, and other items are on display, and because the battle was such a large one, it is necessary to read the material before you set out on the self-guided driving tour. There are markers at each stop that explain what went on during the battle. At the Schuyler House, memorabilia of General Philip Schuyler and his wife show what life was like for people who lived through the battle and the days after. There is even a monument to a leg—Benedict Arnold was wounded in the leg during the battle and became a hero, until he turned traitor later. There are special events, including military encampments, held at the park throughout the year (call for schedule).

SPRINGS

Saratoga is famous for its springs, many of which are still open. A spring tasting guide is available from the Urban Cultural Center (518-587-3241), 297 Broadway, opposite Congress Park. The center is open April through November and also has small exhibits on the history of Saratoga Springs and its commerce. The springs in Saratoga each have their own chemical makeup and characteristics; there are explanatory signs at each spring and, usually, paper drinking cups. Just remember that too much of the springwater might not sit well with your digestive system; try just a sip or two to start.

High Rock Park (go north on Broadway, make a right onto Lake Avenue and a left onto High Avenue). You can sample water from Old Red, the Peerless, and the Governor Springs here. These were the original public springs of Saratoga Springs, and each has its own taste; Old Red, so-called because of its high iron content, was considered good for the complexion.

Congress Park, on Broadway, houses Congress Spring, located underneath an elaborate pavilion. Its waters were some of the first springwater to

Visitors to the Saratoga National Historic Park in Stillwater will find cannons, like this reproduction of one used during the Battle of Saratoga in 1777, scattered about the battlefield. The self-guided 10-mile tour can be taken by car, by bike, on foot, or on horseback, and contains interpreted stops and scenic viewpoints.

be bottled and sold commercially in the early 19th century. Also in the park along the path are the Columbian Spring, Congress 3, and, in the northeast corner, Freshwater Spring. Across from the park, on Spring Street, the Hathorn No. 1 Spring is a popular stop on a hot summer's day; it has a small seating area, and lovely plantings surround it.

Also in Saratoga Springs itself, the **Urban Cultural Park** offers some bottled springwater, and the **Crystal Spa** (at the Grand Union Motel on South Broadway), a private business, offers springwater, mineral baths, and other healthful amenities.

Saratoga Spa State Park (take Route 9 south to the Avenue of Pines and follow that into the park; the site is very well marked) has several springs and bathing facilities (see *Green Space*). Built in the 1930s, the Roosevelt Baths and the Lincoln Park Baths still have mineral baths and massages. The Roosevelt (518-584-2011) is open all year; the Lincoln Park (518-434-3201) is open in the summer months only (call for reservations). The fees are very low. Drinking springs throughout the park include Island Spouter (the only spouting geyser east of the Mississippi), Hayes Well (with an inhaling hole), Orenda Spring, Coesa, and Ferndale. There is a marked walking path to many of the springs, and it is a lovely stroll on a warm summer's afternoon. There is no charge for tasting the springs.

WALKING TOUR

A walk through Saratoga Springs gives visitors a chance to see the great variety of architectural styles in vogue during the 19th and early 20th centuries, but it would be impossible to list all the houses that are worth looking at. A self-guided tour is sometimes available at the information booth near Congress Park or from the Greater Saratoga Chamber of Commerce (518-584-3255), 494 Broadway. Scores of homes offer a look at Italianate, Gothic Revival, Queen Anne, Romanesque, and other styles popular with the upper middle class and wealthy of the city. The **Batcheller House,** corner of Whitney and West Circular, is a fantasy of French Renaissance and Eastern influence; the **Jumel Mansion,** 129 Circular Street, was the summer home of the infamous Madame Jumel, one-time wife to Aaron Burr; the **Adelphi Hotel,** Broadway, recalls the hotels of the past, with tall columns and many arched windows. Several streets and areas you may want to enjoy for their architectural wealth include Broadway, Circular Street, Franklin Square, Clinton Street, Caroline Street, Lake Avenue, and Union Avenue. All the homes are private, but their beauty can easily be appreciated from the sidewalk.

TO DO

FARM STANDS AND PICK-YOUR-OWN FARMS

Among the many things Saratoga is famous for is melon; more specifically, Hand melons, named after the family that first grew them. The **Hand farm stand** is located 13 miles east of Saratoga Springs on Route 29; the melons are usually ready to go in late July through mid-August. The melons are sweet and resemble cantaloupes, and you will see signs for them at many farm stands. A great deal of excellent produce is raised on local farms as well. At **Ariels Vegetable Farm** (518-584-2189), 194 Northern Pines Road, 5 miles north of Saratoga Springs (open April through September), visitors can pick their own berries, buy fruit and vegetables off the stand, or take a tour of the farm.

Bowman Orchards (518-371-7432), Sugar Hill Road, Rexford (open September through November), has pick-your-own apples, as does **Bullards Farm Market** (518-695-3177), Route 29, Schuylerville (open August through February). Both also have well-stocked farm stands.

Riverview Orchards (518-371-2174), Riverview Road, Rexford, has pick-your-own apples, farm tours, lots of produce, and cross-country skiing in the winter.

There is also a nice farmers market held at the Spring Street parking lot in Saratoga Springs every Wednesday evening 3–6 and Saturday 9–1 from May through October.

HORSE RACING

Saratoga Harness Raceway (518-584-2110), Nelson Avenue. Open year-round except December; post time 7:45 PM. Admission fee. This track is often overshadowed by its more sassy cousin, the Saratoga Racetrack, but for anyone who enjoys harness racing, it will provide lots of excitement. Visitors can enjoy watching horses vie for purses on the world's fastest ½-mile trotting and pacing track, which, unlike the "flats," is open all year. If you are in Saratoga Springs between May and early September, call and inquire about the backstretch tours. These take visitors past the paddock, blacksmith shop, and even the horse swimming pool, the only pool in the state located on the grounds of a racetrack and reserved for the use of horses.

Saratoga Racetrack (518-587-5070 or 584-6200), Union Avenue. Open during August meeting only; call for specific dates. Closed Tuesday. Admission fee varies. Saratoga Racetrack is a hub of activity during the month of August, and it is busy from early in the morning until the late afternoon. You can begin with "Breakfast at Saratoga" (7–9:30 AM; get there early), a popular way for people to enjoy the horses and jockeys close up. There is an announcer to keep things lively as the horses and their riders breeze by. Handicapping seminars are held at the track and are announced at breakfast; the seminar times are also posted throughout the track and are very handy for people who are novice bettors. Breakfast is served daily in the clubhouse dining room, in an outdoor tent, and breakfast buffet in the box seats; outside, a continental breakfast is served outside near the clubhouse. Visitors can also enjoy a tour of the backstretch area, where the horses board during the racing season. The tour is escorted, and the area is viewed from an observation "train"; sign up for the tour early during breakfast.

The track opens to the racing crowd at 11 AM weekdays and 10:30 AM weekends. Although there is lots of parking and seating available, remember one thing: The crowds can be large and the track is smaller than many modern racetracks. Get there early for good viewing. You can park in an official track lot or at a private lot. The latter cost more, but the former fill up quickly; again, get there early so at least you have a selection. Bring your own chair, if possible, and remember that both restaurant food and snacks, though usually good, can be very expensive. You are allowed to bring coolers into the track. Both steeplechases and flat races are held throughout the season; check the daily racing forms to see exactly who is racing in what. Races begin (post time) at 1 weekdays, 12:30 weekends, rain or shine.

POLO

You can't play polo unless you have your own string of ponies, but you can watch weekly at Saratoga. The players come from all over the world and are the best in their sport. Matches are held Tuesday, Friday, and Sunday throughout August, but call for hours and a complete schedule (518-584-3255 or 584-8108). There is an admission charge. To get to the polo grounds, go north on Broadway, turn left onto Church Street, go approximately 0.5 mile, and make a right onto Seward Street. Go 1 mile to the railroad overpass and turn right; the polo field is on your left.

GREEN SPACE

Saratoga Spa State Park (518-584-2000), 1 mile south of Saratoga Springs on Route 9. Open year-round. The park is free; there is a small charge for swimming and the bathhouses. This 2000-acre park is a gem: clean, wide open, full of activities to keep visitors busy—and located only minutes from Saratoga Springs. Listed on the National Register of Historic Places, the park is home to the Saratoga Performing Arts Center (see *Entertainment*) and the Gideon Putnam Hotel (see *Lodging*) as well as the Roosevelt Baths and the Lincoln Park Baths (see *Springs*). Recreation opportunities abound in Spa Park: Three pools, tennis courts, streamside trails for walking, and two golf courses (reservations required) are open in the summer; in the winter, cross-country skiing, ice skating, and even a speed skating oval are open for use. Special film evenings, nature walks, tours, and other special events are held throughout the year (call for a schedule of events).

Yaddo (518-587-4886), Union Avenue. Open year-round. Free. The gardens here are superb, and visitors are welcome to walk among the paths and enjoy the fountains, roses, plantings, and quiet seating areas. Yaddo was once a private home and is now an artists' retreat used by both the famous and the someday-to-be-famous; and the site offers a respite from the August frenzy of racing and society.

LODGING

A note on lodging and dining in Saratoga Springs: The Spa City is a wonderful place to visit and spend a day or a week. As in many other resorts, prices range from moderate to expensive. But during the "season"—late July through August, when thoroughbred racing is the main event—prices can go sky high, and accommodations may be difficult to get (some places are booked as early as May). Restaurants can be crowded, expensive, and difficult to get reservations for—that is, unless you know someone. We don't suggest you pass up the excitement that is Saratoga Springs during the summer—it is still the best time to visit—but be prepared to pay top price for lodging and dining. If you are going to visit the area, you may want to consider staying in Albany (see "City of Albany"), which is about 40 minutes away. Hours vary so widely during the different seasons that they have been noted only if they do not change. If you are in doubt, call before you go.

Note: All listings are in Saratoga Springs 12866, unless otherwise indicated.

Chestnut Tree Inn (518-587-8681), 9 Whitney Place. ($$$) Named after the last remaining chestnut tree in Saratoga Springs, this inn offers country ambience within walking distance of the racetrack and other points of interest. The continental breakfast is served on the Victorian porch in summer, and the inn is furnished with antiques. Suites and rooms with shared or private baths are available. Open year-round.

Eddy House (518-587-2340), Crescent and Nelson Avenues. ($$$) The house sits on 1.5 acres of well-tended lawns and gardens, and guests can play badminton or bocce, use the golf net, or just relax. In addition to the five private rooms there are two living rooms, a library, and a screened-in porch for guests' use. A large gourmet breakfast is served daily and may include French toast, eggs, homemade muffins, and other baked goods. Open year-round.

Gideon Putnam Hotel (518-584-3000), Saratoga Spa State Park. ($$$) The hotel is set in the 2000-acre park, a few minutes' walk from the Saratoga Performing Arts Center and minutes away from the track and from downtown Saratoga Springs. In addition to double rooms, there are 18 parlor

Gideon Putnam Hotel

Union Gables Bed & Breakfast

and porch suites available. The service is excellent, and guests may choose to have meals included in the rate. Open year-round.

The Inn at Saratoga (518-583-1890), 231 Broadway. ($$$) This establishment combines the modern comforts of a hotel and the charming touches of an inn. There are 38 rooms and suites, all decorated in Victorian style. A restaurant downstairs serves dinner daily, and the Sunday brunch features live jazz. Continental breakfast is served. Open year-round.

Lombardi Farm (518-587-2074), 34 Locust Grove. ($$) This bed & breakfast is only 1.5 miles from downtown Saratoga Springs and is located in a restored 1850s farmhouse. Guests may enjoy a hot tub, air-conditioned rooms with private baths, and a large gourmet breakfast. There are even Nubian dairy goats to pet. This is a nice, casual farm setting, a change from the rush of Saratoga Springs in August. Open year-round.

The Mansion (518-885-1607), Route 29, Rock City Falls 12863. ($$$) This inn, a dream come true for lovers of Victoriana, has been featured in several publications. The rooms are furnished with period furniture, and the service is elegant, with a full gourmet breakfast included. Guests may use the parlor, walk the grounds, visit the antiques shop, or laze on the porch; the pool is open in summer. All rooms or suites have private baths and air-conditioning; adults only. Open year-round.

Six Sisters Bed and Breakfast (518-583-1173), 149 Union Avenue. ($$$) This charming establishment, named after the six sisters of one of the owners, is located on the flower-bedecked Union Avenue approach to the racetrack. At Six Sisters, guests will enjoy a gourmet breakfast and their choice of guest rooms or suites, all with private baths and air-conditioning. Only minutes from most of the goings-on in Saratoga Springs, this inn is a special place to enjoy a special weekend. Older children welcome. Open year-round.

Union Gables Bed & Breakfast (518-584-1558 or 1-800-398-1558), 55 Union Avenue. ($$) This newly restored Queen Anne Victorian, circa 1901, is a family-owned and -occupied bed & breakfast. Each of the 10 guest rooms is exquisitely decorated to reflect the style of Old Saratoga. Every room has a modern bath, television, telephone, and small refrigerator. The establishment is conveniently located near the downtown area and only 1 block from the thoroughbred racetrack. Children are welcome. Open year-round.

Westchester House (518-587-7613), 102 Lincoln Avenue. ($$$) Built in high Gothic style, complete with towers, crenellations, and oddments, this charming inn is a fairy tale come true. The rooms offer luxury touches like ceiling fans (or air-conditioning), and fresh flowers from the surrounding gardens in summer. Downtown Saratoga Springs is a few minutes' walk away, and guests can enjoy sitting on the porch while looking forward to the morning's breakfast of home-baked goods and fresh gourmet coffee. Open year-round.

WHERE TO EAT

Note: All listings are in Saratoga Springs unless otherwise indicated.

DINING OUT

Adelphi Hotel (518-587-4688), 365 Broadway. ($$) They serve dinner only during July and August, but they will also serve dessert and coffee in the evening year-round, and their pastries are delightful. Entrées may include tuna curry, chicken with corn pudding, or duck with black currant sauce. The Victorian surroundings, which echo the old-time elegance of Saratoga Springs, are delightful. Not recommended for children.

Beverly's (518-583-2755), 47 Phila Street. ($$) Open for breakfast and lunch Monday through Saturday 7 AM–6:30 PM, and Sunday 8 AM–3 PM; dinner Thursday through Saturday 6:30–9:30 during racing season. This small café is tucked down a side street just off Broadway. The food is fresh and carefully prepared, and the baked goods are excellent. They are well known for thick slabs of French toast and will prepare gourmet takeout lunches for picnics trackside (or just anywhere).

Cafe Lena (518-583-0022), 47 Phila Street. ($$) Open Thursday through Sunday from 8 PM. Almost all major folk and folk-rock artists have appeared at this well-known coffeehouse and nightspot over the years. The food is secondary to the performers, although the coffee, including specialties like iced mocha java, is excellent. Worth a stop, no matter who is on the bill. Not recommended for children.

The Caunterbury Restaurant (518-587-9653), 500 Union Avenue. ($$)

Open daily for dinner from 6. Dine by romantic waterfalls or a roaring fire at this delightful spot. Wood-grilled meats and fish, unusual pastas, hearty sandwiches, and salads are some of the popular offerings here. The pesto ravioli is renowned. A variety of wines is available by the glass. Children are welcome.

Eartha's Kitchen (518-583-0602), 60 Court Street. ($$$) Open Tuesday through Saturday from 6. A popular spot with diners in the know, this restaurant serves fresh dishes with a Continental flair, including mesquite-grilled seafood, duck, and steaks. There is a small sidewalk patio, and reservations are a must anytime. Not recommended for children.

Gideon Putnam Hotel (518-584-3000), Saratoga State Park. ($$) Open daily for breakfast 7–11; lunch, noon–2; dinner 6–9. Set in the lovely spa park, this hotel is often packed on the evenings before a concert or ballet. Their Sunday brunch is outstanding and well worth the wait (seatings every half hour 11–2). Jackets are required for dinner, as are reservations.

43 Phila Bistro (518-584-2720), 43 Phila Street. ($$) Open for dinner from 5 PM daily except Tuesday. Sunday brunch 11–3. This New American bistro features dishes from around the world. You can sample such tempting entrées as New Zealand lamb, Maryland crabcakes, and wild boar; there are a number of flavorful vegetarian dishes as well. All the pasta is homemade and the pastry chef creates sensational desserts daily. Children welcome.

Professor Moriarity's (518-587-5981), 430 Broadway. ($$) Open daily for lunch and dinner 11:30–9:30. Victorian in feeling, this café is named after Sherlock Holmes's nemesis. A nice place for lunch, with very hearty sandwiches and homemade soups. Try Dr. Watson's filet mignon; there is no mystery about its popularity. Children welcome.

Siro's (518-584-4030), 168 Lincoln Avenue. ($$$) Open daily for dinner August only. Call for hours, which vary. This is probably the most popular dinner spot with racegoers. Reservations are required, although the bar area is open (and popular). The food here is Continental, with steak and seafood the specialties. Recommended if you want to continue enjoying the horsey atmosphere for the evening.

Sperry's (518-584-9618), 30½ Caroline Street. ($$) Open daily for lunch 11:30–3:30; dinner 5:30–10. This American bistro-style restaurant offers grilled seafood and steak specials, fresh pasta, and soft-shell crabs in season. The homemade pastries and desserts are first rate: the crème caramel was featured in *The New York Times*. One of Saratoga's most reliable year-round gems.

The Waterfront Restaurant and Marina (518-583-BOAT), 3 miles out of town; take Union Avenue to 628 Crescent Avenue, Saratoga Lake. ($$) Open daily from 11:30 for lunch and dinner. The glass-walled dining room and shoreline deck offer an uninterrupted view of Saratoga Lake and make this casual spot special. Steaks, seafood, pasta, and burgers are served in a relaxing atmosphere. Children welcome.

EATING OUT

Bruno's (518-583-3333), Union Avenue, opposite the Saratoga Racetrack. Summer. ($$) Open daily 11 AM–11 PM. Pizza lovers will want to stop by Bruno's and enjoy one from the wood-fired oven. During the August racing season, the restaurant opens early for breakfast, with special egg, bacon, ham, and other creative start-your-day pizzas. Kids are welcome, and the atmosphere is funky '50s.

Country Corner Cafe (518-583-7889), 25 Church Street. ($) Open daily 6 AM–2 PM. The best breakfast in town is served all day in this cozy café. Try the home-baked breads and muffins with preserves or the fresh fruit pancakes with maple syrup. The hearty soups and sandwiches make this a popular lunch spot with local residents.

Hattie's Chicken Shack (518-584-4790), 45 Phila Street. ($) Open from breakfast till dinner daily except Tuesday, 11–8. This is *the* place for great fried foods: chicken, fish, potatoes. There are also nice pancake breakfasts, and biscuits with everything. For lovers of the lost art of the deep-fry. Children welcome.

Old Bryan Inn (518-587-2990), 123 Maple Avenue. ($) Open daily at 11 AM. This unpretentious country inn is a nice stop for lunch and dinner. The burgers are hearty, the salads are fresh, and the steaks are grilled. Try the hot spinach salad or deep-fried cheese sticks with an unusual raspberry sauce. Children welcome.

The Parting Glass (518-583-1916), 40 Lake Avenue, Saratoga Springs. ($) Open daily from 11 AM until the early morning hours. An Irish pub–style restaurant, try their Guinness and black bean soup for a hearty meal. There is entertainment on Wednesday and Saturday nights, and the place is a favorite with the racetrack crowd. Great fun if you enjoy pubs; they have a vast selection of beers and even have a serious dart shop. Not recommended for children.

PJ's Bar-b-q (518-583-CHIK), Route 9S, Broadway. Open noon for lunch and dinner. Call for hours. Real, thick, smokey ribs and chicken. Spicy and satisfying for take-out or eat-in-the-parking-lot.

Scallions (518-584-0192), 404 Broadway. ($) Open daily 11–9. A gourmet eatery with a cheerful café atmosphere. Try the unique sandwich combinations, homemade soups, and specialty chicken and pasta dishes. Desserts are first rate: The carrot cake is the best around. A great place to take out a meal for a picnic if you are heading to SPAC or the track.

ENTERTAINMENT

ARTS

Saratoga Performing Arts Center (SPAC) (518-587-3330), Saratoga Spa State Park, off Route 9, Saratoga Springs. Open from Mother's Day through early September; schedules, performances, and ticket prices

Saratoga Performing Arts Center

vary. Each summer there are performances by the Philadelphia Orchestra and the New York City Ballet, jazz, rock, and folk concerts, and more with matinee and evening shows. You can bring a picnic, select foods from the gourmet food carts, or stop at one of the restaurants in town and arrange for an elegant take-along dinner. There is a covered, open-air seating area as well as lawn seats under the stairs, and plenty of parking. SPAC is but a few minutes' drive from the center of town, but beware: A popular concert can create bottlenecks, so plan to get there early. Lawn tickets can be purchased the night of most performances, but it is a good idea to call ahead and inquire about ticket availability.

SELECTIVE SHOPPING

Celtic Treasures (518-583-9452) and **Saratoga Science Fiction & Mystery Bookshop** (518-583-3743) can both be found in a mall at 454 Broadway in downtown Saratoga Springs.

Lyrical Ballad Bookstore (518-584-8779), 7 Phila Street, Saratoga Springs, is a classy antiquarian shop.

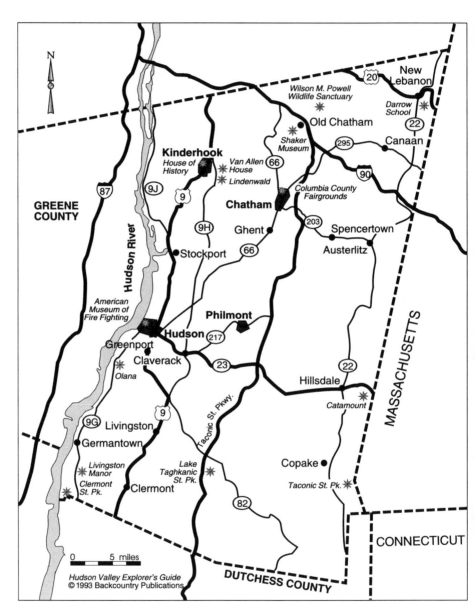

Columbia County

Columbia County

First the home of the Native Americans who greeted Henry Hudson, Columbia County later attracted Dutch, German, and New England settlers with its river and its fertile land. Whaling became a major industry, with the ships moving up the Hudson River and unloading their international cargo at Hudson in the 1830s. The city echoed with the noises of shipping, rope making, and trading. Fine homes resembling the extravaganzas of Maine and Massachusetts were built for men and women of substance and sophistication. The unusual is the rule here: a colorful museum filled with firemen's equipment, and a library that was once a lunatic asylum. The Shakers built settlements here and led their sober lives, which were also filled with song, dance, and fine craftsmanship. Across the county antiques glow in the windows of well-appointed shops, while the simplicity of Shaker furniture offers its own comment on life and living. Martin Van Buren lived in Columbia County (in fact, the term *OK* is thought to have originated from Van Buren's nickname, "Old Kinderhook"). Thoroughbred race horses are bred, raised, and trained in Columbia County, and each year the state's oldest county fair brings folks of all ages together in celebration of the harvest's best.

GUIDANCE
Columbia County Tourism (518-828-3375), 401 State Street, Hudson 12534.

GETTING THERE
Columbia County be reached from the Taconic State Parkway or Routes 9 and 9H; the Massachusetts Turnpike also cuts directly across the county from west to east.

MEDICAL EMERGENCY
Columbia-Greene Medical Center (518-828-7601), 71 Prospect Avenue, Hudson.

TO SEE

American Museum of Fire Fighting (518-828-7695), Harry Howard Avenue, Hudson. Open April 1 to November 1 daily except Monday. Admission fee. Take a step back in time to the glory days of fire fighting, at this fascinating museum located next door to the Firemen's Home. You will discover the oldest and broadest collection of fire-fighting gear and memorabilia in the United States. Hundreds of pieces of horse-drawn and steam- and gas-powered equipment are on display, some dating back to the 18th century. Greeting you as you enter the museum is a wooden statue of a volunteer fire chief dressed in patriotic red, white, and blue, complete with stars and golden trumpet. The museum is divided into two halls that house fire-fighting pumps, mobile apparatus, and engines, as well as paintings, clothing, banners, photographs, and other memorabilia. There is a Newsham engine, which was used to quench flames in Manhattan houses in 1731 and saw more than a century and a half of use. A delicate silver parade carriage from Kingston is topped by the figure of a fireman holding a rescued baby. Throughout the museum you will see lots of gleaming brass, bright red paint, and an oddity or two, like the ornate firemen's parade trumpets, the hand grenade-style fire extinguishers, and the brass fire markers, which indicated which fire company had the right to fight a particular fire. There are even modern fire clothes, which show the difference in fire-fighting techniques through the years. There are several special events held at the site, all involving displays of the firefighter's skills. Call for schedule.

Louis Paul Jonas Studios (518-851-2211), Miller Road, Churchtown. By appointment only. Free. Discover dinosaurs lurking in Churchtown. This workshop produced the dinosaurs that were displayed at the 1963 New York World's Fair, and they still make full-sized and smaller versions of the reptilian wonders. Although not open to the general public, with advance notice group tours may be welcome. It's worth the call.

The Shaker Museum and Library (518-794-9100), Shaker Museum Road, off County Route 13, Old Chatham. Open May 1 to October 31; library open by appointment at other times. Admission fee. Although there are several Shaker museums in the country, this one owns the foremost study collection of Shaker cultural material. In the late 18th century, a group of English men and women immigrated to the colonies with the hope of being allowed to practice their communal religion. Called Shakers because they danced and moved during worship services, the group established settlements throughout their new country and became as well known for their crafts and innovations as for their unusual celibate lifestyle. Industry, thrift, and simplicity were their bywords. In their workshops, chairs, seed packets, tin milk pails, and jams were made with equal skill and care, and today Shaker-made items are still valued for their beauty and grace. This museum is located in a restored barn and outbuilding; the collections were gathered by both Shakers and non-Shakers, with the goal of preserving a life that is almost gone. All the major Shaker industries are represented at the museum—trip-hammer and washing machine manufacturing as well as clothing and broom making. The Shakers are credited with inventing the circular saw and the revolving bake oven, although they rarely took

The American Museum of Fire Fighting in Hudson

out a patent, preferring that the world benefit from their work. The museum also houses a fine collection of furniture and household items from the various settlements. Special events are held throughout the season, including crafts workshops, lectures, and concerts.

Columbia County Museum (518-758-9265), 5 Albany Avenue, Kinderhook. The museum, owned by the Columbia County Historical Society, is open May through October. The exhibits here include paintings, textiles, and other items that help to tell the story of Columbia County.

HISTORIC HOMES

Clermont (518-537-4240), located on Route 6 just off Route 9G, in Germantown. Open late May through October; tours Wednesday through Sunday. The grounds are open year-round. Admission fee. Standing on land that was awarded to the Livingston family in 1686, this Georgian mansion remained in the family for nearly three centuries. The Livingstons' illustrious history—Judge Robert Livingston wrote the letter of protest to King George just before the Revolutionary War, and Chancellor Robert R. Livingston helped draft the Declaration of Independence—is evident throughout the house. Although Clermont itself was burned by the British during the war, it was later rebuilt around the old walls and foundation. Alterations and additions were made into the late 19th century, so the house today reflects changes wrought by several generations. Clermont's 35 rooms are furnished with family heirlooms and fine examples of period furniture and decorative accessories. A crystal chandelier from 1700 hangs above the drawing room, where you will also find a French balloon clock made to commemorate the Montgolfier brothers' ascent. Family portraits decorate the hallways and help visitors sort out the confusing Livingston family tree, and there are exquisite examples of cabinetmaking throughout the mansion. But as lovely as Clermont is, the setting makes it more so. The views up, down, and across the Hudson River are magnificent; the family purchased as much land as possible in order to preserve the setting. Tradition holds that the black locust trees flanking the house were planted by the builder of Clermont in the mid 18th century. The roses in the English box garden transform the month of June into an enchanting time. There are special events from April through December at Clermont, including a sheep-shearing festival, which recalls Chancellor Livingston's interest in agriculture; a croquet day, complete with musical entertainment; Independence Day, which has featured hot-air balloons and costumed Colonial soldiers; the annual Hudson River Steamboat Days; and a Christmas open house.

Lindenwald (518-758-9689), Route 9H, Kinderhook. Open May through October, Wednesday through Sunday 9–4:30. Admission fee. Built in 1797, the house was renovated in 1849 as the retirement home of Martin Van Buren, eighth president of the United States. The resulting structure was a blend of Federal, Italianate, and Victorian styles. Van Buren was born in Kinderhook (Dutch for "children's corner"), the son of a tavern keeper. He studied law and from Kinderhook embarked on a 30-year political career. At Lindenwald, visitors will see the house Van Buren returned to in order to look back upon three tumultuous decades of public service. Named after the trees on the property, the graceful building—complete with shutters, double chimneys, and arched windows—is today a National Historic Site; it was recently renovated in order to remove or lessen the impact of certain Victorian "improvements." The grounds offer an escape to the peace of rural 19th-century America, but it is inside that the recent renovations are more evident. A center stairway winds upward through the house, the hundreds of turned spindles polished so they gleam. The old wallpaper was stripped and replaced with paper appropriate to the era, and furniture and decorative objects finally look as if they belong to the home. The house contains a fine collection of Van Buren memorabilia, and a visit is an excellent way to become acquainted with the president known as the Little Magician, because of both his size and his political acumen.

Luykas Van Alen House (518-758-9625), Route 9H, Kinderhook. After visiting Lindenwald, you may want to stop at the Luykas Van Alen House, which is operated by the Columbia County Historical Society and is a brick Dutch farmhouse of the early 18th century. It has been

Lindenwald, home of President Martin Van Buren

restored to reflect its heritage. The site contains the Ichabod Crane School House—a restored, one-room schoolhouse open to the public and named after the character in Washington Irving's tale. In fact, Irving based Crane on a local schoolteacher who worked in this schoolhouse.

Olana (518-828-0135), Route 9G, 1 mile south of Rip Van Winkle Bridge, Greenport. Open May through October daily except Monday and Tuesday. The house is viewed by guided tour only, and group size is limited; you can call to reserve tickets before you go. The grounds can be viewed without a guide. Admission fee. Frederic Edwin Church was one of America's foremost artists, a painter who captured the grandeur and mystery of the nation in the 19th century. Church first gained acclaim for his vision of Niagara Falls, a painting that won a medal at the 1867 Paris International Exposition. In 1870, Church and his wife, Isabel, returned from their travels in the Middle East and Europe to their farm in Hudson and began the planning and building of the Persian fantasy that would become known as Olana. Hand-painted tiles on the roof and turrets of the 37-room mansion, situated 460 feet above the river, add touches of pink and green to the sky. Church called his style "personal Persia," and inside you will discover hand-carved, room-sized screens, rich Persian rugs, delicate paintings, decorative pottery and china, and even a pair of gilded crane lamps that look as if they stepped out of an Egyptian wall painting. Olana is also rich in examples of Church's paintings, including *Autumn in North America* and *Sunset in Jamaica*. His studio is still set up as it was in his time. During the holiday season the house is decorated with elaborate greenery, and Yuletide confections grace the tables. Visitors can hike year-round along the carriage paths and roadways that wind through the property. The house tour is not recommended for younger children.

James Vanderpoel House (518-758-9265), Board Street, Kinderhook. Open Memorial Day to Labor Day, Tuesday through Saturday 10:30–4:30, Sunday 1:30–4:30; weekends only in September and October. Admission fee. This site is also called the House of History, and indeed it does present some fine exhibits of life in Columbia County, especially the era when the area was a bustling industrial and whaling center. Built around 1819 for lawyer and politician James Vanderpoel, the Federal house is characterized by delicate ornamentation including plasterwork ceilings, graceful mantelpieces, and a wide staircase that seems to float to the second floor. The work of New York cabinetmakers, a blend of American pride and European style, is displayed throughout the rooms. A fine selection of paintings, including many by country artists, depicts Columbia County life. The Vanderpoel House holds several special events throughout the year, including a Christmas greens show and a coaching competition.

HISTORIC SITE

Mt. Lebanon Shaker Village (518-794-9500), Route 20, New Lebanon. Open daily Memorial Day to Labor Day; weekends only Labor Day through October. Hours vary with the season, so call ahead. Admission fee. Located on the site of a former Shaker settlement and now part of the Darrow School, the village tour includes an introductory slide show about the Shakers and a walking tour through several buildings, including the stone dairy barn and meetinghouse.

SCENIC DRIVES

It is difficult to avoid taking a scenic drive in Columbia County—wherever you look, you can see rolling, bright green meadows, misty ponds, and quiet villages that look the same as they did a century ago. You may find yourself on a bluff overlooking the Hudson River or in a city that recalls the glory of the whaling industry. The roads are well maintained, and you can't get lost for very long.

For a sampling of the county's charms, Route 9 and Route 9H will take you through Hudson, Kinderhook, and Valatie, with plenty of museums, shops, and restorations to explore. Other routes worth a drive include Route 82, Route 7, and Route 22, all of which take you through the western part of the county. A road that has actually received an award for its scenic beauty—Route 11 between Routes 23 and 27, near Taghkanic—has been declared a National Beautiful Highway.

WALKING TOURS

The city of Hudson, located on Route 9G, is rich with the traditions and cultural heritage of its settlers: first the Dutch, then seafarers from

Olana, a Persian-style mansion, was home to Hudson River School painter Frederic Church.

Massachusetts and Rhode Island, and Quakers and whalers. Carefully designed in the 1780s as a shipping center, with straight streets and "gangway" alleys, ropewalks, wharves, and warehouse, Hudson was the first city to receive a charter after the Declaration of Independence. Soon whaling and industry took over as the mainstays of the economy, and although Hudson has had its ups and downs since, the city is now in the full flower of a renaissance. On a walking tour of Hudson you'll see dozens of architectural styles and hundreds of commercial buildings and homes that have been maintained or restored to their earlier glory. A visitor to the city may want to stop in at the Chamber of Commerce, 729 Warren Street, and pick up a detailed walking guide. Columbia County Tourism (518-828-3375), at 401 State Street, may be a source for the walking guide. But whether or not you follow a specific tour, a walk around several main streets will reveal the architectural heritage of the area.

From Route 9G, follow Warren Street to Front Street and park. At Front Street, you will see the Parade, an 18th-century park that was kept open for use by the city's inhabitants. From the park, also called Promenade Hill Park, you'll have a dazzling view of the Hudson River and the Catskill Mountains, and of the Hudson-Athens Lighthouse, built in 1874 and used to warn ships off the Hudson Middle Ground Flats. Inside the park, you will find a statue of St. Winifred, donated to the city by a man who felt that Hudson needed a patron saint.

The easiest walk in Hudson is along Warren Street, which is also an antiques mecca (see *Selective Shopping*). The architectural styles to be found here include Greek Revival, Federal, Queen Anne, and Victorian. At the Curtiss House, 32 Warren Street, look up at the widow's walk, which was built by the whaling owner in the 1830s to provide a sweeping view of the river. Some of the houses here sport "eyebrow" windows—narrow windows tucked under the eaves, which often appear at floor height from within the houses. The Adams-style house at 116 Warren Street is considered a rare remnant from the early 19th century and boasts an enclosed private garden.

The 1811 Robert Jenkins House (518-758-9873 or 828-9764), 113 Warren Street, is open to the public in July and August, Wednesday 1–4 and Sunday 1–3 or by appointment. The house serves as the headquarters of the local Daughters of the American Revolution chapter and was built by an early mayor of Hudson. The exhibits offer a look at the city over the past two centuries and contain material on whaling and genealogy, paintings by Hudson River School artists, and other historic items.

Another good walking area is around State Street. At the Hudson Area Library Association, 400 State Street, you will find an 1818 stone building guarded by stone lions. The structure has also served as an almshouse, a lunatic asylum, a young ladies' seminary, and a private home. If the building is open, stop in at the second-floor History Room, which has some local memorabilia, prints, and books.

You'll notice the *Register Star* newspaper building, with its tiny park, at 354 North 4th Street. Like many other of the buildings here, it has served several purposes: It was a dance hall, an opera house, a county jail, and an assembly hall. Continue south down Warren Street and spend some time looking at the fine 18th- and 19th-century buildings, many of which are undergoing restoration.

Other walking areas include Union Street, Court Street, and East Allen Street.

TO DO

AIRPLANE RIDES, BALLOON RIDES, AND WATERWORKS

There is no better way to see Columbia County than from the air. The area's ever-changing land- and riverscapes are colored with the seasons.

To arrange an airplane flight, call **Richmor Aviation** (518-828-9461), Columbia County Airport, Route 9H in Ghent.

Balloon flights are available from **American Balloon Works, Inc.** (518-766-5111), in Kinderhook.

Those craving a quieter trip may wish to kayak the Hudson River or visit a tidal marsh, which are among the tours provided by **High Adventure Quiet H$_2$O Farms.**

FARMS

There are some farms in Columbia County that allow visits and/or offer some unique products. **The Berry Farm** (518-392-4609), Route 203, Chatham, is a haven for berry lovers, raising everything from gooseberries and currants to boysenberries, strawberries, and even kiwi fruit! Call the farm to find out when the crops are ready.

Gourmet goat cheese is produced at **Coach Farm** (518-398-5325), Mill Hill Road, Pine Plains. With advance notice, they will allow visitors into the milking parlor for the afternoon milking.

Fans of venison may enjoy a visit to **Highland Farm** (518-537-6397)—call for directions—where deer are pasture-raised. The farm has tours by appointment and also has buffalo and llamas on site.

FARM STANDS AND PICK-YOUR-OWN FARMS

Not only are the lush, rolling farmlands of Columbia County a lovely place to visit, but you'll find a remarkably large variety of farm stands and pick-your-own farms here as well. Along with the traditional apple orchards and berry fields, discover the county's vineyards, melon patches, and cherry orchards, where the selection of the fruit is left up to you. If you go to a pick-your-own farm, bring along a container, a hat to shade you from the sun, and a long-sleeved shirt to protect you from insect bites, sunburn, and scratches. The delightful thing about the smaller farm stands, which sprout as fast as corn in the summer, is that many of them carry unusual or hard-to-get varieties of corn, apples, and tomatoes.

In Germantown, **Hettling Farmlands** (518-537-4152), Route 9, open year-round, lets you pick your own grapes, while **Wintje Farms** (518-537-6072), Route 9G, lets you buy or pick apples, cherries, melons, berries, squash, plums, and more.

A truly special farm is found in Ghent on Route 9H, north of Hudson: **Loveapple Farm** (518-828-5048), open July through November, lets you pick your apples, but they also sell pears, prunes, cherries, and more than a dozen varieties of peaches at the roadside market.

Kinderhook is home to **Samascott Orchard** (518-758-7224), Sunset Avenue (open June through November), which has more than a dozen pick-your-own harvests, including grapes, pears, plums, strawberries, and a dozen varieties of apples.

Near Claverack you'll find **Hotalings** (518-851-9864), Route 9H, which lets you pick cherries, apples, and strawberries; **Phillips Orchards** (518-851-6351), Route 9H, with pick-your-own apples and pears; **Cardinales Orchard** (518-851-7390), Route 9H, for apple and plum picking; and **Bryant Farms** (518-851-9061), Route 9H, which is strictly a roadside market but offers a huge selection of fruits, vegetables, and local products.

The region around the city of Hudson is filled with seasonal farm stands including **Taconic Orchards** (518-851-7477), Route 82, where you can pick berries and buy everything else imaginable; **Meisner's Farm Stand** (518-851-3714), junction of Routes 9 and 23; **Kleins Kill Fruit Farm** (518-828-6082), Route 10, which has sweet, deep red cherries; **Don Baker Farms** (518-828-5890), Route 14 (follow signs), with more than seven varieties of apples, both standard and heritage; and **Stone Bridge Farm** (518-828-0261), Middle Road, with apples and pumpkins in season.

Valatie is home to **Golden Harvest Farms** (518-758-7683), Route 9, with pick-your-own apples and a large roadside stand, and **Yonder Farms** (518-758-7011), Maple Lane, with pick-your-own apples, blueberries, raspberries, and strawberries.

HIKING

Wilson M. Powell Wildlife Sanctuary (518-794-8811), off County Route 13 on Hunt Club Road, Old Chatham, is a small nature site and bird sanctuary with a lovely view of the mountains. A marked trail leads you on a 0.5-mile walk to the observation area. Open year-round.

Lake Taghkanic State Park (518-851-3631), Route 82 at Taconic Parkway, is open year-round and includes fitness trails and areas for hiking.

There are hiking trails and a nature center at **Taconic State Park** (518-329-3993), Route 344, off Route 22, Copake Falls, where you can enjoy the outdoors in all seasons.

CROSS-COUNTRY SKIING

Cross-country skiing in Columbia County is centered in the state parks, where well-marked trails are uncrowded—and free—and natural surroundings are breathtaking. You must bring your own equipment.

Lake Taghkanic State Park (518-851-3631), Route 82 at Taconic Parkway, 11 miles south of Hudson, has skiing and ice skating.

Clermont State Park (518-537-4240), Route 6 off Route 9G, has skiing, as does **Taconic State Park** (518-329-3993), east of Route 22 in Copake; **Rudd Pond** (518-789-3059), off Route 22 near Millerton; and **Olana State Historic Site** (518-828-0135), in Hudson.

DOWNHILL SKIING

Catamount (518-325-3200), in Hillsdale, straddling the borders of New York and Massachusetts, is popular with downhill skiers of all ages, beginner to expert, and offers many services, including snowmaking, dining, lessons, rentals, and even RV and camping facilities. In summer, Catamount has grass skiing and mountain coasters, a sort of bobsled on tracks.

ICE FISHING

Ice fishing is allowed at **Lake Taghkanic State Park** (518-851-3631), Route 82 at Taconic Parkway, 11 miles south of Hudson, and **Rudd Pond** (518-789-3059), off Route 22 near Millerton.

GREEN SPACE

Crailo Gardens (518-329-0601), Route 82, Ancram. Open May through September, Sunday afternoon or by appointment. Free. Fans of the world of horticulture should make a stop at this unusual site, which was founded in 1960 by Edwin R. Thomson. A member of the American Conifer Society, Thomson planted more than 450 varieties of rare and dwarf conifers throughout the exhibit gardens. Visitors can walk along the paths and enjoy discovering singular trees, all of which carry identifying markers. The owner also stocks a wide variety of plants for sale.

LODGING

The following establishments welcome visitors to the Columbia County area, but if you have special requirements, or you just want to know more about bed & breakfasts in the region, contact American Country Collection of Bed and Breakfasts (518-439-7001), 4 Greenwood Lane, Delmar 12054.

Inn at Blue Stores (518-537-4277), Route 9, Hudson 12534. ($$$) Built in 1908, this lovely, luxurious inn is one of the nicest in the region and is located on a working farm. Guests can enjoy the pool, take a nap on the veranda, or have a cozy chat in front of the fireplace. Decorative accents include stained glass, a clay-tile roof, and black oak woodwork throughout the house. Four rooms have king-sized beds and private or shared baths, and a full gourmet breakfast is included in the fee. Open year-round.

The Inn at Green River (518-325-7248), 9 Nobletown Road, Hillsdale 12529. ($$) Set on an acre of lawn and gardens above a meadow where Cranse Creek flows into the Green River, this 1830 Federal house is a beautiful place for a relaxing weekend. The Green River is a good spot to fish or cool off in summer. Tanglewood, in the Berkshires, is just 20 minutes away. A full breakfast is elegantly served in the dining room or on the screened porch. The lemon-ricotta pancakes and honey-spice French toast are house specialties. Two rooms have private baths; two share a bath. Open year-round.

Inn at Shaker Mill Farm (518-794-9345), off Route 22, Canaan 12029. ($$) This restored Shaker gristmill was built of fieldstone and sits alongside a waterfall on a quiet country lane, a perfect romantic spot. The inn is surrounded by woodland trails just right for walking. You can take breakfast or the Modified American Plan (MAP) package. Dining is informal and provides a way to meet other guests. Twenty rooms with private bath; two suites. Children are welcome. Open year-round.

The Inn at Silver Maple Farm (518-781-3600), Route 295, Canaan 12029. ($$) This 10-room inn is located in a converted barn with wide-board pine floors and exposed beams. There are 10 acres of woodlands surrounding the inn and all rooms have countryside views. The owners live in a house next door. An outdoor hot tub on the deck is in use year-round. Breakfast includes homemade breads, muffins, fresh fruit, and quiche. No smoking or pets. Children welcome. One room is accessible to the disabled; all have private baths. Open year-round.

L'Hostellerie Bressane (518-325-3412), Routes 22 and 23, Hillsdale 12529. ($$$) An outstanding example of Dutch Colonial architecture, this inn was built in 1783 by an officer in the Revolutionary War. There are three Palladian windows, a museum-quality corner cupboard, and eight fireplaces with original mantelpieces. Each of the six guest rooms is decorated differently, and the furniture includes many period pieces. A continental breakfast is served at 8:30, and the restaurant serves dinner daily (see *Dining Out*). Four rooms share a bath; two others have private baths. Open year-round except March and April.

Kinderhook Bed and Breakfast (518-758-1850), Route 9, Kinderhook 12106. ($$) This majestic classical Greek Revival house is near all the historic homes in Kinderhook. If you have never slept in a featherbed, it is one pleasure of country living you may want to try here. All three guest rooms have private baths; two rooms have air-conditioning. There is a comfortable sitting room where you can socialize with other guests or just relax. A continental breakfast is served in the spacious country kitchen. Children are welcome. Open year-round.

Palmer House (518-794-9385), Route 22, New Lebanon 12125. ($$) Two interesting buildings make up this bed & breakfast: an 1821 farmhouse with five cozy rooms (one room has a private bath; the other four share two baths), and a renovated creamery with three suites (all with private baths). This is a great spot for a family reunion or wedding party. A full breakfast is served. Pets and children are welcome. Open year-round.

Wolfe's Inn (518-392-5218), RD #2, Ghent 12075. ($$) A white, 19th-century farmhouse with black trim and red doors, this inn is nestled on 10 acres and has a large fishing pond. A hearty breakfast is served. Onesuite suite and one double room with private bath. Open all year except Christmas Day.

Woodbine (518-781-4748), Whitings Pond Road off Route 295, Canaan 12029. ($$) This lovely Colonial farmhouse on a scenic country road dates back to 1763. It is filled with period furniture but has all the modern comforts. Four rooms share two baths. A full breakfast with home-made breads and muffins is served 8–10. Open year-round.

WHERE TO EAT

DINING OUT

Blue Plate (518-392-7711), Central Square, Chatham. ($$) Open Wednesday through Sunday for dinner from 5. Closed Monday and Tuesday. This American bistro housed in a Victorian building serves a variety of pastas, steaks, seafood, and salads. Wednesday is Mexican night, and on Thursday there is an array of pasta specials. Make sure to notice the antique copper bar and wonderful murals. This spot has earned a fine reputation with both local residents and travelers.

Carolina House (518-758-1669), Route 9, Kinderhook. ($$) Open daily for dinner at 5. A log cabin restaurant with a large fieldstone hearth in the dining room. The cuisine is American Southern, and specialties include ribs, Chesapeake crabcakes, blackened beef steak, and crispy catfish. For those who enjoy warm biscuits and other traditional southern favorites, this is the place to go.

Charleston (518-828-4990), 517 Warren Street, Hudson. ($$) Open daily except Tuesday and Wednesday for lunch 11:30–2:30; dinner 5:30–9:30. The eclectic international menu emphasizes grilled entrées. The grilled shrimp with spicy Mexican sauce is popular, and the restaurant grows many of its own vegetables and herbs. Selections such as fall apple chicken as well as many game dishes (including venison and buffalo) are seasonal.

Hillsdale House (518-325-7111), Anthony Street, Hillsdale. ($$) Open daily for lunch 11:30–2; dinner 5:30–9 (10 on Friday and Saturday). Regional American cuisine is served here in an informal atmosphere. Mussels are a house specialty, and they are served several different ways. The pasta is made fresh daily. They also have a wood-fired oven for breads and pizza.

La Gonia's Fire Hill Inn (518-392-5510), Route 203, Austerlitz. ($$) Open Wednesday through Saturday at 5, Sunday at 3. Relax in a casual atmosphere in a dining room overlooking a lovely pond. Northern Italian cuisine is served, with several Continental dishes to choose from as well. The chef recommends the zuppa de pesce with either red or white sauce, a house favorite. All pasta is made on the premises; there is a live lobster tank where you can choose your own dinner!

L'Hostellerie Bressane (518-325-3412), Routes 22 and 23, Hillsdale. ($$) Open for dinner Wednesday and Thursday at 6:30, Friday through Sunday at 5:30. Open Tuesday in July and August. Closed March and April. Classical French cuisine is the specialty here. Located in a 1783 brick Dutch Colonial house, this restaurant's warmth and character are the result of meticulous refurbishing. For the seafood lover there's fillet of sole with puree of scallops, while veal fans will enjoy veal chop Orloff.

The dinners are outstanding. Call for reservations. Not recommended for children.

Old Dutch Inn (518-758-1676), Route 9 at the village square, Kinderhook. ($$) Open for lunch 11:30–2:30 Tuesday through Sunday; dinner Tuesday through Saturday at 5, Sunday at 1. The dining room here is country in feel and overlooks Kinderhook's square. Linen, crystal, and old-fashioned prints add to the charming atmosphere, and specials range from seafood to steak and veal. The tavern room is also open Friday and Saturday nights for light fare and entertainment. Well-behaved children only.

Paramount Grill (518-828-4548), 225 Warren Street, Hudson. ($$) Open for lunch Monday through Saturday 11:30–3; dinner Thursday through Saturday 5:30–9:30. Closed Sunday. The international cuisine here features an eclectic mix of dishes including Cajun shrimp and chicken fajitas. The restaurant is housed in a beautifully restored brick building in downtown Hudson. The ambience is casual yet elegant.

7th Street Cafe (518-822-9011), 11 North 7th Street, Hudson. ($$). Open for lunch Monday through Saturday 11–3; dinner served Thursday through Saturday 5–10. There's live jazz here on Friday and Saturday nights 7–10. Continental cuisine is served in an informal atmosphere. Children are welcome.

Shuji's Japanese Restaurant (518-794-8383), Routes 20 and 22, New Lebanon. ($$) Open Tuesday through Sunday 6–9. Closed Monday. This superb Japanese restaurant is located in a Victorian house that dates back to 1897. The sushi, sashimi, and teriyaki are all beautifully presented and made with the freshest ingredients. Diners can also order lobster, shrimp, crab, prime rib, chicken, and pork loin cooked in the Japanese style.

Swiss Hutte (518-325-3333), Route 23, Hillsdale. ($$) Open daily for lunch at noon; dinner Monday through Saturday at 5, Sunday at 5:30. Overlooking the slopes at the Catamount ski area, the dining rooms here are wood-paneled, and the three fireplaces make them warm and cozy. The Swiss chef-owner is both a master chef and a ski racer. The menu features French-Swiss dishes and home-baked pastries.

The Vanderbilt Inn (518-679-9993), Main Street, Philmont. ($$) Open daily for dinner 5–10, this establishment serves home-cooked American foods and is a great stop on a summer tour.

EATING OUT

The Cascades (518-822-9146), 407 Warren Street, Hudson. ($) Open daily 8–4. This café/gourmet deli has just about every type of fresh bagel imaginable. It is a terrific stop for a simple, healthful breakfast or lunch and features homemade soups, salads, and sandwiches. The desserts are sumptuous (try the chocolate silk pie).

Chatham Bakery and Coffee Shoppe (518-392-3411), 1 Church Street, Chatham. ($) Open Monday through Saturday 5 AM–8:30 PM, Sunday 5 AM–noon. An institution in Chatham, this family-run restaurant is famous for its baked goods. Other specialties include Wallyburgers, served on homemade bread, and pumpkin doughnuts in the fall. The soups, sandwiches, and coffee are great. The perfect stop for breakfast or lunch, and great for children.

The Claverack Food Mart (518-851-9164), Route 9H, Claverack. ($) Open daily 8–8, Sunday until 2. The place to go for enormous sandwiches made with high-quality meats and salads.

The Columbia Diner (518-828-9083), 717 Warren Street, Hudson. ($) Open daily 6 AM–9 PM, Sunday until 3. For a taste of vanishing Americana—good diner food—stop here for breakfast or lunch.

The Cottage Restaurant (518-392-4170), Route 295, East Chatham. ($) Open daily except Tuesday, at 8:30 AM. Enjoy the peaceful country atmosphere and friendly service at this restaurant where all soups, breads, and desserts are prepared fresh every day. Specials include stir-fried shrimp, Cottage chili, and pastrami surprise (hot pastrami, mushrooms, and cheese on rye). A good place for children.

Country Cuisine Catering and the Bakery (518-758-7247), 3030 Main Street, Valatie. ($) Open Thursday through Saturday 7 AM–6 PM, Sunday until 1. The ambience here is Victorian, with stenciled walls and antique oak-and-glass display cases. Sample Scottish scones, cranberry crunch pie, chocolate mousse cake, and a huge daily selection of doughnuts. Also a great stop for gourmet take-out treats.

Mama Rosa's Pizza Palace (518-828-6324), 614 Warren Street, Hudson. ($$) Open Tuesday through Saturday 11–11. Don't be fooled by the name of this establishment: There is much more on the menu than pizza. An informal Italian American restaurant, it offers all the traditional favorites, from lasagne and pasta dishes to pizza and sub sandwiches, so you can enjoy a full dinner or a light meal.

Random Harvest (518-325-5103), Route 23, Craryville. ($$) Open daily. This charming combination of gourmet shop and country store is an oasis on Route 23. It is filled with fabulous cheeses, salads, breads, and all kinds of tempting baked goods—the perfect stop if you are planning a picnic. You can also browse through the fine selection of cookbooks and regional books.

The Red Barn (518-828-5550), Route 9H, West Ghent. ($) Open May through September daily except Wednesday, noon–10; April and October, Friday through Sunday, noon–9. Closed November through March. They make their own ice cream and toppings here, which are worth a stop in themselves, but hungry diners will want to try the salads, homemade soups, and hearty sandwiches.

ENTERTAINMENT

THEATER

In Columbia County there are several places to go for good summer stock and concerts. The **MacHaydn Theatre** (518-392-9292), Route 203,

Chatham, specializes in musicals like *Red, Hot and Cole!* and *Barnum!*

Ancram is home to the **Ancram Opera House** (518-329-3300), Route 7, a restored Victorian theater that offers concerts and other special events, including a bluegrass festival.

At **The Spencertown Academy** (518-392-3693), Route 203, Spencertown, built in 1847 as a private school, visitors will enjoy shows, concerts, and other cultural events.

SELECTIVE SHOPPING

ANTIQUES

When searching for antiques in Columbia County, expect to discover rare and lovely items at shops that are often as well stocked as many museums. You'll see everything from severe Shaker rockers to ornate English sideboards, from fine examples of American folk art to the just plain odd. Quality antiques and shops are located throughout the county, but you may have to look around for bargains; many of the dealers here carry only the best, with prices to match. This is not to say that an English hunt table isn't worth several thousand dollars; just don't expect to find a Shaker table at a yard sale, since sellers have become savvy about their goods. Shop hours vary widely and by season, so call before you go.

In the city of Hudson, a sort of antiques hub, Warren Street and nearby blocks are a popular antiques haunt, with more than 30 shops located in a 5-block area. Irish antiques can be seen at **The Irish Princess** (518-828-2800), 612 Warren Street, where the stock includes furniture, jewelry, and silver as well as some lovely gift items. **The Hudson Antiques Center** (518-828-9920), 536 Warren Street, carries the wares of more than a dozen dealers. You'll find everything from clothing and jewelry to toys, games, and even cast-iron garden furniture. At **Watnot Shop** (518-828-1081), 525 Warren Street, the emphasis is on home furnishings, and their ever-changing stock is sure to suit all tastes and budgets. The same is true of **Bobbie's Flea Market** (518-828-1274), 510 Warren Street. **Townhouse Antiques** (518-828-7490), 307 Warren Street, housed in a Hudson Valley town house, has a funky selection of antiques and collectibles.

While in Hudson stop in at the following Warren Street shops: **Brandow's Antiques** (518-828-2661), 337 Warren; **Only Yesterday** (518-828-6824), 608 Warren; **Pavillion** (518-828-4750), 521 Warren; **PJ's Flea Market** (518-828-2271), 348 Warren; **Days Gone By**, 530 Warren; **Doyle Antiques**, 711 Warren; **Lou Marotta, Inc.**, 430 Warren; **Foxfire, Ltd.**, 538 Warren; **Atlantis Rising**, 545 Warren; and **Uncle Sam's Antiques** (518-828-2341), 535 Warren.

In the Chatham area, **The Librarium** (518-392-5209), Route 295, is a book barn that stocks more than 20,000 used books at great bargains. **Rich-**

ard and Betty Ann Rasso (518-392-4501), Route 295, specialize in Shaker items and American folk art. **Robert and Mary Lou Sutter** (518-392-4690), 59 Frisbee Street, carry 18th- and 19th-century decorative items; they also have a small tool museum open by request only. On County Route 9, two shops offer a varied selection: **Greenwillow Farm Gallery** (518-392-9720) and **Skevington Back Antiques** (518-392-9056). On Main Street, above the theater, quilt lovers will want to stop in at **Sarris Quilts** (518-392-6323).

In Malden Bridge, **Spencertown Art and Antiques Company** (518-392-4445) sometimes offers rare Shaker items; they welcome visitors, but by appointment only. Malden Bridge shoppers should also look for **Willard Vine Clerk Antiques** (518-766-2516). **Blue Stores Antiques** (518-537-6518), Route 9 in Livingston, will yield treasures. Country is the focus, and a half dozen rooms are packed with everything from collectibles to antique accessories.

BOOKSTORES

Blackwood & Brouwer Booksellers (518-758-1232), 7 Hudson Street, Kinderhook, is a general bookshop located in an attractive old building.

Rodgers Book Barn, Rodman Road, Hillsdale. A renowned stop for book collectors.

SPECIAL EVENTS

If you are in Hudson in June, you might get to see the **Hudson River Shad Festival,** which is held annually in honor of this river fish so important to the area's early economy and diet. There is a shad bake, music, and entertainment at the Hudson Boat Launch. Call Columbia County Tourism (518-828-3375) for information.

Columbia County Fair (518-828-4417), County Fairgrounds, Routes 66 and 203, Chatham. Held Labor Day weekend. Admission fee. The oldest continuously held fair in the country, the Columbia County Fair is still as lively as ever. This 5-day celebration is less raucous and somewhat smaller than some county fairs, but just as much fun. Horses, sheep, cows, and other animals are all displayed proudly by 4-H members, while prize-winning vegetables and fruits are shown off in the grange buildings. Handmade quilts and needlecrafts make a colorful display. Sheep-to-shawl demonstrations and antique gas engines enliven the fairgrounds throughout the week; modern farm machinery has its place here also. But the fair is more than just exhibits—it's also entertainment in the best country tradition. Bluegrass bands, folksingers, and country and western stars entertain the crowds in the evening, and because the fairgrounds are also the training area for more than 100 trotters and pacers, you'll see some fine racing as well. Children should love this fair and all the rides.

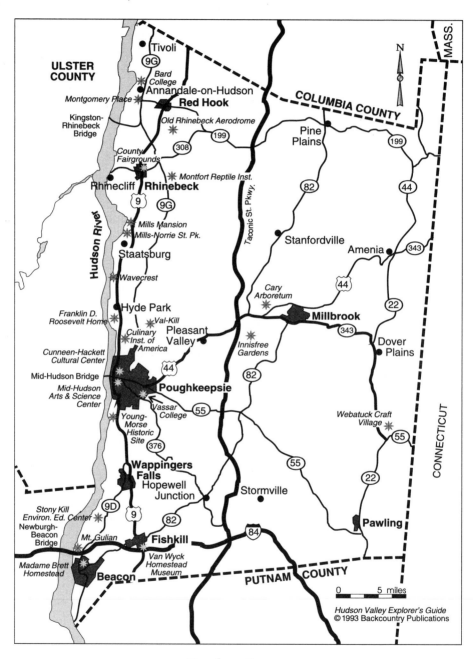

Dutchess County

Dutchess County

When Henry Hudson sailed up the river that bears his name, one of his crew described the region known today as Dutchess County as "as pleasant a land as one can tread upon." With an area of 800 square miles, Dutchess boasts more than 30 miles of Hudson River shoreline and thousands of acres of farms and fields. The generous forests, impressive mountains, and abundance of wildlife attracted the Dutch first, but the county was named for the duchess of York, later Queen Mary of England. Powerful families controlled local industries like farming, lumbering, and mining and built elegant stone and wood manors overlooking the river and mountains. Today, much of the county's past is still visible in the grand homes overlooking the Hudson, the gracious villages, and the historic restorations that dot the region.

GUIDANCE

Tourism Council (914-463-4000 or 1-800-445-3131), 3 Neptune Road, Poughkeepsie 12601.

Rhinebeck Chamber of Commerce, Route 9, PO Box 42, Rhinebeck 12572.

For detailed tour information, call the **Dutchess County Tourism Promotion Agency** (914-464-4000 or 1-800-445-3131).

GETTING THERE

Dutchess County can be reached via I-84, the Taconic State Parkway, or Route 9.

MEDICAL EMERGENCY

St. Francis Hospital (914-431-8220), North Road, Poughkeepsie.

TO SEE

Craft Village at Webatuck (914-832-6464), Route 55 and Dogtail Corner Road, Wingdale. Open year-round, but the hours change with the seasons. Free, although admission is charged for some special festivals. Webatuck is a village of artists' studios and workshops that lies along the Ten Mile River. Visitors can watch craftspeople in action, and there are glassblowers, weavers, furniture makers, and more at work. Special events include an Americana festival, a nature festival, and a medieval fair, which offer color and action on the site itself.

The Culinary Institute of America (914-452-9600), Route 9, Hyde Park. Open year-round except for vacation periods in July and December. No admission charged. Founded in 1946 as a place where returning veterans could learn useful culinary job skills, today the school is regarded as a premier training institute for those in the food-service and hospitality industries. Housed in a former Jesuit seminary, the grounds of the institute provide visitors with a sweeping view of the Hudson. Tours can be arranged only for prospective students or for groups (12 or more people) with reservations at one of the restaurants. Still, the courtyard has a fine display of carved pumpkins for Halloween and ice sculptures in winter; the bookstore is filled with culinary gifts, cookbooks, and a selection of baked goods and foods made by the students. (Also see *Dining Out*.)

Old Rhinebeck Aerodrome (914-758-8610), Stone Church Road, off Route 9 in Rhinebeck (watch for signs). Open daily May 15 through October 31, 10–5. Tours Monday through Friday in July and August at 1; Saturday and Sunday air shows June 15 through October 15 at 2:30. Admission fee. Viewing stands for the air shows are outside; dress appropriately. One of the most unusual history museums around, the aerodrome is the site for air shows, displays, and demonstrations of aeronautic history. But the finely restored airplanes (or copies with original engines) are not earthbound—they are frequently taken for a spin over the Hudson Valley or used in a make-believe dogfight. Fokkers, Sopwiths, and Curtiss airplanes are found in the museum, which offers guided tours. On Saturdays, daring men and women reenact flights from the pioneer and Lindbergh eras; World War I battles are saved for Sundays, complete with nefarious villains, beautiful damsels, and brave fighter pilots.

Omega Institute (914-338-6030 September through May; 914-266-4301 May through September), Lake Drive, off Route 19 in Rhinebeck. Open mid-June through mid-September. Course fees charged. One of the country's foremost learning/retreat centers for adults, Omega Institute offers more than 200 weekend and week-long summer workshops and seminars. Taught by leaders in the fields of holistic health, psychology, preventive medicine, fitness, the arts, and spiritual studies, the courses range from dancing to painting in the Hudson River School style. The 80-acre site fronts a lovely lake. Day visitors should call ahead.

MUSEUMS

Bard College (914-758-6822), Route 9G, north of Rhinebeck in Annandale-on-Hudson. Open year-round. No admission charged to the campus, but there are fees for various programs. Founded in 1860 as a men's school, today Bard College is a coeducational institution known for its support and encouragement of the creative arts. Special programs open to the public include lecture series, art shows, performances, and concerts. There are several changing exhibits each year in the gallery of the

The Culinary Institute of America

Edith C. Blum Art Institute; the Avery Center for the Arts focuses on modern artists. The centerpieces of the campus are two Hudson River estate houses: Blithewood and Ward Manor. There are also gardens and a Victorian gatehouse nearby, which make the campus a nice stop in summer and fall.

Franklin Delano Roosevelt Home and Library (914-229-8114), Route 9, Hyde Park. Open year-round Wednesday through Sunday 9–5 except Thanksgiving, Christmas, and New Year's Day. Admission fee. Springwood, a Victorian house embellished with Georgian touches, was the boyhood home of Franklin Delano Roosevelt. Here, Eleanor and Franklin raised their family, entertained heads of state, and shaped world history. The site includes the house, the first presidential library, the rose garden, and the site of the Roosevelts' graves. In the house itself, once jokingly called the Summer White House by Roosevelt, family memorabilia, including photos, antiques, and the possessions of Franklin's iron-willed mother, Sara, are displayed. The museum has both permanent and changing exhibits that reflect the impact both Eleanor and Franklin had on their times and world events during the first half of the 20th century. The rose garden is exquisite in June.

Val-Kill (914-229-9115), Route 9G, Hyde Park. Open 9–5 Wednesday through Sunday, May through October; weekends only November, December, March, and April; closed January and February. Admission fee. Call for information. The site offers a shuttle bus in conjunction with the FDR museum (see above). The only National Historic

Site dedicated to the memory of a first lady, Val-Kill was a favorite spot for Roosevelt picnics; in 1924 FDR deeded the land to Eleanor for a personal retreat. A Dutch-style stone cottage was built (it now serves as a conference center), and an existing building was converted into a factory as part of Eleanor's efforts to encourage rural economic development. The factory was later remodeled into a house, which now houses the museum. Visitors can see a film about Mrs. Roosevelt, tour her home, and walk the grounds.

Vassar College and **Art Gallery** (914-437-7000), Raymond Avenue, Poughkeepsie, off Route 44/55. Hours vary; call for information or appointment. When Matthew Vassar founded the college in 1861, he not only broke new ground by making it a women's college, he also made it the first college to have an art gallery and museum. The gallery now owns more than 8000 pieces, including Hudson River School landscapes, Whistler prints, and European coins, armor, and sculpture. Shows and exhibits change on a regular basis, and after enjoying the art, visitors can walk around the campus, with its lakes, gardens, amphitheater, and rare trees. Stop in at the chapel to see the Tiffany windows. Also on the campus is the Warthin Geological Museum (Ely Hall, open year-round; summer hours by appointment), which houses a large collection of mineral, gem, and fossil exhibits.

Wavecrest (914-229-7107), Route 9, Hyde Park. Hours vary with the season. Admission fee. A privately owned home overlooking the Hudson, Wavecrest is the site of the Edwin A. Ulrich Museum, which has a permanent exhibit of the paintings and drawings done by the Waugh family. Edward Ulrich, who assembled the collection, which includes sea- and landscapes, cartoons, and portraits by this painting dynasty, takes you around himself, and his stories about the Waughs are fascinating.

WINERIES

A wine sampling is a nice way to spend an afternoon, and there are several wonderful places to choose from in Dutchess County. Two award-winning wineries welcome visitors with tours, demonstrations, and tastings: **Cascade Mountain** (914-373-9021), Flint Hill Road, Amenia (open daily year-round), is a respected winery that has won accolades from both wine lovers and diners. Visitors can take a tour of the winery and dine indoors or outdoors in a country setting. **Clinton Vineyards** (914-266-5372), Schultzville Road, Clinton Corners (open weekends 9–5 year-round), is a small, family-run winery that specializes in seyval blanc. You can take a tour, but please call them before you go.

Millbrook Vineyards (914-677-8383), Wine Road, Millbrook, (open daily except holidays, noon–5), is the largest 100 percent vinifera vineyard in the Hudson River region. Production follows French techniques. Go for a tasting and a tour.

Amberleaf Winery (914-831-4362), River Road North, Wappingers Falls (open weekends), overlooks the Hudson River. Call for tour and tastings information.

HISTORIC HOMES

Madame Brett Homestead (914-831-6533 for general information; 914-896-6897 to arrange tours, which are by appointment), 50 Van Nydeck Avenue, Beacon. Open May through October, Saturday and Sunday 1–4. Admission fee. When Catheryna and Roger Brett moved to the area now known as Beacon in 1708, they built a homestead of native stone graced with scalloped cedar shingles, and sloped dormers. The house is one of the oldest in Dutchess County and was the center of a 28,000-acre estate. During the Revolutionary War, the homestead was believed to have been a storage place for military supplies, as well as a stopping point for such luminaries as Washington, Lafayette, and the Baron von Steuben. The house remained in the family until 1954, when it was purchased by the Daughters of the American Revolution. Today it offers visitors a look back to the time when the home had lodgings for slaves and what is now the front door was the rear: As the town grew around the house, the main street formed at the back of the building, so the doors were switched for the convenience of callers. There was even a well accessible from inside the house—a major convenience in the 18th century. In summer, the herb and formal gardens are lovely.

Mills Mansion (914-889-4100), Old Post Road, off Route 9, Staatsburg (watch for signs). Open May through October; hours vary with the season so call ahead. Admission fee. One of the grand old Hudson River estates, the Mills Mansion has its origins in the 18th century, when Morgan and Gertrude Lewis built a home on the site. The house was destroyed by fire in 1832 and was rebuilt by Ruth Livingston Mills in 1896. Rooms were gilded and plastered, with ornamental balustrades, ceilings, and pilasters. The size of the rooms is still overwhelming, as are the furnishings: dining tables that take 20 leaves; carved, gilded, and floral furniture in the style of Louis XIV, XV, and XVI; and many fine paintings and elaborate tapestries. Ironically, the house was used primarily as an autumn retreat and stood unused most of the year.

Montgomery Place (914-758-5461), River Road, off Route 199 in Red Hook. Open daily 10–5 April through October; limited hours the rest of the year. Admission fee. A magnificent, Federal-style mansion, Montgomery Place was once the home of Janet Livingston Montgomery, wife of the Revolutionary War general Richard Montgomery. Begun in 1802 and completed three years later, the mansion is the centerpiece of an estate that includes waterfalls, footbridges, gardens, and Hudson River views. The building was remodeled in the 1860s by the great architect Alexander Jackson Davis and was home to the Livingstons until the 1980s. Purchased and restored by Historic Hudson Valley, the mansion reflects the family's history rather than one specific era. Gilbert Stuart portraits, Persian tile chairs, Czechoslovakian chandeliers, family china, and rare books are only some of the treasures to be seen on tour. Walking the grounds, visitors might enjoy watching ships on the Hudson or imagine having tea in a "ballroom" of evergreen trees. Special events throughout the year include holiday tours, concerts, and art shows.

Vanderbilt Mansion National Historic Site (914-229-9115), Route 9, Hyde Park. Open Wednesday through Sunday 9–5 year-round. Admission fee. This imposing Beaux-Arts mansion was used by Frederick Vanderbilt and family as a spring and fall home. A fine example of Gilded Age living, the mansion was the focus of a large Hudson River estate and was built at a cost of $660,000. Lavish furnishings, fine art, and decorative items from around the world are on view throughout the spacious rooms (the living room is 30 feet by 50 feet); visitors can also stroll garden pathways and take in the breathtaking river panorama.

Van Wyck Homestead (914-896-9560), at the intersection of Route 9 and I-84, 1 mile south of Fishkill. Open Memorial Day to Labor Day, Saturday and Sunday 1–5, or by appointment. Admission fee. Guides in period costume escort visitors through the Dutch Colonial house, built in 1732 by Cornelius Van Wyck and untouched by any changes after the 1757 addition. During the Revolution, the house served as a depot and courtroom, and it is also believed to have been the inspiration for the setting of James Fenimore Cooper's *The Spy*. The homestead is furnished with 18th-century pieces, and visitors can examine artifacts recovered from surrounding archaeological sites or watch costumed Colonial craftspeople at work.

Wilderstein (914-876-4818), Morton Road (off Route 9), Rhinebeck. Open May to October, Thursday through Sunday, noon–4. Admission includes tea, served at 3. The history of this country seat begins in 1852, when Thomas Suckley purchased this riverfront site and commissioned an architect to build an Italianate villa. He named the property Wilderstein (wild man's stone) in reference to an Native American petroglyph by a cove on the property. For over 125 years and three generations, Wilderstein was owned by the Suckley family. It is filled with their furniture, paintings, antiques, and other effects, which attest to the lively social history of the estate and the family's relationship to the Hudson Valley. The main floor rooms were designed by J.B. Tiffany, and Calvert Vaux was responsible for the landscape art. There is an intricate network of drives, walks, and trails throughout the property, so make sure to explore a few of them when you visit. This National Historic Landmark is a gem and will intrigue both scholars and those interested in life in the region during the 19th century.

Wing's Castle (914-677-9085), Bangall Road, off Route 57 in Millbrook (call for detailed directions). Open May 31 through October 31, Wednesday through Sunday 10–5. Admission fee. A weird and intriguing site, the "castle" has been under construction for more than 20 years, and work is still in progress. Salvaged materials have gone into the towers, crenellations, cupolas, and arches—don't be surprised if a Victorian birdbath turns up as a sink or a cauldron as a bathtub. There are some special events throughout the summer, and children especially will enjoy a castle tour and owner Peter Wing.

Young-Morse Historic Site (914-454-4500), Route 9, Poughkeepsie. Open Memorial Day weekend through September, Wednesday through Sunday 10–4; weekends in October. Admission fee. Situated along the old stagecoach route, this site, also known as Locust Grove, was the summer home of Samuel Morse. An artist and scientist who changed the way the world communicates, Morse purchased the country residence in 1847 and, under the tutelage of Alexander Jackson Davis, began to transform the house into a Tuscan villa with extensive gardens. The octagonal house boasts a four-story tower, a skylighted billiard room, and a false stone exterior. Throughout the house decorative items (including the then elegant and new fabric known as "denim"), furniture, paintings by Morse and George Caitlin, and John James Audubon's *Birds of America* can be enjoyed. In the basement gallery there is a collection of telegraphs, Morse's most famous invention. The formal herb gardens, giant floral urns, and a wildlife sanctuary offer a lovely setting in which to spend an afternoon.

SCENIC DRIVES

In Dutchess County almost any drive is a scenic one. Even the Taconic Parkway, which is now over 50 years old, is more a country drive than a major highway here, and there are commanding views of distant mountains and lovely vistas along its length. The roads of Dutchess County are very well marked, both with direction and historic site signs, and the **Tourism Council** publishes a series of detailed, self-guided tours that are keyed to roadside markers. Write to them at PO Box 2025, Hyde Park 12538, or call (914-229-0033 or 1-800-445-3131) for the free maps. The following roads will take you through farmland and villages and along the river, but for detailed trips, we do suggest a map.

Route 9 is the old stagecoach road that once was the main route to New York City; there are many restorations and historic sites along it. Route 9G (also known as River Road) takes you past old homes and gracious stone walls. Route 44/55 catches up with the Taconic, which is, despite it being a parkway, a lovely road. Route 199 runs across the state toward Connecticut, and the views are more New England than New York.

DRIVING TOURS

Poughkeepsie. The city has several historic districts that are fascinating to drive through. Garfield Place (go south off Montgomery Street) was a residential area in the 1850s and has been popular ever since. The houses boast turrets, towers, cupolas, and Hudson River bracketing, and they span several periods. Academy Street from Montgomery to Holmes Street is a gracious residential area with ornate Victorian houses, as is the Union Street Historic District (cross Market Street and continue down Union to Grand Street). In the 1760s, Union was a path to the river, and later it was the German–Irish area of town. Notice the cast-iron details on the brick-and-clapboard buildings. Lower Mansion Avenue, off North Bridge Street, has fine examples of 19th-century architecture, although there are many modern buildings as well. Clinton House, on the corner of Main and North White Streets, is the headquarters of the Dutchess County Historical Society, where visitors can see exhibits of local history (open Monday through Friday 9–4); they also maintain the Glebe House Historic Site.

Rhinebeck. The village of Rhinebeck is rich in architectural delights, and a walk through town can make the history of families like the Roosevelts, Livingstons, and Beekmans come alive. The Beekman Arms, in the center of town, is one of the oldest inns in the United States (see *Lodging*); across the street, the department store is housed in a Civil War–era building. The post office was reconstructed in 1938 under the direction of Franklin Delano Roosevelt; it is a replica of a 1700 Dutch house and contains murals by local artists. If you amble down Route 9 and along the side streets, you will discover Gothic Revival homes, Georgian-style churches, and homes with mansard roofs, arched windows, and Second Empire touches. For more information on tours of Rhinebeck, contact the Chamber of Commerce (914-876-4778).

TO DO

BOAT CRUISES

Spend a day on the Hudson River sailing by elegant old estates, being dazzled by autumn's painted trees, and stopping at a riverside festival or two. There's a cruise for all budgets, from 1-hour introductory sails to daylong extravaganzas complete with champagne.

Riverboat Tours (914-473-5211), Rinaldi Boulevard Dock, Poughkeepsie, allows you to explore the Hudson on a motor launch with a decorative sternwheel. The *River Queen* is available for special tours, which can include trips to West Point for football games or to riverside festivals in Greene County.

One of the most famous of the ships plying the river is the sloop ***Clearwater*** (914-454-7673), 112 Market Street, Poughkeepsie. A fixture at festivals up and down the Hudson River, the *Clearwater* stops at many sites, and private tours and sailings can be arranged. The ***Woody Guthrie*** (914-297-7697) is operated by the Beacon Sloop Club and sails the Hudson on summer weeknights with up to a dozen guests. It is a sister ship to the *Clearwater* and allows volunteers to join the crew.

FARM STANDS AND PICK-YOUR-OWN FARMS

June's ripe strawberries, summer blueberries, and jewellike raspberries are three of the most popular crops in Dutchess County. But the harvest doesn't end with the berries: There are asparagus, apples, and big-bellied orange pumpkins for the choosing. Farm stands sprout like corn along the back roads; many are homey little places where fresh cider and doughnuts lure you inside. Pick-your-own farms often have roadside signs indicating which crop is ready for harvest. For your own comfort, bring along a hat, sunscreen, and a container for the pickings (although you can usually buy buckets and boxes at the farms). Harvest times vary with the weather and the temperature, so please call before you go.

Montgomery Place Orchards (914-758-6338), Back River Road, Annandale-on-Hudson. Here you can pick fruit in an orchard that has been operating for more than two centuries (see *Historic Homes*).

Blueberry Park (914-724-5776), County Route 21, Wingdale, lives up to its name—stocking only pick-your-own blueberries, in July and August. Farm tours are offered as well.

Fishkill Farms (914-897-4377), East Hook Cross Road, Hopewell Junction, stocks its farm stand with luscious tomatoes, corn, plum beans, berries, and more. The apples are pick-your-own, and there are more than a dozen varieties to choose from. Freshly pressed cider can be sampled in the fall along with hot malt cider.

Johnson Farms (914-221-7940), Carpenter Road, Hopewell Junction, lets you harvest snap peas and raspberries on your own.

Kohlmaier Farm (914-226-5068), Route 376, carries a broad selection of vegetables and fruits, including cherries, melons, and grapes from local growers. The farm also specializes in German yellow potatoes and offers tours by appointment.

Dykeman's (914-855-5166), Route 22, Pawling. Open May 1 through November 1. Pick your own strawberries in the spring, and pumpkins in the fall. Get some of the best fresh corn here.

Piggots Farm Market (914-297-3993), Spring Road, Poughkeepsie, stocks fruit and vegetables along with local maple syrup, eggs, and honey. Tours of the farm can be arranged with a phone call.

Adams Fairacre Farm (914-454-4330), 195 Dutchess Turnpike, Poughkeepsie, is a fantastic farm market with a gift shop.

Lewis Country Farms (914-452-7650), Overlook Road, Poughkeepsie, has fresh produce, homemade baked goods, and a large gift shop.

Greig Farm (914-758-5762), Pitcher Lane, Red Hook (follow the signs), has acres of fields that are available for self-harvesting. Berries, beans, apples, pumpkins, and peaches are only some of the seasonal treats; they also have a greenhouse, farm market, and extensive herb and cut-your-own flower gardens on the site.

Oriole Orchards (914-758-9355), Route 9, Red Hook, specializes in pick-your-own plums, pears, and apples.

When in Rhinebeck, stop at **Breezy Acres** (914-876-2402), Route 9G, and select from apples, peaches, and nectarines. **Wonderland Farm** (914-876-4981), Hilltop Road, carries coveted springtime asparagus in addition to other harvests.

A specialty grower of strawberries, **Secor Strawberries, Inc.** (914-452-6883), Robinson Lane, Wappingers Falls, despite its name, has pumpkins in the fall and hay rides.

Those interested in the new "crop art" may wish to write to the Dutchess

County Tourism Promotion Agency, 3 Neptune Road, Poughkeepsie 12601, for the locations of new works. Crop art is created by artist-farmers who plant, cut, and trim fields into acres of art; one "picture" of the American flag was created from more than 3000 impatiens plants. Each year, new art flourishes and visitors can enjoy a unique agricultural event.

GOLF

There are several courses open to the public in Dutchess County; since hours change with the seasons, courses may be more or less challenging, and there may be a waiting list, we suggest calling ahead. All charge use fees.

Beekman Country Club (914-226-7700), 11 Country Club Road, Hopewell Junction, has 27 holes and a clubhouse, restaurant, and lounge.

Dutcher Golf Course (914-855-9845), East Main Street, Pawling, is the oldest public course at the same location in the country.

Golfers should also try **College Hill Golf Course** (914-486-9112), North Clinton Street, Poughkeepsie; the **Dinsmore Golf Course** (914-889-4751), Route 9, Staatsburg; **Vassar Golf Course** (914-473-1550), Vassar College, Poughkeepsie; and the **James Baird State Park Golf Course and Driving Range** (914-452-1489), Freedom Road, Pleasant Valley.

HIKING

The **Appalachian Trail** passes through several state parks in the southeastern portion of Dutchess County and 30 miles of it is open to day-hikers.

Edward R. Murrow Park (914-855-1131), Lakeside Drive, Pawling, has hiking trails, camping for Appalachian Trail hikers only, and picnic facilities.

Wilcox Park (914-758-6100), in Stanfordville, open year-round, has the amenities of a large park, along with marked hiking trails suitable for a family outing.

Pawling Nature Reserve (914-855-1569), Quaker Lake Road, Pawling, covers more than 1000 acres and has several trails; guided nature walks are also offered.

Mills-Norrie State Park (914-889-4100 or 4626), Route 9, near the Mills Mansion in Staatsburg, has hiking trails, campgrounds, a well-marked fitness trail, playgrounds, picnic areas, and a golf course.

CROSS-COUNTRY SKIING

Dutchess County was made for cross-country skiing, with low hills that slope down toward the river, open meadows turned liquid silver by moonlight, and secret paths that cross streams and disappear into the pines. Many of the area's trails are maintained by towns and villages, and many are quiet even on a winter's day. Multiple-use sites dot the Dutchess countryside, offering camping and hiking in summer and skiing in winter, although you have to bring your own equipment. Be sure you know the area you are planning to ski, so you'll avoid being caught on private property.

Mills-Norrie State Park (914-889-4100 or 4646), Route 9, near the Mills Mansion in Staatsburg, has several miles of well-marked trails, some of which have Hudson River views. The park also has picnic and sledding areas.

Wilcox Park (914-758-6100), Route 199, Stanfordville, offers more than 600 acres of land to explore; trails are not marked.

Bowdoin Park (914-758-6100), Sheafe Road, Poughkeepsie, is a 300-acre site that allows skiing and sledding throughout the winter.

James Baird Park (914-452-1489), Freedom Road, Pleasantville, is open all winter for outdoor fun, as are **Lafayetteville State Multiple Use Area** (914-677-8268), Route 199, Milan; **Roeliff Jansen Kill State Multiple Use Area** (914-677-8268), Route 44, Millbrook; **Stissing Mountain State Multiple Use Area** (914-677-8268), Hicks Hill Road, Stanford; and **Ferncliff Preserve,** Astor Road, Rhinebeck.

GREEN SPACE

Innisfree Gardens (914-677-8000), Tyrrell Road, 1 mile from Route 44, Millbrook. Open May through October, Saturday and Sunday 11–5, Wednesday through Friday 10–4; closed Monday and Tuesday. Free. Inspired by the Eastern cup garden, these individual "garden pictures" draw the attention to a particular object, setting it apart by establishing an enclosure around it. Inspired by Oriental artists, garden founder Walter Beck set to work sculpting the land. Using natural formations, as well as the additions of terraces, walls, and paths, Beck followed his vision and kept specific areas in "tension," believing that moving rocks or plants only an inch or so would destroy the effect. Visitors can stroll these public gardens and enjoy this visual laboratory and garden notebook.

Mary Flagler Cary Arboretum (914-677-5359), Route 44, Millbrook. Open May through September, Monday through Saturday 9–4, Sunday 1–4. Free, but stop at the visitors center for an access permit. There are more than 1900 acres of nature trails and plant collections at this educational and research facility. Public ecology programs, perennial gardens, and a tropical greenhouse (where you'll find pineapples and banana trees) highlight a stop at these lovely grounds.

Omega Institute for Holistic Studies (914-266-4444), Lake Drive, Rhinebeck. Fee. Call for booklet. This is not for day-trippers but for visitors who wish to spend a weekend or a week exploring the arts, culture, health, or spiritual studies. Outstanding, world-renowned instructors and guides make this a superb place to explore new ideas and skills, from music making to descriptive writing and painting. There are workshops for individuals and families throughout the summer and fall.

Stony Kill Environmental Education Center (914-831-8780), Route 9D, Wappingers Falls. Open year-round; house hours vary. Part of a 17th-century estate owned by Gulian Verplanck, this nature center was later used as a farm. Today Stony Kill is fulfilling its mission to provide agricultural and natural history programs to the public. The trails are relatively short (the longest is 2 miles) and there are places to study pond life, deciduous forests, swamps, and fields. The bird observation area is a great place to view migrating and native birds, and special events and family-oriented workshops are held throughout the year.

Trevor Teaching Zoo (914-677-8261), Millbrook School, Route 44, Millbrook. Hours vary with school semesters. Free. Started as a teaching zoo in 1936 with the hope that children would better appreciate wildlife if they were familiar with it, the zoo is now a 4-acre site that offers close-up looks at a variety of animals. Red-tailed hawks, coati, otters, swans, and badgers are only some of the zoo's guests. There is a self-guided nature walk and a boardwalk that overlooks a lively marsh.

LODGING

A Cat in Your Lap (914-677-3051), Millbrook 12545. ($$) All rooms at this charming home have private baths, and the village of Millbrook is within walking distance. A hearty breakfast is served. Open year-round.

Beekman Arms (914-876-7077), 4 Mill Street, Rhinebeck 12572. ($$$) The oldest inn in America, the Arms is steeped in history and antiques. Located on the main road, it is within walking distance of many attractions and includes a courtyard annex. If you want a quieter place, ask about the Delamater House, a gingerbread fantasy that dates to 1844. Private baths. Open year-round.

Belvedere Mansion (914-889-8000), PO Box 785, Route 9, Rhinebeck 12572. ($$$) Belvedere means "beautiful view," and there is a wonderful one from this restored Greek Revival mansion overlooking the Hudson River. In addition to the lavish accommodations, there are outside cottages within a separate building facing the mansion. All have individual entrances and private bathrooms. Each cottage has a unique character and is decorated with antiques and American folk art. During the winter months a hearty country breakfast is served fireside in the main dining room. In the warmer weather, breakfast is served alfresco in a pavilion gazebo overlooking the fountain and pond. There is also an outdoor in-ground pool. Open year-round.

Bykenhulle House (914-221-4182), Bykenhulle Road, Hopewell Junction 12533. ($$$) A Georgian Colonial, this house has four large bedrooms featuring poster beds and antiques (one shared and two private baths). There are six fireplaces, a sun room, a flower garden, and a swimming pool. A full country breakfast served on fine china. Open year-round.

Calico Quail Inn (914-677-6016), Route 44, Mabbettsville (near Millbrook) 12545. ($$$) This lovely, classic 1830s farmhouse is set on park-like property that has a Chinese bridge and a pond, complete with a boat. Service is the watchword here, and guests enjoy fresh flowers,

antiques, homemade pastries, and breakfast in the Tavern Room. Two rooms, shared bathroom. No children. Open all year except March.

Castle Hill Bed and Breakfast (914-298-8000), Wappingers Falls 12590. ($$$) A tree-lined drive leads to this brick Victorian mansion, once the home of Henry Yates Satterlee, the designer of the National Cathedral in Washington. Four bedrooms and two suites are furnished with antiques; both shared and private baths. Continental breakfast. In the summer, the large outdoor pool is at the disposal of guests. Open April through November; children not permitted.

Le Chambord Inn (914-221-1941), Route 52 and Carpenter Road, Hopewell Junction 12533. ($$$) A charming inn tucked away in the woods, Le Chambord offers elegance and relaxation with the convenience of a restaurant downstairs. The rooms are furnished with antiques and a continental breakfast is served by the fireplace. Private baths. Children are welcome. Open year-round.

Hammertown Inn (518-398-7539 or 398-7075), Hammertown Road, Pine Plains 12567. ($$$) This elegantly restored Colonial is filled with antiques and sits on 2 lovely acres. The owners also run a country gift and antiques shop next door, and guests may visit the family's dairy farm. There are two guest rooms, with a shared bathroom. A full country breakfast is served. Children are welcome.

Inn at the Falls (914-462-5770), 50 Red Oaks Mill Road, Poughkeepsie 12603. ($$$) This inn blends the luxury of a plush resort and the atmosphere of a country estate. Nestled next to a waterfall, the inn has rooms decorated in English, Oriental, and American country styles. A continental breakfast is delivered to your room. Twenty-four rooms and 12 suites have private baths, phones, and TV. Children welcome. Open year-round.

Lakehouse Inn on Golden Pond (914-266-8093), Shelley Hill Road, Stanfordville 12581. ($$$) There are four separate buildings around a lovely lake on this 22-acre estate. The 13 guest rooms offer all the modern conveniences, including private bath and deck, color TV, and air-conditioning. Many rooms have Jacuzzis and some have fireplaces. This is a wonderful spot to enjoy swimming and fishing in the summer months. Guests can take one of the rowboats out on the lake. A full gourmet breakfast is served. Open year-round.

Mansakenning Carriage House (914-876-3500), 29 Acker Hook Road, Rhinebeck 12572. ($$) This home is on the National Register and has three suites with private bathrooms, air-conditioning, fireplaces, and stereo. A six-course gourmet breakfast is included, and there are faxes and photocopy machines on hand for the executive. Open year-round.

Mill at Bloomvale Falls (914-266-4234), Route 82, Salt Point 12578. ($$) Located in the heart of hunt country, this house was once a stone cider mill. Guests can swim and splash under the nearby falls or hike the 24 acres surrounding the house. Inside, fireplaces and antiques greet guests; fountains, dining decks, and an antiques shop are on the site as well. There is a master suite and four guest rooms. Adults preferred. Open year-round.

Old Drovers Inn (914-832-9311), Dover Plains 12522. ($$$) This inn is coupled with a fine restaurant downstairs (see *Dining Out*). There are antiques in the three rooms, and private baths. Breakfast is served in the Federal Room. Well-behaved children only. Open Thursday through Sunday; closed part of December.

The Pines (518-398-7677), North Main, Pine Plains 12567. ($$$) This spacious Victorian mansion was built in 1878 and boasts walnut, cherry, and chestnut woodwork throughout. The rooms are furnished with period furniture. Breakfast consists of eggs, fresh fruit, and homemade bread. Two rooms have private baths; three others share a bath. Children not permitted. Open year-round.

The Pynes on Hudson (914-757-2323), Box 99, Tivoli 12583. ($$$) There are spectacular views from most rooms of this luxurious, historic house on the Hudson River. The five guest rooms have private bathrooms and air-conditioning. A full breakfast is served in the cozy dining room. Closed December through March.

Sheraton Civic Center Hotel (914-485-5300), 40 Civic Center Plaza, Poughkeepsie 12601. ($$$) A full-service hotel, the Sheraton, commanding spectacular views of the Hudson, boasts 213 rooms and an on-site health club with sauna. Several suites have Jacuzzis. Guests will enjoy the fine restaurant on the premises and Banana's, a live comedy club open Friday and Saturday nights. Open year-round.

The Residence Inn (914-896-5210), Route 9, Fishkill 12524. ($$$) Part of the Marriott hotel chain, this inn offers suites with fireplaces, kitchens, and continental breakfast. There is a pool, whirlpool, and a health club on site. All 104 suites have private bathrooms. Children welcome. Open year-round.

Simmon's Way Village Inn (518-789-6235), Route 44, Millerton 12546. ($$$) Built in 1854, the Village Inn was remodeled in 1892 and now boasts rooms filled with down pillows, fine linens, antiques, and canopied beds. Enjoy a continental breakfast in your suite, in the dining room, or on the front porch. There is an excellent restaurant on the premises as well. Eleven rooms with private baths. Children are welcome. Open year-round, except for 2 weeks in March.

Troutbeck (914-373-9681), Leedsville Road, Amenia 12501. ($$$) This English country estate on 422 acres is an executive retreat during the week, but on weekends it's a relaxed getaway. Fronted by sycamores and a brook, the slate-roofed estate has leaded-glass windows, walled gardens, antiques, and an outdoor pool and tennis courts. Twenty-six bedrooms and five suites, all with private baths, some with fireplaces. Not recommended for children. Open year-round, weekends only.

Village Victorian Inn (914-876-8345), 31 Center Street, Rhinebeck 12572. ($$$) Located in a lovely Victorian house, this inn is but a short walk from the center of town, with all its shops and galleries. The rooms have private baths and are furnished with romantic period antiques and artwork (and the pieces are for sale). A sumptuous, full breakfast is served as well as afternoon tea or sherry. No children under 17. Open year-round.

Whistlewood Farm (914-876-6838), 11 Pells Road, Rhinebeck 12572. ($$) This distinctive B&B is also a working horse farm, and animals abound. The living room has a stone fireplace and a view of the paddock area, and there are antiques, including a player piano, throughout the house. A hearty farm breakfast with home-baked muffins, breads, and jams and jellies is served daily. One master bedroom with private bath; three bedrooms share a bath. Children are welcome. Open year-round.

WHERE TO EAT

DINING OUT

Dining in Dutchess means country settings and the finest food. Since many of the restaurants have hours that change with the day or the season, we recommend calling and checking on times and reservation requirements.

Allyn's Restaurant & Cafe (914-677-5888), Route 44, Millbrook. ($$) Open daily except Tuesday, for lunch 11:30–3, dinner from 5:30; Sunday brunch 11:30–3. Regional specialties and Continental favorites are served in two dining rooms—one elegant, the other informal. The restaurant tends to get crowded on weekends so you may want to make a reservation.

Beekman Arms (914-876-7077), 4 Mill Street, Rhinebeck. ($$) Open daily for breakfast, lunch, and dinner; Sunday brunch 10–3. This Hudson Valley institution is housed in the oldest inn in America (see *Lodging*) and dates back to 1766. Hearty breakfasts and weekend brunch are particularly good. The new owner, chef Larry Forgione, of An American Place, has given a modern lift to traditional food.

Caesar's Ristorante (914-471-4857), 2 Delafield Street, Poughkeepsie. ($$) Open daily 4–11. Located in a historic district of the city, this first-rate Italian restaurant has art deco decor and a piano bar. Specialties include homemade pasta, veal, and Caesar salad. Not recommended for children.

Coppola's Restaurant (914-452-3040), 825 Main Street, Poughkeepsie. ($$) Serving Italian cuisine for lunch and dinner, Tuesday through Sunday 11–9.

Culinary Institute of America (914-471-6608), Route 9, Hyde Park. ($–$$$) Hours vary; call for reservations. There are four first-rate restaurants at this world-famous culinary institution, where the food is prepared and served by the students under the guidance of world-class chefs. Except for weekdays at St. Andrew's Cafe, reservations are essential and should be made several weeks in advance; the wait is well worth it. American Bounty Restaurant offers the best in the way of American regional cuisine: smoked turkey with black pepper pasta and cream or a Mississippi riverboat for dessert. Caterina d'Medici Restaurant specializes in northern Italian food, like tricolor pasta diamonds with prosciutto or chestnut soup. Escoffier Restaurant has classical haute cuisine, such as pheasant with morels and fillet of sole with lobster mousse. St. Andrew's Cafe is informal and has healthful dishes that are delicious as well, like grilled salmon fillet with tomato-horseradish sauce or chocolate bread pudding soufflé. They will also provide diners with a computer printout of the food's nutritional analysis.

Fine Foods Cafe (914-855-3785), 10 Charles Colman Boulevard, Pawling. ($$) Open for lunch Tuesday through Friday 11:30–3; for dinner Tuesday through Sunday 6–9:30; Sunday brunch 9–2. This old-fashioned, high-ceilinged storefront café has exposed brick walls, a mix of booths and tables, and lots of local memorabilia in the decor. The eclectic cuisine includes such unusual treats as grilled shrimp with Thai peanut sauce over angelhair pasta, and breast of duck with peppercorns and applejack-soaked figs. An excellent bakery operates out of the café, so don't skip dessert. Sour cream apple pie and raspberry linzer torte are just a couple of the tempting creations. There is an Oktoberfest beer-tasting dinner, and wine tastings as well.

La Fonda Del Sol (914-297-5044), Old Route 9, Wappingers Falls. ($$) Open daily for dinner 3–10. The menu here is extensive, and the Mexican cuisine is excellent. Downstairs La Cantina offers nightly entertainment, and the food includes Mexican specialties and paella.

Greenbaum & Gilhooley's (914-297-9700), Route 9, Wappingers Falls. ($$) Open daily for dinner 4–10. Lavish portions of traditional favorites are served at this popular steakhouse, including aged New York sirloin, prime rib, and jumbo lobster. Try the mud pie for dessert.

Guidetti's (914-832-6721), Pleasant Ridge Road, Wingdale. ($$) Open Wednesday through Sunday for dinner 5–10. This restaurant serves fine northern Italian cuisine.

Harrald's (914-878-6595), Route 52, Stormville. ($$$) Open Wednesday through Saturday for dinner from 6. The dining here is prix fixe and five star. Set in a 200-year-old Tudor-style house, this restaurant offers candlelight atmosphere and specials like Maryland jumbo lump crabmeat cakes and trout meunière. Children must be well behaved.

Hudson's Ribs and Fish (914-297-5002), Route 9, Fishkill. ($$) Moderately priced steaks and seafood dishes with an excellent selection of specials daily. Open daily for dinner from 5.

The Inn at Osborne Hill (914-897-3055), 150 Osborne Hill Road, Fishkill. ($$) Open for lunch Monday and Friday 11:30–2:30; for dinner Monday through Saturday 5–10. *Connoisseur* magazine raved about this restaurant; the creative husband/wife team that runs it both graduated from the Culinary Institute of America. The American regional cuisine is particularly imaginative and includes such selections as breast of pheasant with cranberries and green peppercorns and linguine with rock shrimp, scallions, mushrooms, and tomatoes in lobster cream sauce. The wine cellar is extensive, with many difficult-to-find selections.

Le Pavillon (914-473-2525), 230 Salt Point Turnpike (Route 115), Poughkeepsie. ($$) Open Tuesday through Friday for lunch, noon–2; dinner Monday through Saturday 5:30–10; reservations required. This 200-year-old brick farmhouse provides an elegant dining setting. Serving French country cuisine, the specialties are game, fish, and seasonal dishes. Not for children.

Le Petit Bistro (914-876-7400), 8 East Market Street, Rhinebeck. ($$) Informal dining with a French touch, and a nice place to stop for dinner (5–10 PM). Closed Tuesday and Wednesday.

Old Drovers Inn (914-832-9311), Dover Plains. ($$$) Open Thursday through Tuesday, lunch noon–2, dinner 5–10. Long ago this former tavern catered to the drovers who transported cattle to New York for sale. Today, the 240-year-old building is home to an appealing restaurant that serves dishes such as cheddar cheese soup, breast of pheasant in champagne sauce, and chocolate truffle cake. Well-behaved children are welcome.

Rolling Rock Cafe (914-876-ROCK and 876-ROLL), Route 9, Rhinebeck. ($$) Open daily 11:30 AM–2 AM. This American bistro serves hearty portions at reasonable prices. The Cajun chicken salad and blackened Delmonico steak are both excellent. There is a huge selection, with pizza, pasta, and a great children's menu.

Santa Fe (914-757-4100), 52 Broadway, Tivoli. ($) Dinner daily except Monday, 5-10. Enjoy traditional Mexican favorites like tacos and enchiladas in a festive atmosphere. The goat cheese in the enchiladas is locally made.

Stoney Creek (914-757-4117), 76 Broadway, Tivoli. ($$) Open daily for dinner from 5 PM. This lovely restaurant features Continental favorites in an elegant atmosphere.

EATING OUT

American Spoon Foods Cafe, 51 East Market Street, Rhinebeck. ($) Lovers of condiments, jellies, jams, and other treats made with wild and fine fruit must stop at chef Larry Forgione's shop. These are the best: wild thimbleberry preserves, cherry spoon fruit, to-die-for granola. Taste-test, stock up, and then sample a pastry and coffee at the tiny café on the premises. A delight for food lovers.

Cafe Pongo (914-757-4403), 69 Broadway, Tivoli. ($) Open daily except Monday, 8–6. Excellent baked goods, and a large selection of hearty soups and sandwiches made on their renowned freshly baked breads.

Calico Restaurant & Patisserie (914-876-2749), 9 Mill Street, Rhinebeck. ($$) Open Wednesday through Sunday 11:30–6. This establishment is great for takeout or for an elegant lunch. We recommend the smoked salmon with capers and the chicken salad sandwich. The pastries are first rate.

The Cornerstone Restaurant (914-896-8050), Route 9 at Route 52, Fishkill. ($$) Open daily for lunch at 11:30, dinner 5–9. Traditional German food in a greenhouse setting, with many daily specials.

Foster's Coach House Tavern (914-876-8052), 22 Montgomery Street, Rhinebeck. ($) Open daily except Monday for lunch and dinner 11–11. Decorated with lots of horse collectibles, this is a great place to stop for a hamburger and homemade fries.

Jamo's Restaurant and Ice Cream Parlor (914-677-5108), Church Street, Millbrook. ($) Open Monday through Saturday for breakfast and lunch. A great place for breakfast or to satisfy a desire for an old-fashioned ice cream specialty.

Julia & Isabella (914-876-7168), 43 East Market Street, Rhinebeck. ($) Open Monday through Saturday 10–6, Sunday 11–4. Offering fresh, homemade Italian and Mediterranean foods, this spot is famous for its specialty sandwiches: naturally smoked turkey with Brie and honey mustard; imported provolone, roasted peppers, and artichoke hearts with olive oil and oregano; hummus, couscous, lettuce, and tomato.

La Parmigiana (914-876-3228), 37 Montgomery Street, Rhinebeck. ($$) Open daily except Tuesday, for lunch and dinner, noon–10. Italian cuisine, including fine pasta and pizza from a wood-fired oven.

Lia's Mountain View (518-398-7311), Route 82, Pine Plains. ($) Open daily except Monday, for lunch and dinner 11:30–10. Italian home cooking combined with a lovely view of the mountains. Try spidini, white pizza, calzones, and excellent desserts.

River Station Restaurant (914-452-9207), 25 Main Street, Poughkeepsie. ($$) Open for lunch and dinner daily. Enjoy American and Continental cuisine overlooking the Hudson River. There is a light menu featuring burgers, tacos, and pizza; the full dinner menu includes fresh fish, steaks, pasta, and salads.

Schemmy's Ltd. (914-876-6215), 19 East Market Street, Rhinebeck. ($) Serving breakfast and lunch daily, this old-fashioned ice cream parlor features homemade soups and salads.

Town Crier Cafe (914-855-1300), Route 22, Pawling. ($) Open Thursday through Monday for dinner; call for hours. Hear top-name folk, jazz, and blues performers while you enjoy Southwestern and Creole food.

Village Diner (914-758-6232), 39 North Broadway, Red Hook. ($) Open daily for breakfast, lunch, and dinner 6 AM–midnight. The only diner in the state on the National Historic Register, this art deco structure was built in 1927 and is family owned and operated. They serve hearty home-cooked meals and are known for their breakfasts, doughnuts, soups, and egg creams.

ENTERTAINMENT

Bardavon Opera House (914-471-5313), 35 Market Street, Poughkeepsie. Built in 1869, this opera house is one of the oldest theaters in the country. The building stands on the site of former lumber and coal yards and was remodeled in 1921 in response to the public's desire for a grand movie palace. Today it is a major center for the performing arts. Tours of the theater are available by appointment; write to them (Pleasant Valley 12569) for performance schedules.

Mid-Hudson Civic Center/McCann Ice Arena (914-454-5800), Civic Center Plaza, Poughkeepsie. This multipurpose recreation and entertainment center also hosts a number of conventions. There is ice skating October through March and a variety of programs ranging from rock and pop concerts to consumer and trade shows and cultural events.

ART GALLERIES

Barrett House (914-471-2550), 55 Noxon Street, Poughkeepsie, exhibits distinguished Hudson River School and other American artists.

Cunneen-Hackett Cultural Center (914-471-1221), Vassar Street, Poughkeepsie, has theater, dance, and art shows on its schedule. The center is housed in restored Victorian buildings, and regional art and artists are usually featured.

Howland Center (914-831-4988), 477 Main Street, Beacon, sponsors exhibits, concerts, and workshops year-round.

John Lane Gallery (914-471-2770), 31 Collegeview Avenue, Poughkeepsie, stocks magnificent prints and original art by American artists; the shop is as much a tiny gem of a museum as it is a gallery.

Mid-Hudson Arts & Science Center (MASC) (914-471-1155), 228 Main Street, Poughkeepsie, is housed in the old city hall, which once had fish stalls and an open market on the first floor. Now the site is a showcase for lectures, exhibits, and workshops, and it is a lively place to visit.

Mill Street Loft (914-471-7477), 20 Maple Street, Poughkeepsie, is a multi-arts center, which sponsors shows, workshops, and a unique art camp.

If you plan to stroll through Rhinebeck, don't miss the following galleries, all in walking distance of one another; many carry locally made fine arts and crafts: **Connoisseur Gallery** (914-876-6994), 9 Mill Street; **John Lane Gallery** (914-876-2441), 28 East Market Street; **Eleven West Rhinebeck Craft Gallery** (914-876-2728), 11 West Market Street; **Hummingbird Jewelers** (914-876-4585), 14 East Market Street.

SELECTIVE SHOPPING

J.B. Peel, Inc. (914-758-1792), 55 North Broadway, Red Hook, has one of the best coffee selections available in the country. The aroma in the store is fantastic and so is the coffee-making equipment.

ANTIQUES AND AUCTIONS

Lovers of antiques and collectibles will have a field day in Dutchess County, where it seems that every village and hamlet boasts a selection of fine antiques shops. Clocks, vintage clothing, fine china, Hudson River School paintings, and rare jewels are all waiting for a home, and it's easy to spend an afternoon looking for that one-of-a-kind treasure. The search is made even easier at antiques centers that offer a cluster of dealers under one roof and regular hours year-round.

Amenia Antique Center (914-373-7845), Route 22, Amenia, stocks the wares of dealers in Americana, books, nostalgia, and other categories.

The Annex Antiques and Accessories (914-758-2843), 9 South Broadway, Red Hook, is filled with Victorian and country furniture, jewelry, collectibles, and Americana.

Beekman Arms Antique Market (914-876-3477), Route 9, is behind the Beekman Arms Hotel (see *Lodging*).

Cider Mill Antiques (914-876-0684), Route 9, Rhinebeck, has country furniture and accessories, teddies, and quilts.

Country Fare Antiques, Arts Center and Auction Barn (914-868-7107), Route 82, Stanfordville, is a unique café/antiques shop/auction gallery where a wide variety of goods may be purchased.

DePeyster Common Antique Center (914-757-3781), 75 Broadway, Tivoli, offers diverse antiques and collectibles.

At **The Hyde Park Antiques Center** (914-229-8200), Route 9, Hyde Park, there are more than 50 dealers and a very large range of specialty collectibles and antiques.

At the **Millbrook Antique Mall** (914-677-9311), Franklin Avenue, Millbrook, there are many 18th-century-furniture dealers, and the **Millbrook Antiques Center** (914-677-3921), 789 Franklin Avenue, has nearly 50 different "minishops." Don't miss Millbrook's **Village**

Petting zoo at the Dutchess County Fair

Antiques Center (914-677-5160), 388 Franklin Avenue, with 50 quality dealers and offerings in categories as diverse as decorative items and sporting collectibles.

There are 10 dealers at the **Thee Carpenter Antique Center** (914-855-5907), Route 22 in Pawling, and 28 dealers at **The Antique Center** (914-855-3611), Route 22. If you like auctions, call the **Pleasant Valley Auction Hall** (914-635-3169), South Avenue, for their auction schedule.

Rinaldi Auctions (914-485-5252), 133 Bedell Road, Poughkeepsie, holds sales year-round.

Rock City Relics (914-758-8603), Route 199, Rock City, has country collectibles and old finds.

At the **Vassar Antique Center & Wynwood Ltd.** (914-473-8260), 7 Collegeview Avenue, Poughkeepsie, there are 20 dealers who stock everything from vintage clothing to books, estate jewelry, and small furnishings.

At **The Village Antique Center at Hyde Park** (914-229-6600), 69 Albany Post Road, Route 9, Hyde Park, dealers stock pine and oak furniture, silver, glassware, books, and more.

BOOKSTORES

Merritt Books (914-677-5857), Front Street, Millbrook, is a general bookstore that offers an expansive selection of new books, an upstairs art gallery, reading events, and a good selection of local guidebooks.

Oblong Books & Music (518-789-3797), Main Street, Millerton. A full-line store that has a good music selection upstairs and an attached children's bookshop.

Red Hook and Rhinebeck each have a bookshop that will be useful for local information and perhaps a mystery to read in your B&B: **Book Center** (914-876-2303), 15 East Market, Rhinebeck; and **The Bookery** (914-758-4191), 16 East Market, Red Hook. Also see The Culinary Institute of America under *To See.*

SPECIAL EVENTS

Dutchess County Fair (914-876-4001), County Fairgrounds, Route 9, Rhinebeck. Last week in August; open daily. Admission fee. For the biggest—and some say the best—county fair in the Hudson Valley, a stop at the Dutchess County Fair is in order. The fairgrounds include large display buildings, show arenas, a racetrack, food stands, and even an "old-fashioned village" where kids can play. Plenty of livestock is displayed, and name entertainment is offered. The colorful, noisy midway attracts all ages, and the rides will please the adventurous and the not-so-adventurous. The fairgrounds are also home to the New York State Wool Festival, held in October. This is an outstanding exhibit and great fun for all ages, especially if you like sheep, llama and alpaca.

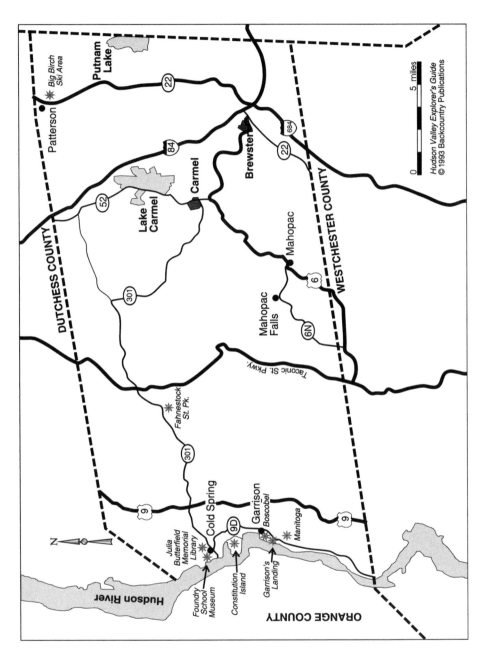

Putnam County

Putnam County

One of the gateways to the Hudson Highlands, Putnam County offers splendid river views, lots of outdoor entertainment, and a chance to see small-town America before it disappears. In Cold Spring, the tiny shops and riverside gazebo are charming reminders of a more leisurely past. Up north, the Federal mansion called Boscobel, which came within hours of being demolished, has been restored to its former elegance. A walk through the gardens there offers thousands of flowers in full color, blooming with scent. There are also thousands of acres of wetlands, lakes, forests, and meadows in Putnam beckoning the hiker, walker, and nature lover. A very different outdoor environment was created at Manitoga, where industrial designer Russell Wright built Dragon House, a unique home built into the wall of a quarry. In Putnam, you can drive along rustic roads, smell apple blossoms, see houses that date back to before the Revolution, stop at an art gallery, or just laze away an afternoon watching the Hudson. Route 9D from the Bear Mountain Bridge goes past many historic areas. Route 9 is the old Albany Post Road and has been in constant use for more than two centuries. Just an hour from New York City, Putnam County can seem a century away, with a pace and a grace all its own.

GUIDANCE
   Cold Spring Chamber of Commerce (914-265-9060), Main Street, Cold Spring 10516.

GETTING THERE
   Putnam County can be reached via I-84, the Taconic State Parkway, or Route 9.

MEDICAL EMERGENCY
   Putnam Hospital Center (914-279-5711), Stoneleigh Avenue, Carmel.

VILLAGES

Cold Spring. This lovely river town was founded in the 18th century and, according to local folklore, got its name from George Washington's comment on the water found at a local spring. Cold Spring received an economic boost in the 19th century, when it became the site of one of the largest iron foundries in the United States. The town's West Point

Foundry produced everything from weapons to some rather unusual furniture, some of which can be seen at the Tarrytown home of Washington Irving in Westchester County.

On Main Street you can visit **"antiques row,"** where many dealers own or share shops that specialize in everything from rare books to vintage clothing to brass beds. Be sure to stop in at the **Hudson Valley Visitors Center** (914-265-3066), 72 Main Street, which specializes in local crafts as well as regional books and maps. If you continue down Main Street to the railroad tracks, you will find a plaque commemorating Washington's visit. The bandstand here was constructed for riverside concerts—now it provides a wonderful place to look across the river to Storm King Mountain, which, true to its name, is the center of many storms. At the corner of Main and West Streets, follow West Street south to Market to see the **Chapel of Our Lady** (914-265-2781). This one-room Greek Revival chapel was built in 1834 for workers at the foundry; it is the oldest Roman Catholic church in the region and was one of the most popular subjects for painters and artists of the Hudson River School. The chapel looks across the river, but you may have to wait to get in on weekends, because it's popular for weddings.

Garrison. The Landing, which overlooks the Hudson River at the railroad station, is the town's hub. Walk down to the riverside gazebo, which was used as the set for the filming of *Hello Dolly*. The Landing is also home to the Garrison Art Center (914-424-3960), which holds exhibits, auctions, workshops, and special events, including an art fair, throughout the year.

TO SEE

Foundry School Museum of the Putnam Historical Society (914-265-4010), 63 Chestnut Street, Cold Spring. Open March through December, Wednesday 10–4 and Sunday 2–5. Free. The original Foundry School served the children of Irish immigrants and apprentices who were employed at the West Point Foundry; today the 1820 building is a small museum. The exhibits offer a look at local history, including the Civil War artillery weapons (the Parrott gun was developed by a West Point officer) that were constructed here, and there are also small collections of paintings and furniture. There is even a horse-drawn cutter, once owned by Julia Butterfield, who is said to have received the sleigh from the tsarina of Russia.

Mahopac Farm Museum (914-628-9298), US Route 6, Baldwin Place, Mahopac. Open daily 10–5 April through November. Admission fee; admission to country store is free. This jumble of collections is a fun stop if you are traveling with children: There are antique cars, automatic musical instruments, costumes, bone-shaker bicycles, and other items of everyday 19th-century life. The small country store has an ice cream parlor.

Southeast Museum (914-279-7500), Main Street, Brewster. Open March through December, Tuesday through Thursday 2–4, Saturday and Sunday, noon–4. Free. This Victorian-style building houses a small museum with an eclectic local collection. There are permanent exhibits on the Borden Dairy Condensory (condensed milk was developed by a Putnam County citizen), the construction of the Croton Water System (a project remarkable for engineering innovations), the Penn Central Railroad, and a large collection of minerals from local mines. Local history is also a focus of this museum.

Putnam Art Council Art Center (914-628-3664), Kennicut Hill Road, Mahopac. Open year-round; call for hours. Fee charged for workshops. This cultural organization has a gallery with annual and changing exhibits, as well as workshops on performance and art for children and adults. There are concerts, lectures, and special events offered throughout the season.

HISTORIC HOMES

Boscobel Restoration (914-265-3638), Route 9D, Garrison-on-Hudson. Open April through October, Wednesday through Monday 9:30–4:30; March, November, and December, Wednesday through Monday 9:30–3:30. Admission fee. Standing on a bluff overlooking the Hudson River, the country mansion known as Boscobel looks as if it had spent all of its 180 years in peace and prosperity. But appearances can be deceiving. States Morris Dyckman, a Loyalist of Dutch ancestry, began building the mansion in 1805, but he died before it was completed; his wife, Elizabeth Corne Dyckman, lived there with their family. Designed in the Federal style, Boscobel was furnished with elegant carpets, fine porcelain, and furniture from the best workshops in New York. The house remained in the family until 1888; from then on it had various owners, including the federal government. In 1955 the government decided it no longer needed Boscobel and the house was sold for $35 to a contractor, who stripped it of many of its architectural details and sold them off. Local people were so incensed that they tracked down the sections that had been sold, salvaged and stored the other parts of the house, and, finally, purchased land on which to re-erect the building. Today, visitors to Boscobel will see the house as it was, complete with elegant staircase, fine decorative objects, and period furniture made by New York craftspeople. (It is requested that visitors wear broad-heeled walking shoes to tour the house; it helps to preserve the floors and rugs.) Boscobel's grounds are enchanting as well. At the Gate House, you can see the home of a middle-class family of the era and explore the Orangerie, a 19th-century greenhouse. In spring and summer, the gardens at Boscobel blaze with thousands of flowers, including tulips, daffodils, roses, pansies, and wildflowers. Special events are held all season, including a rose festival, concerts, candlelight holiday tours, and workshops in horticultural and American crafts.

HISTORIC SITES

Old Southeast Church (914-279-6576), Route 22 (Old Croton Turnpike), Brewster. Open June to Labor Day, Sunday 2–5. Free. Founded in 1735 by Elisha Kent, this is the church that most of the tenant farmers attended in the 18th century; the present building was built in 1794. Guides in period dress take visitors through the structure in the summer.

Town of Carmel Historic Center (914-628-0500), Old Town Hall, Carmel. Open April through December, Wednesday and Sunday 1–4. Free. An interesting stop for history buffs, the center was donated by a general of the Civil War. Displays include a general store, an exhibit on local history, and decorative accessories of the period.

TO DO

BOAT CRUISES

The 32-foot ketch **Claddagh** will take up to six people on a private cruise of the Hudson River May through October. Piloted by one of the few female Coast Guard captains on the Hudson, the *Claddagh* was named after an ancient center for boating in Ireland. The ketch disembarks from the Ring Maritime Dock at Garrison's Landing (914-424-3546), Old West Point Road, Garrison.

FARM STANDS AND PICK-YOUR-OWN FARMS

Green Chimneys Farmstand (914-279-2996), Putnam Lake Road, Brewster, is open June through September, Wednesday through Saturday 3–6, and offers organically grown vegetables raised by the students of the Green Chimneys School.

Maple Lawn Farm Market (914-424-4093), Route 9, Garrison, is open daily March through December and stocks seasonal produce, baked goods, cider, and Christmas trees.

Christmas trees and flowers are found at **Philipstown Farm Market** (914-265-2151), Route 9, Cold Spring, along with fruit, vegetables, and imported foods; open daily March through December, 8–7.

Ryder Farm (914-279-3984), Starr Ridge Road, Brewster, has 125 acres of organically grown raspberries on its pick-your-own family farm, in operation for 200 years.

For a wide selection of local fruit and vegetables, stop in at **Salinger's Orchards** (914-279-3521), Guinea Road, Brewster, where a cider mill and bakery offer seasonal treats to visitors. Open daily June 1 to August, 9–6.

GOLF

The lush greens of Putnam County golf courses lure golfers from novice to expert. You may want to call before you go, since some of the courses are semiprivate and may have special events scheduled. All charge fees for use and cart rentals.

Garrison Golf Club (914-424-3604), Route 9, Garrison, is open daily 8–7 April through November.

This is the guest chamber at Boscobel Restoration, decorated for the Christmas season. The fireplace mantel is adorned with a variety of fruits and nuts interspersed with evergreens. Cyclamen and narcissus plants edge the hearth.

Highlands Country Club (914-424-3727), Bear Mountain Bridge Road, Garrison, is open daily April through December.

Putnam Golf Course (914-628-3451), Hill Street, Mahopac, has 18 holes and is 6750 yards in length; open daily April through November.

Vails Grove Golf Course (914-669-5721), Route 121, Brewster, has nine holes. Open to the public weekdays and weekends after 2, April through November.

DOWNHILL SKIING

Located in Patterson, **Big Birch Ski Center** (914-878-3181) is especially fun for families and beginners. The snowmaking here means there's skiing from morning till night throughout the winter, and the triple chair lift keeps the lines short. There are rental shops on site.

GREEN SPACE

BIRD WATCHING AND NATURE WALKS

Thousands of acres of Putnam County are dedicated to public use and outdoor education. Most parks are free, but some charge use fees for special events, camping, and swimming; activities include nature studies, birding, hiking, walking, ski touring, and boating.

Constitution Marsh Wildlife Preserve (914-265-3119), access off Route 9D, .25 mile south of Boscobel. Open May through November. Visitors must make reservations for a tour. A National Audubon Society haven for nature lovers who enjoy birding along the river and spotting rare wildflowers in spring. There is a boardwalk to make viewing easier and a self-guided nature tour.

Taconic Outdoor Education Center (914-265-3773), Clarence Fahnestock Memorial State Park, 12 Dennytown Road, Cold Spring. Free. This state-run center is situated on 500 acres and holds classes and workshops year-round. Boat, swim, fish, or just stay overnight in one of the park's cabins and enjoy the fellowship at Highland Lodge (reservations for camping required).

Other parks include **Hudson Highlands State Park** (914-225-7207), Route 9D, Cold Spring; **Pudding Street Multiple Use Area** (914-831-3109), Pudding Street, Putnam Valley; **California Hill Multiple Use Area** (914-831-3109), Gordon Road, Kent; **White Pond Multiple Use Area** (914-831-3109), White Pond Road, Kent; **Big Buck Mountain Multiple Use Area** (914-831-3109), Farmers Mills and Ressique Road, Kent; **Ninham Mountain Multiple Use Area** (914-831-3109), Gypsy Trail and Mt. Ninham Roads, Kent; and **Cranberry Mountain Wildlife Management Area** (914-255-5453), Stagecoach Road, Patterson.

Clarence Fahnestock Memorial State Park (914-225-7207), Route 301, east of the Taconic Parkway, Carmel. Open year-round. Free. This 12,000-acre park consists of swamp, lake, forest, and meadow and was assembled through donations of land from private and state organizations. Several hiking trails, including part of the Appalachian Trail, weave in and out of the park; there are also fishing ponds, Canopus Beach, boat rentals, ice-skating areas, and cross-country ski trails. Fees are charged for boats and for swimming, and you must bring your own equipment for winter sports and for fishing and hiking. The park also sponsors performing arts programs and has provisions for camping, although you must call ahead to make reservations. The park's 1.5-mile Pelton Pond Nature Trail is a marked trail that follows the perimeter of a pond formed when an old mine shaft was dammed. You can picnic in this area or watch the woods from a small pavilion. Hikers will want to look for the 8-mile stretch of Appalachian Trail that crosses the park; the Three Lakes Trail, with its varied wildflowers and views; and Cat-fish Loop Trail, which cuts through the abandoned settlement once known as Dennytown. Since many of these trails cross one another, you should look for signs and trail blazes along the main park roads, which include Route 301, Dennytown Road, and Sunk Mine Road. If you plan to go fishing in the park, you will need a state license. When you visit, be sure to stop at the park headquarters first, where you can pick up a list of special events (some nice programs for children are offered in the summer) and free maps and fishing guides. Some facilities are accessible to the disabled.

Graymoor (914-424-3671), Route 9D, near Route 403, Garrison. Open daily 10–5 year-round. Free. Founded by the Episcopal Church in 1898, this historic site is home of the Franciscan Friars of the Atonement. Today the site is an ecumenical retreat center, with nature trails and access to the Appalachian Trail.

Manitoga, Man with Nature Center (914-424-3812), Old Manitou Road and Route 9D, Garrison. Open year-round, but hours vary. Admission fee. The name of this center is taken from the Algonquin word for "place of the spirit," and the philosophy of Manitoga lives up to its name. Here people and nature are meant to interact, and visitors are encouraged to experience the harmony of their environment. The center was designed by Russell Wright, who created a 5-mile system of trails that focus on specific aspects of nature. The Morning Trail is especially beautiful early in the day, the Spring Trail introduces the hiker to wildflowers, and the Blue Trail wanders over a brook and through a dramatic evergreen forest (the trail system hooks up with the Appalachian Trail). You will find a full-sized reproduction of a Native American wigwam, which was constructed with traditional methods and tools. The site is used as an environmental learning center, and many special programs are offered here. There are workshops in art, poetry, photography, and botany, along with guided nature walks and concerts of music and dance. You can even visit Dragon Rock, the glass-walled cliff house built by Wright. Manitoga is a place where human design and the natural world reflect and inspire each other.

LODGING

Unless otherwise noted, all of the following inns are in the $$$ range, although some of them offer special packages; call for reservations and rate information. You can also contact Westchester Bed & Breakfast Association (914-271-4663), 92 Old Post Road South, Croton-on-Hudson 10520, for hundreds of other selections.

The Bird and Bottle Inn (914-424-3000), Route 9, Garrison 10524. For history buffs, this is a great place to stay. Built in 1761, the building has had a romantic and colorful past. Each room has a fireplace and period furnishings that include a canopied or four-poster bed. A full breakfast is served to guests in the restaurant dining room downstairs (see *Dining Out*). Two double rooms with private baths; one suite and one cottage. Children not permitted. Open year-round, except part of January.

Hudson House Inn (914-265-9355), 2 Main Street, Cold Spring 10516. The second-oldest continuously operating inn in New York State, Hudson House is completely restored and filled with antiques. In addition to quaint bedrooms, there's a cozy lounge, river views, and an exquisite garden. Eleven rooms with private baths; two suites. Full breakfast on weekends; continental breakfast during the week. Children welcome. Open year-round, except January.

Traditional tulips at Boscobel Restoration

Olde Post Inn (914-265-2510), 43 Main Street, Cold Spring 10516. Built in 1820, this inn is listed on the National Register of Historic Homes. The decor is Early American, and a large, comfortable living room, patio, and garden are available to guests. A continental breakfast is served in the dining room, which boasts its original exposed-beamed ceilings and wide-plank floors. A tavern in the stone-and-brick cellar offers entertainment in the evenings. Six rooms share two baths. Children not permitted. Open year-round.

One Market Street (914-265-3912), Cold Spring 10516. This handsome brick town house offers guests a suite close to the river, the train station, and the shops. Open year-round.

Pig Hill Bed and Breakfast (914-265-9247), 73 Main Street Cold Spring 10516. This Georgian brick town house is a most unusual place to stay. Each guest room is furnished in a different style and all have fireplaces—and if you fall in love with the rocking chair or anything else in your room, you can buy it. All breads and cakes are homemade. Breakfast in bed is offered, as is a morning meal in the dining room. You can even make reservations for a picnic lunch. Four rooms with private baths; four others share two baths. Open year-round.

Plumbush Inn (914-265-3904), Route 9D, Cold Spring 10516. Now you can stay at this famous restaurant on an 1867 estate. Period furnishings fill the rooms, and, of course, the food is superb (see *Dining Out*). Three rooms, private bath. Open year-round; closed Monday and Tuesday.

The Village Victorian (914-265-9159), Route 9D, Cold Spring 10516. ($$) This rambling Victorian mansion dates back to the 1860s. The cozy living room has a fireplace and is furnished with antiques. All the rooms have canopied beds where breakfast will be served to you on request. Four guest rooms share two baths. Open year-round.

WHERE TO EAT

DINING OUT

The Arch (914-279-5011), Route 22, Brewster. ($$$) Open for lunch Wednesday through Friday and Sunday, noon–2:30; dinner Wednesday through Sunday 6–10. An elegant, intimate spot filled with antiques and separated into three small dining rooms with fireplaces and lots of airy windows. The chef specializes in Continental cuisine with a French touch. The menu changes seasonally; game is the specialty in the fall. Reservations and jackets for men are required. Not for children.

Bavarian Inn (914-739-0702), Route 9, Garrison. ($$) Dinner daily except Wednesday, at 5, Sunday at 1. Music and dancing are featured at this landmark restaurant, which specializes in old-fashioned German cuisine, including sauerbraten and schnitzel.

The Bird and Bottle Inn (914-424-3000), Route 9, Garrison. ($$) Open for lunch Thursday through Saturday, noon–2:30; brunch Sunday, noon–2:30; dinner Wednesday through Sunday 6–9. Established in 1761 and originally known as Warren's Tavern, this restaurant was a major stagecoach stop between New York and Albany. The inn still retains a Colonial ambience with wood-burning fireplaces, beamed ceilings, wide-plank floors, and authentic antiques. Lunches are reasonably priced and include a tankard of draft beer. Brunch and dinner are both prix fixe; the dinner specialties include salmon Wellington and a dessert soufflé with whiskey-butter sauce. Reservations suggested; jackets required for men. Not recommended for children.

Breakneck Lodge Restaurant (914-265-9669), Route 9D, Cold Spring. ($$) Open daily for lunch, noon–2:30; dinner 5–9, until 10 Friday and Saturday; Sunday, noon–8:30. This cozy restaurant has been in business since 1935. Set at the foot of Breakneck Mountain, it looks out over the Hudson River. Featuring German-Swiss and Austrian cuisine, specialties include veal, beef, venison, and homemade pastries.

Capriccio (914-279-2873), Route 22, Brewster. ($$) Open daily except Tuesday, for lunch, noon–3; dinner 6–9:30. Enjoy a lake and countryside view from this fine restaurant, which is housed in a large, white clapboard house. Northern Italian specialties include pasta, shrimp, and lamb. Reservations are required on weekends; men must wear jackets. Not recommended for children.

Hudson House Restaurant (914-265-9355), 2 Main Street, Cold Spring. ($$) Open for lunch and dinner Monday through Saturday, noon–3 and 5:30–9; Sunday 11:30–2:30 and 4:30–8. Country touches fill this charming 1832 landmark building, and the dining rooms have Hudson River views. Specialties include dishes like star-spangled salad, nesting chicken, and superb peanut butter and chocolate pie. Children welcome.

Long Pond Inn (914-628-0072), Long Pond Road, Mahopac. ($$) Open Tuesday through Sunday for dinner at 6; reservations suggested. In a casual, country inn overlooking a lake, Continental and American entrées are served with flair. Red pepper and Brie soup, medallions of pork with curried pear sauce, and an excellent wine selection.

Northgate at Dockside Harbor (914-265-5555), 1 North Street, Cold Spring. ($$) Open Wednesday through Sunday for lunch 11:30–3; dinner 5–10. The emphasis here is on American regional cuisine, and there are steaks and seafood as well as pasta dishes. This is a great stop in the summer since most tables have a magnificent view of the Hudson River. There is outdoor dining, weather permitting.

Plumbush Inn (914-265-3904), Route 9D, Cold Spring. ($$) Open for lunch Wednesday through Saturday, noon–2; dinner Wednesday through Sunday at 5:30; Sunday brunch noon–3. Closed Monday and Tuesday. A restored Victorian home, complete with antiques and cozy paneled rooms. Both dining rooms have fireplaces and candlelight. During the summer, dine on the spacious porch overlooking the grounds. There is a live trout tank and lots of attention to service. Jackets for men required on weekends; not recommended for children.

Riverview Restaurant (914-265-4778), 45 Fair Street, Cold Spring. ($$) Open daily except Monday, for lunch, noon–3; open daily for dinner 5:30–10; Sunday brunch from noon. The Italian cuisine here is hearty and the place is popular with locals. The wood-fired brick oven pizza is the specialty; Wednesday night is pizza night and everything on the menu is reduced in price. Enjoy the river view while dining on the terrace, weather permitting.

Vintage Restaurant and Bar (914-265-4726), 91 Main Street (courtyard), Cold Spring. ($$) Open daily for lunch, noon–2:30; dinner 6–9:30. Sunday brunch. A quirky, fun dining establishment, with fresh American cooking the specialty. Hudson Valley ingredients are emphasized, and great pastas. There are even gameboards for each table. Reservations suggested.

Xaviar's Restaurant (914-424-4228), Route 9D, Garrison, at the Highland Country Club. ($$$) Open for dinner Friday and Saturday 6–9; brunch served Sunday, noon–3. A prix fixe six-course meal is offered at Xaviar's, one of the finest restaurants in the region. Tables are set with flowers, crystal, and silver, and the menu, which changes continually, features such entrées as grilled quail on pasta and medallions of rabbit with grapes and mustard. Reservations required. Jackets recommended for men. Not recommended for children.

EATING OUT

Cold Spring Depot Restaurant (914-265-2305), 1 Railroad Avenue, Cold Spring. ($) Open daily for lunch 11:30–4:30; dinner 4:30–10. A casual restaurant housed in a restored train station where, to the delight of rail fans, trains still pass by. Burgers and fries are hearty, and there is an antique ice cream and soda fountain.

Karen's Kitchen (914-265-1083), 55 Main Street, Cold Spring. ($) Open daily 9–9. Naturally healthy foods (low fat, whole grain, and tasty) are the specialty here, prepared in the spirit of regional America. Home-baked goods and hearty, fresh soups are prepared daily; the peanut butter sandwiches are made with natural honey and fresh peanut butter. There is a gourmet health food store on the premises. The restaurant can get crowded on weekends.

Papa John's Pizzeria and Restaurant (914-265-3344), Route 9, Garrison. ($) Open daily 11–10. This family restaurant featuring pizza, pasta, sandwiches, and fantastic calzones is patronized by local residents who enjoy hearty Italian food at reasonable prices.

Texas Taco (914-878-9665), Route 22, Patterson. ($) Open daily 11:30–9:30. Open for over 20 years, this unique Tex-Mex restaurant has a talking parrot and a monkey who lives out back. Owner Rosemary Jamison is from Texas and started out with a pushcart in front of New York's Plaza Hotel. The chili dogs, franks and chips, and burritos are delicious.

SELECTIVE SHOPPING

BOOKSTORES
Salmagundi (914-265-4058), 66 Main Street, Cold Spring, is where to stop for an intriguing and idiosyncratic selection of new books. The emphasis is on nonfiction, local books, and antiquarian works. There's a separate children's bookroom.

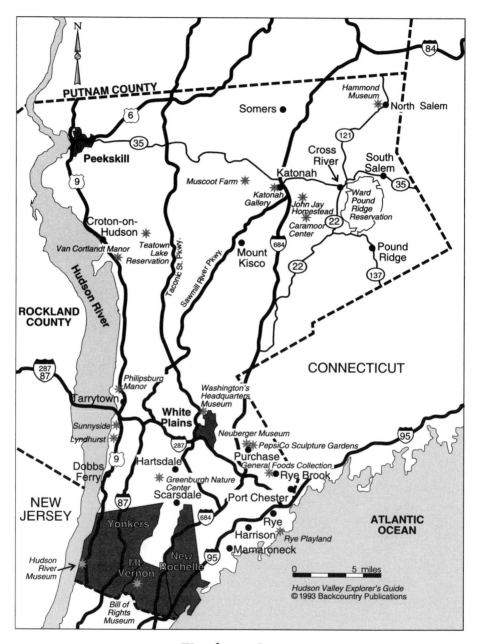

Westchester County

Westchester County

Home of the unexpected, Westchester, which calls itself "the Golden Apple," can be a nature preserve, a riverfront mansion, a 17th-century Dutch house tucked just off the old Post Road, or a bustling shopping district. The county has made extraordinary attempts to preserve both its history and its natural environment. Although Westchester borders urban New York, it is an area replete with parks and nature preserves that offer an enormous selection of children's activities and special events for visitors. Washington Irving described the enchantment of Westchester in his short stories, immortalizing Tarrytown and the Headless Horseman. On historic Route 9, visitors will be awed by the Gothic castle called Lyndhurst and the working Dutch mill at Philipsburg Manor. From the Pinkster Festival in spring to December's candlelight tours of historic homes, Westchester is fun to visit year-round.

GUIDANCE
Westchester Tourism (914-948-0047), 148 Martine Avenue, White Plains 10610.

GETTING THERE
Westchester is accessible from I-87, I-95, Route 684, and Route 9.

MEDICAL EMERGENCY
White Plains Hospital Medical Center (914-681-0600), Davis Avenue at East Post Road, White Plains; **Peekskill Community Hospital** (914-737-9013), 1980 Crompond Avenue, Peekskill.

TO SEE

Bill of Rights Museum (914-667-4116), St. Paul's Church, South Columbus Avenue, Mount Vernon. Open Tuesday through Saturday year-round. Hours and holidays vary, so call ahead. Free. Few people realize that the 18th-century libel trial of John Peter Zenger led directly to the establishment of the Bill of Rights in 1791; fewer still know that this all took place in Mount Vernon, and that an unusual museum preserves the story. Begin your visit with a tour of St. Paul's Church, which was founded in 1665 (the present building dates from 1763). The church has a highly carved bishop's chair from 1639 as well as one of the oldest working church organs in the country. You will also see the Freedom

Bell, sister of Philadelphia's Liberty Bell, which was cast at the same time in the same London foundry. At one time the church was used as a courthouse during the week, and lawyers, including Aaron Burr, presented their cases here. The Bill of Rights Museum is located in the former carriage house and has exhibits that recall young America's drive to guarantee essential freedoms. Displays include historic dioramas and panels, a working printing press, and papers and prints that describe America's historic dedication to individual rights. There are self-guided sections of the museums, and guided tours are available as well. Special events include holiday tours and printing demonstrations.

Jasper F. Cropsey Home and Studio (914-478-1372), 49 Washington Avenue, Hastings. Open weekdays by appointment only. Free. Although you have to make an appointment to view this site, it is well worth the extra time. Cropsey was a member of the Hudson River School of painters as well as an architect (he designed part of the New York City railroad system), and his Gothic home has about 100 of his works, including paintings, sketches, and studies. The furniture spans those styles that appealed to the Victorian taste, and the artist's studio is part of the tour. Maintained by a private foundation, the site also offers visitors a short film about the life and times of Cropsey.

Hudson River Museum (914-963-4550), 511 Warburton Avenue, Yonkers. Open Wednesday through Saturday at 10; Sunday, noon–5; some tours by appointment only. Admission fee. When financier John Bond Trevor built a 19th-century mansion called Glenview on a rise overlooking the Hudson River, he probably never envisioned it becoming a museum; but when the house was purchased by the city of Yonkers, that is what happened. And a lucky thing, too. Period artwork, clothing, furniture, and decorative accessories are displayed throughout the mansion; the museum is located in a new wing and contains science and art exhibit areas. The Red Grooms bookstore is a favorite stop with visitors, and the Andrus Space Planetarium (the only public planetarium in the area and one of the few in the Northeast) can take you on a journey through the universe with its Zeiss star machine. There are special events at this site all year, so it is best to call ahead for a schedule. You can even plan a birthday party for young people in the planetarium; call for reservations.

Katonah Museum of Art (914-232-9555), Route 22 at Jay Street, Katonah. Open Tuesday through Friday 1–5; Saturday 10–5; Sunday 1–5. Free. This lively "teaching" museum was founded in 1953 to display the best art of the past and present and to foster art education. There are exhibits by museum members, an annual local studio tour, and changing displays, which might range from a look at the creations of fashion designers to Navaho rugs or modern art. Special events and shows are held year-round at this museum, which is well worth a stop.

Neuberger Museum (914-251-6133 or 251-6100), SUNY Purchase Campus, Anderson Hill Road, Purchase. Open Tuesday through Friday 10–4, Saturday and Sunday 11–5; closed Mondays and Thanksgiving, Christmas, and New Year's. Children welcome. Masterpieces of modern art by Avery, Hopper, O'Keeffe, and others are displayed in several galleries at this extraordinary teaching museum. There is also an important collection of African art, and selections from Nelson Rockefeller's collection of ancient art are also exhibited. Special shows and events are held all year; call for their schedule.

Peekskill Museum (914-737-6130), 124 Union Avenue, Peekskill. Open Saturday and Sunday year-round 2–4; an appointment may be necessary during winter months. Free. This local history museum is housed in a Victorian home that offers visitors a look at how well-to-do New Yorkers lived in the "country." Exhibits focus on Peekskill's religious, social, and Native American history, and locally made cast-iron items, including some Revolutionary War cannons, are on display.

Somers Circus Museum (914-277-4977), junction of Routes 100 and 202 in Somers. Open Fridays 2–4, or by appointment. This unusual museum is located in the historic Elephant Hotel, probably the only hotel in the world built in memory of an elephant. Recalling the birth of the American circus in the 18th century, the hotel was erected by showman Hachaliah Bailey (a distant relation of the Bailey of Barnum & Bailey), who imported the first elephant to America in 1796. Called Old Bet, the elephant journeyed with Bailey up and down the eastern seaboard as part of a traveling menagerie, until it was shot by a suspicious farmer in Maine. Today the former hotel houses a museum full of circus memorabilia, posters, photographs, a miniature big top, and exhibits of local history.

Square House Museum (914-967-7588), 1 Purchase Street, Rye. Open year-round Tuesday and Saturday 12:30–4:30, Wednesday, Thursday, Friday, and Sunday 2:30–4:30. Closed Monday. Admission fee. This 1760 Federal farmhouse and tavern once hosted George Washington, and today the restored rooms offer a fascinating look at 18th-century life. In the tavern room, visitors learn that the term *bar and grill* derives from the fact that barkeepers secured a wooden covering over the bar at night in order to avoid having the liquor stolen. In the kitchen, a beehive oven (the interior was shaped like an old-fashioned bee skep) and open hearth are still used by museum staff. There was also an early medical office in the building, and you'll discover that the barber, who was also the doctor, would wrap bloody cloths around a stick to indicate he was open for business: the origin of the striped pole still used by barbers today.

Town of Yorktown Museum (914-962-2970), 1974 Commerce Road, Yorktown Heights. Open year-round Monday through Friday 9:30–

4:30; Saturday and Sunday 1–4. Free, but donations accepted. A unique collection of dollhouses and miniature landscapes depicting Victorian homes, street scenes, and stores are on display, as are exhibits of Native American life, railroad memorabilia, and local history. Antiques shows and special events are held throughout the year.

Washington's Headquarters Museum (914-949-1236), Virginia Road, North White Plains. Open Wednesday through Sunday 10–4. Free. Take the self-guided tours of this small farmhouse museum and visit the rooms where Washington planned the strategy for the battle of White Plains. On display here are unusual items such as one of the great general's boots (or at least his reputed boot), which appears very large until you discover that insulation was tucked inside to keep his feet warm. There's a rifle pellet still embedded in a piece of furniture (a remnant of the Revolutionary War), an early washing machine that was "child and stick" powered, and uneven floors that have been raised by the roots of a 300-year-old sycamore tree. This is an old-fashioned, fun museum, with many special events throughout the year.

***Reader's Digest* Tour** (914-241-5125), Route 117, Pleasantville. Tours are offered Monday through Friday at 10:30 and 2; reservations are required. Not too many people know that the headquarters of *Reader's Digest* also houses an outstanding collection of Impressionist and Postimpressionist artworks. Paintings by Monet, Renoir, Chagall, and others and sculpture by masters like Modigliani and Brancusi are on view throughout the building. This is a special stop for an art lover but not recommended for children.

North Salem Vineyard (914-669-5518), Hardscrabble Road, North Salem (watch for signs). Open year-round Saturday and Sunday 1–5. Free. This small, privately owned vineyard produces several wines and welcomes guests to sample their products. There is a short tour and a wine- and snack shop on site. A picnic area is available.

HISTORIC HOMES

Caramoor Center for Music and the Arts (914-232-5035), Girdle Ridge Road, off Route 22 in Katonah. Open year-round, but hours vary so call for a schedule. Admission fee. Built in the 1930s by lawyer and banker Walter Tower Rosen, this 117-acre estate was meant to be the setting for Rosen's magnificent collection of fine art from Europe and the Orient. The house itself was created by combining entire rooms (55 in all) from European villas with an American "shell"; the result is a unique, magical building that provides an architectural tour of the world in a few hours. Rosen's bedroom, for example, was taken from an Alpine cottage; in his wife's room is a headboard made for Pope Urban VIII; the music room is from a 16th-century Italian villa; portions of the outdoor theater are from the south of France. Throughout the house are thousands of breathtaking pieces of priceless needlework, tapestries, porcelain, furniture, and art, some of which date from the Middle Ages and

China's golden age. Tours are offered, and lectures are given by art historians who illustrate their talks with pieces from the collections. Don't miss the exquisite gardens at Caramoor, where fine statuary is set among evergreens and flowers. Caramoor is also the site of a world-renowned music festival, which is presented each summer. The Venetian Theater is a showcase in itself and was built around 15th-century Venetian columns; operas and concerts take center stage on warm evenings, while chamber concerts are offered in the Spanish Courtyard. Concertgoers are allowed to picnic on the grounds before the shows. Special events are also held throughout the year, including Renaissance Day, crafts and antiques shows, and holiday tours.

John Jay Homestead (914-232-5651), Route 22, north of Bedford Village. Open mid-April through October, Wednesday through Sunday. Hours vary, so call ahead. Admission fee. This 18th-century farmhouse was home to five generations of Jays. As president of the Continental Congress, first chief justice of the Supreme Court, Minister to Spain, and Foreign Affairs Secretary, John Jay, the most famous member of the family, held some of the most influential appointments in the new country's government. He retired to this homestead in 1801, and the house reflects the changes wrought by his descendants. Family portraits grace the walls, and the kitchen has an impressive beehive oven along with the hearth. Various styles of furniture and decorative items can be viewed, and the tour adds an interesting dimension to America's early years. The homestead also hosts special events, including candlelight tours during the winter holidays.

Kykuit (914-631-9491), Route 9, North Tarrytown. Tours begin from Philipsburg Manor. Open May 1 through November 1, 10–5. Admission fee. John D. Rockefeller, the founder of Standard Oil, delegated the task of building Kykuit, his home, to his son John D. Rockefeller Jr. The neo-Classical country house and its gardens were completed in 1913, and Kykuit remains one of the finest and best-preserved Beaux Arts homes in America. Governor Nelson Rockefeller lived here from 1960 to 1979. The gardens contain masterpieces by Henry Moore, Alexander Calder, and Louise Nevelson. The tour lasts 2 hours.

Lyndhurst (914-631-0046), Route 9, Tarrytown. Open March through October, Tuesday through Sunday 10–4:15; November and December, Saturday and Sunday 10–3:30; closed Thanksgiving and Christmas. Admission fee. The words *Gothic Revival* may bring to mind castles, turrets, and crenellations, but they won't prepare a visitor for the wealth and magnificence of Lyndhurst. Built in 1838 for William Paulding, a former New York City mayor, the house and grounds were enlarged by the Merritt family. Lyndhurst was later owned by the notoriously wealthy Jay Gould. Much of the furniture, paintings, and decorative accessories are original to the mansion, which was owned by the Goulds until 1961, when it was given to the National Trust. The rooms are sumptuous, and many are decorated in "faux" material—a substance made to resemble something else. Ironically, in the case of marble, to imitate it with wood and paint often cost more than real marble would have (some of the mineral "marble" was actually limestone quarried at Sing Sing Prison). Each room is filled with rare furniture, paintings, and decorative accessories; Tiffany glass and windows are outstanding highlights. Outside in the gardens there are roses, a children's playhouse, and nature paths among the dozens of different trees. Special events here include antiques shows, concerts, and a children's day.

Sunnyside (914-631-8200), Route 9, at Tarrytown-Irvington line. Open daily except Tuesday, 10–5; March, weekends only 10–4; closed Thanksgiving, Christmas, and New Year's Day. Admission fee. Washington Irving once referred to it as being "as full of angles and corners as an old cocked hat," and indeed the charming, wisteria-draped home of the author of "The Legend of Sleepy Hollow" and "Rip Van Winkle" is an original. Irving purchased the small estate in 1835 and soon began to remodel it, adding weather vanes, gables, and even an oriental-style tower. There is much locally made furniture, and some furnishings from Irving's time, including his desk and many of his books, remain. The kitchen was considered a modern wonder; a large hot-water heater was fed from the nearby pond by a gravity-run system. Every year Sunnyside is lovingly decorated for the holiday season and candlelight tours are held, recalling Irving's pleasure at seeing his home bustling with relatives and guests. The grounds are carefully attended and overlook the Hudson and the railroad tracks; Irving made a deal with the railroad,

Washington Irving's Home, Sunnyside, in Tarrytown

allowing it to pass through his land if they would stop to pick him up for the trip to New York. Visitors can also stroll the paths, picnic near the Little Mediterranean (a pond) and watch the swans, and see the icehouse, root cellar, and "necessary."

Van Cortlandt Manor (914-631-8200), Route 9, Croton-on-Hudson. Open daily 10–5, although winter hours vary; closed Thanksgiving, Christmas, and New Year's Day. Admission fee. This manor originally consisted of 86,000 acres of land. The main floors of the present manor house were built in 1748 and remained in the Van Cortlandt family until the middle of this century. As supporters of the American Revolution, the Van Cortlandts were hosts to such luminaries as Washington, Franklin, and Lafayette. Inside the house, there is a blend of styles and periods, reflecting the history of the family. One of the most impressive items is the fowling gun, a huge firearm that was fired into a flock of birds and reduced hunting time considerably! Outside, the gardens beckon the flower lover, and the Long Walk, a brick path that leads to the Ferry House, a nearby inn and tavern, wanders by well-maintained flower beds and herb gardens. Special events are held throughout the year, with Autumn Market Days, candlelight tours, and colonial crafts workshops among the most popular. The Ferry House has been restored and furnished with Hudson Valley pieces and offers a rare look into the social life of the colonial period. Notice the familiar white clay pipes that were for rent; the ends were broken off for each new smoker. The Ferry House is open for tours as well.

HISTORIC SITES

Muscoot Farm (914-232-7118), Route 100, Somers. Open 10–4 daily year-round except Thanksgiving, Christmas, and New Year's Day. Free, but certain workshops charge a fee. A showplace for the farming techniques of the 19th century, this 700-acre farm is now run by the county. Built in 1885 by a pharmacist, Muscoot's farmhouse and outbuildings were once—and fortunately still are—the heart of a well-run, progressive agricultural enterprise. Such events as cooking demonstrations are held in the Main House, while the farm is a great place to tour. The huge dairy barn was a model of innovative construction in its day, with its hay chutes and natural insulation, and the corn crib kept the feed clean and (almost) rodent-free. Out in the carriage shed, exhibits show what it was like to depend on horses to get from the farm to the town. The duck pond still fills with ducklings in the spring, and the herb and vegetable gardens are still stocked with heirloom varieties. Children will love to meet the farm animals up close, and the horses, sheep, and cows are good-natured. Special programs may involve a blacksmith or pony rides or even a beekeeper. Muscoot also has a series of trails that wind through ferns and wildflowers, along which animals and an amazing number of birds make their homes; there are ponds, wetlands, and meadows to explore as well.

Philipsburg Manor looks very much as it did 100 years ago.

Philipsburg Manor and the Upper Mills (914-631-8200), Route 9, north of Tarrytown. Open April through December daily except Tuesday, 10–5; March, weekends only 10–4; closed January and February, as well as Thanksgiving and Christmas. Admission fee. Once the center of a 17th-century estate of more than 50,000 acres, Philipsburg Manor was founded by Frederick Philipse, an immigrant Dutch carpenter. The manor was in the middle of a bustling commercial empire, which included milling and trading concerns. For almost a century the Philipses were respected colonists; then the family fled to England as Loyalists during the Revolution, and their land holdings were broken up. Today tours of the manor begin with a short film that traces its history; visitors then cross the wooden footbridge that spans the Pocantico River and walk to the main site. At the two-story stone house and office building, the rooms have been restored to their earlier simplicity. The house was not the main residence of the family, so it was not furnished lavishly, but there are several bedrooms, a kitchen, and the counting office to explore. The next stop is the mill, still run by waterpower, still grinding meal for the kitchen (you can purchase the flour in the gift shop). The resident miller explains the intricacies of a millwright's job, how waterpower turns corn into flour, all the while working the dusty, noisy machinery. Then it's outside again to the barn and the outbuildings, where costumed guides go about the business of working a small farm. Special events are held throughout the year, including sheep shearing and spinning demonstrations (call for schedule).

Old Dutch Church (914-631-1123), Route 9 near Philipsburg Manor, Tarrytown. The cemetery is open year-round, but the church has infrequent tours; call for hours. Free. One of the oldest churches in New York State, this stout stone building was erected in the late 17th century and is still used, albeit infrequently, for services. Surrounding the church is the fascinating Sleepy Hollow Cemetery, where visitors can read old Dutch and English tombstones. Washington Irving is buried here (his grave site is a National Historic Landmark), and the cemetery was reputed to be the spot where a headless Hessian ghost resided, giving rise to "The Legend of Sleepy Hollow."

Old Marble School (914-793-1900), 388 California Road, Eastchester. Open by appointment. Admission fee. Although you have to make arrangements with the Eastchester Historical Society to visit this site, if you are interested in seeing a school of the past, by all means go. The school, built of locally quarried "marble" (actually limestone), is furnished in the style of the last century, with many antique toys and games still available for playtime. A good collection of children's books from the past is also contained in the society's archives.

Union Church of Pocantico Hills (914-631-8200), Route 9 to Route 448 (River Road), Pocantico Hills. Call for tour hours. Admission fee. Art lovers may wish to schedule a stop here; there are church windows by Henri Matisse and Marc Chagall (the only complete set of his windows in the United States), which are exquisite on a sunny day. Chamber concerts are given during the year.

FOR FAMILIES

Playland (914-921-0370), Playland Parkway, off I-95, Rye. Different sections of the park are open year-round, although the rides end around Labor Day; hours vary, so call for schedule. Admission fee. A true old-fashioned amusement park, Rye Playland is an architectural gem. Built in 1928, Playland was the first amusement park constructed according to a complete plan, where recreational family fun was the focus. Fortunately, the park's family atmosphere and art deco style are still here to be enjoyed. Set on the beaches of Long Island Sound, Playland offers a famous 1200-foot boardwalk, a swimming pool, gardens, a saltwater boating pond (paddleboats can be rented), a beach, and, of course, the rides and amusement area. There are seven original rides still in use; among them are the carousel (with a rare carousel organ and painted horses), the Dragon Coaster (a rare wooden roller coaster), the Derby Racer (horses zip around a track). Fireworks and special entertainment, along with an amusement area, are active all summer; in winter, the ice-skating rinks at Rye are open to the public.

TO DO

BICYCLING

If bicycling is your sport, plan to take part in **Bicycle Sundays** (May through September except holiday weekends, 10–2), when the Bronx River Parkway is closed to vehicular traffic.

Call 914-285-PARK and request the trail maps for the Bronx River Pathway, North County Trailway, and Briarcliff-Peekskill Trailway, which have free bike paths that are open year-round.

FARM STANDS AND PICK-YOUR-OWN-FARMS

Even though Westchester is more built up than many other Hudson River counties, farm stands provide fresh local produce during the summer and fall harvest seasons.

Outhouse Orchards (914-277-3188), Hardscrabble Road, Croton Falls, offers tours; you can pick apples in the fall or shop at their stand year-round.

Pataki Farms (914-737-6720), Frost Lane, Peekskill, offers the best of the local harvest June through December.

Ryder Farm (914-279-3984), Star Ridge Road, North Salem, is open from July 4th to Labor Day for pick-your-own raspberries.

Stuarts Fruit Farm (914-245-2784), Granite Springs Road, Granite Springs, is open year-round.

Westchester Greenhouse (914-592-4610), 701 Dobbs Ferry Road, White Plains, open April through December, has tours and organic produce, maple syrup, and honey.

Wilkens Fruit Farm (914-245-5111), 1313 White Hill Road, Yorktown, has a farm stand, and pick-your-own apples and peaches in season.

GOLF

Westchester is famous for some of the professional golf tourneys hosted in the county, but there are also five county-owned courses that are open to the public (other courses are sometimes for members only): **Dunwoodie** (914-476-5151), Wasylenko Lane, Yonkers; **Maple Moor** (914-949-6752), North Street, White Plains; **Mohansic** (914-962-4065), Baldwin Road, Yorktown Heights; **Saxon Woods** (914-723-0949), Mamaroneck Road, Scarsdale; and **Sprain Lake** (914-779-5180), Grassy Sprain Road, Yonkers. For general information about greens fees, tournaments, and special events, call 914-428-0760.

HIKING

Franklin Roosevelt State Park (914-245-4434), Route 202 and the Taconic Parkway, has hiking and cross-country ski trails and a huge outdoor pool that is also accessible to the disabled.

Indian Brook Assemblage (914-232-9431), Mount Holly Road, Lewisboro, is really a "collection" of smaller parks and preserves maintained by The Nature Conservancy. Lakes, waterfalls, ponds, and trails form a perfect getaway for the outdoors lover, and the hiking ranges from a leisurely walk to a challenging outing.

Marshlands Conservancy (914-835-4466), Route 1, Rye. Marked trails take the hiker through fields and woods and along the seashore. This is a great spot for birdwatchers, and a small nature center has exhibits on the natural history of Long Island Sound.

More hiking is found at the **Mianus River Gorge** (203-322-9148 for a guided Saturday hike), Mianus River Road, Bedford, and along the **Old Croton Aqueduct** (914-271-2196), Route 129, to the Croton Dam Plaza. The latter hike is a total of 30 miles, but both hikers and bicyclers can follow as much or as little of the trail as they want. Stop at the plaza spillway, which was considered an engineering marvel in its day.

HORSEBACK RIDING

Horseback riders can rent horses and use the trails at **Rudan Stables** (914-636-9371), 960 California Avenue, Eastchester. This county-run facility is open daily except Monday year-round.

SWIMMING

Those who want to go to the beach can enjoy the one at Playland in Rye (see *For Families*).

Croton Point Beach and Park (914-271-6858), Croton-on-Hudson, overlooks the Hudson River and has special events all summer.

Blue Mountain Reservation Beach (914-737-2194), Welcher Avenue, Peekskill, has beaches, a pool, and extensive recreation areas.

WALKING

There are **Healthwalking Clinics** along the Bronx River Pathway Saturdays at 9 AM year-round, weather permitting. Walkers meet at the Westchester County Center parking lot in White Plains. Call Westchester Tourism for directions and details.

ICE SKATING

There are indoor rinks at Rye's Playland (see *For Families*), and at the **Hommocks Park Ice Rink** (914-834-1069), Boston Post Road, Larchmont. Call for hours. Skaters should be aware that many parks offer lake and pond skating; call the individual site to check on conditions and rentals (see *Green Space*).

GREEN SPACE

Westchester may be a bustling region for big business, but you'll also find dozens of lovely public parks and outdoor facilities throughout the county.

Blue Mountain Reservation (914-737-2194), Welcher Avenue, Peekskill. Open year-round. Situated in the northwest part of the county, this recreation area has a large lake for swimming in summer and ice skating during winter. There are facilities for hiking, fishing, and picnicking. Camping is available in the Trail Lodge, which has a dining hall with a fireplace.

Cranberry Lake Preserve (914-428-1005), Old Orchard Street (off Route 22), North White Plains. Open year-round. This lovely preserve consists of 135 acres of unspoiled wetlands and hardwood forests. The park has a 10-acre pond with trails and boardwalks so visitors can observe life in an aquatic habitat. There is fishing, cross-country ski trails, and hiking. A small lodge offers interpretive programs and seasonal exhibits.

Croton Point Park (914-271-3293), Croton Avenue (off Route 9), Croton. Open year-round. This park is located along the banks of the Hudson River. There is a pool, canoe launching area, recreation hall, and ball fields. The location is ideal for fishing, hiking, and picnicking. There are also cabins, lean-tos, and facilities for tents and trailers available.

Greenburgh Nature Center (914-723-3470), Dromore Road, off Central Avenue in Scarsdale. Open daily year-round. Situated on 32 acres, this innovative nature center offers visitors a chance to explore several environments, including woodlands, a vineyard, orchards, and cultivated gardens. There are more than 30 different species of trees in the preserve, along with wildflowers, ferns, and a host of songbirds. At the center's museum, Nunataks, an Eskimo word meaning "hill of stone," there are animal exhibits and descriptive displays that explain some of the area's natural history. You can also pick up maps here to use on the self-guided nature walks. Many special events are held at the nature center, from concerts on the lawn to art exhibits; there is even a Honey Harvest Brunch (the museum has a glass beehive!).

Hammond Museum and Oriental Stroll Gardens (914-669-5135), Deveau Road, off Old Route 124 in North Salem. Open weekends May through October, 11–5; call for other times. Admission fee. A chance to step back into the Edo period of Japanese history. Created by Natalie Hays Hammond in memory of her parents, these gardens are actually 15 small landscapes, including waterfall, Zen, azalea, and fruit gardens. Each section is lovely and has a symbolic meaning: In the reflecting pool, for example, five water lilies, beautiful on their own, represent humanity, justice, courtesy, wisdom, and fidelity. There is also a small museum here, with a mix of art, antiques, and collectibles, but it is the gardens that must not be missed. Reservations are necessary for lunch at the small restaurant on the site.

Marshlands Conservancy (914-835-4466), Route 1, Rye. Open year-round. There is an environmental education center with changing exhibitions and four saltwater aquaria at this 137-acre wildlife sanctuary. The unique character of the conservancy lies in the diversity of habitats preserved within its boundaries, including woods, fields, freshwater ponds, a salt marsh, and shore. There are paths throughout to these points of interest.

PepsiCo Sculpture Gardens (914-253-2000), Anderson Hill Road, Purchase. Open daily 9–5 year-round. Free. Located at the world headquarters of PepsiCo, this site is properly called the Donald M. Kendall Sculpture Gardens. Here, on more than 100 acres, visitors will see more than 40 large sculptures by Rodin, Giacometti, Nevelson, Moore, and Noguchi. Carefully landscaped with paths, reflecting pools, and fountains, the gardens, a sight in themselves, bloom from early spring until fall. Picnicking is permitted.

Rye Nature Center (914-967-1549), 873 Boston Post Road, Rye. Open daily 9–5 year-round. A "small" nature center, under 50 acres, this is a nice stop if you are traveling with children. A small museum has exhibits of local animals and plants, and there are several mini-exhibits about nature. Take the (2.5-mile) nature walk, which is described in guidebooks you can pick up at the museum. There is a picnic area.

Teatown Lake Reservation (914-762-2912), Spring Valley Road, Croton. Take Exit 134 on the Taconic, then take Grant's Lane to Spring Valley Road. Open daily year-round; museum open Tuesday through Saturday 9–5. Free. This 400-acre reservation has marked nature walks and hiking trails, a museum, and outdoor exhibits. Wildflowers are abundant here in the spring, and there is an unusual selection of fences. Visitors can enjoy viewing waterfowl and other animals at a large lake, and inside the museum there are live exhibits of local animals and plants.

Ward Pound Ridge Reservation (914-763-3493), Routes 35 and 121, Cross River. Open year-round. Ward Pound Ridge is the largest park in Westchester County, covering more than 4700 acres. There are miles of trails for cross-country skiing, sledding, snowmobiling, hiking, and horseback riding. There are also several places to go fishing and to picnic. You can easily spend a day here. On weekends there are often nature programs for families and children.

Westmoreland Sanctuary (914-666-8448), Chestnut Ridge Road, Mt. Kisco. Open year-round 9–5 Monday through Saturday, Sunday 10:30–5. Free; fees for some workshops and special events. The sanctuary is an active site, with more than 15 miles of walking and hiking trails, wildlife displays, and exhibits of local natural history. There are workshops, lectures, and events all year, including "Building Bathhouses," seasonal hikes, birdsong identification walks, Earth Day celebrations, even a search for the first ferns of spring! An excellent site for a family visit.

LODGING

Westchester County is home to many conference centers and four-star hotels, which offer visitors everything from saunas to fine dining. Visitors who prefer B&B establishments (and these can range from mountain-top estates to cozy town houses) must make their reservations through the Westchester Bed & Breakfast Association, 92 Old Post Road South, Croton-on-Hudson 10520 (914-271-4663). Unless otherwise noted, the establishments in this section are open year-round.

Crabtree's Kittle House (914-666-8044), Route 117, Mt. Kisco 10549. ($$$) This 200-year-old building has been an inn since the 1930s, when it attracted film stars like Henry Fonda and Tallulah Bankhead. One of the few inns in Westchester, the Kittle House is moderately priced for the area. Continental breakfast is served, and children are welcome. There are 12 rooms with private baths, telephones, and cable TV, and a fine restaurant on the premises (see *Dining Out*).

Alexander Hamilton House (914-271-6737), 49 Van Wyck Street, Croton-on-Hudson 10520. ($$$) This Victorian house dates back to 1889 and has 10 luxurious rooms: 3 have Jacuzzis and 7 have fireplaces. The bridal chamber is on the third floor and has a king-sized bed, skylights, and a pink marble fireplace. All rooms have private baths, TV, and telephones. A full breakfast is served. In-ground pool.

HOTELS AND CONFERENCE CENTERS
The following full-service hotels and conference centers welcome individual guests as well as groups.

Arrowwood (914-939-5500), Anderson Hill Road, Rye Brook 10573. ($$$) This full-facility resort is located on 114 wooded acres. There is a nine-hole golf course, indoor-outdoor pools, tennis, and squash, along with a sauna and Universal gym. The atrium dining room is a multilevel restaurant that overlooks the grounds and gardens and serves excellent food. Weekend packages are available during the spring and summer. Children are welcome.

Holiday Inn Crowne Plaza (914-682-0050), 66 Hale Avenue, White Plains 10601. ($$$) This hotel has 400 guest rooms and an indoor pool, whirlpool, sauna, and exercise room. The Post Road Cafe offers breakfast, lunch, and dinner daily.

La Reserve Suites (914-761-7700), 5 Barker Avenue, White Plains 10601. ($$$) This all-suite hotel has 120 guest suites, a fitness room, a lounge, and the Corniche Restaurant, which serves fine Continental cuisine.

The Rye Town Hilton Inn (914-939-6300), Westchester Avenue, Port Chester 10573. ($$$) This hotel has 440 guest rooms, indoor and outdoor pools, saunas, a whirlpool, tennis courts, and an exercise room. There are two restaurants: Tulip serves Continental cuisine; Penfield's serves American cuisine.

The Stouffer Westchester Hotel (914-694-5400), 80 West Red Oak Lane, White Plains 10601. ($$$) A 364-room full-service hotel with an indoor pool, sun deck, sauna, exercise room, tennis courts, and volleyball courts. There are excellent dining facilities in The Woodlands Restaurant and 24-hour room service, and transportation within a 5-mile radius of the hotel is provided. Special weekend rates. Children welcome.

The Tarrytown Hilton (914-631-5700), 455 South Broadway, Tarrytown 10591. ($$) Guests have a choice of 236 rooms and the use of indoor and outdoor pools, exercise rooms, tennis courts, and jogging trails. Fine Continental cuisine is served in the Dutch Treat and Pennybridge restaurants.

Westchester Marriott (914-631-2200), 670 White Plains Road, Tarrytown 10591. ($$$) The Marriott has 444 guest rooms, indoor and outdoor pools, saunas, and a fitness center. Allie's Restaurant serves Continental cuisine; Kona Kai features Polynesian dining.

WHERE TO EAT

DINING OUT
Westchester is lucky enough to have hundreds of restaurants, in all price ranges and for all tastes. The following were selected from personal experience and are only a few of the fine choices available to the visitor. Don't be afraid to try the broad range of restaurants, from Jamaican to Continental, that you will find on just about every street and back road in the county.

Abhilash India Cuisine (914-235-8390), 30 Division Street, New Rochelle. ($$) Open daily for lunch (11:30–2:30) and dinner (5–10). Authentic Indian cuisine is served in an atmosphere of Indian decor and music. The menu features such tandoori specialties as chicken dhaka-sag and vegetable fritters and exotic desserts like frozen milk with cashews, raisins, and saffron.

Auberge Argenteuil (914-948-0597), 42 Healy Avenue, Hartsdale. ($$$) Open daily except Monday, for lunch (11:30–2:30) and dinner (5–9:30). Set in a building that was a speakeasy in the 1920s, this restaurant is hidden high up in a wooded area above Central Avenue. Specialties include lobster bisque, veal with wild mushrooms, and a superb ice cream bombe. Not recommended for children.

Auberge Maxime (914-669-5450), Route 116, North Salem. ($$$) Open daily except Wednesday, for lunch at noon and dinner at 6. Enjoy classical French cuisine with a nouvelle touch in this lovely country inn. Comfortable chairs and beautifully appointed tables grace the dining room, and the six-course prix fixe dinner includes such treats as duck with pear or fresh ginger sauces and hot and cold soufflés. Children are welcome.

Benny's (914-591-9811), 6 South Broadway, Irvington. ($$) Open daily for lunch 11:30–2:30; dinner 5–10. This well-known spot is popular with local residents and has been serving fabulous fresh fish entrées since 1943. There is a down-home, friendly atmosphere, and many of the waiters have been working in the restaurant for years. The trout, lobster, crab legs, and halibut are all first-rate.

Buffet De La Gare (914-478-1671), 155 Southside Avenue, Hastings-on-

Hudson. ($$$) Open for lunch Tuesday through Friday from noon; dinner Tuesday through Saturday from 6. Enjoy classical French cuisine in a relaxing ambience. Everything here is prepared to order and the desserts should not be passed up. The fine reputation of this establishment, long a favorite with local residents, has spread throughout the country.

La Camelia (914-666-2466), 234 North Bedford Road, Mt. Kisco. ($$) Open daily except Monday, for lunch at noon and dinner at 6. One of the best Spanish restaurants you will find anywhere, La Camelia is located in a landmark, 140-year-old building. Northern Spanish cuisine is the specialty and includes gazpacho, shrimp Catalan, squid with angelhair pasta, and homemade desserts. Children welcome.

Chart House Restaurant (914-693-4130), High Street, Dobbs Ferry. ($$) Open for dinner Monday through Saturday at 5; Sunday brunch at 11, dinner at 4. This contemporary restaurant has a magnificent view of the Palisades, the Tappan Zee Bridge, and the New York City skyline. Specialties include prime rib, thick steaks, and an enormous selection of seafood dishes. Their mud pie is famous throughout the area. Children are welcome.

Le Chateau Restaurant (914-533-6631), Route 35, South Salem. ($$) Open daily except Monday, for dinner at 6. This French restaurant with old-world charm is situated on 32 wooded acres and offers magnificent sunset views and lavishly decorated dining rooms. House specialties include wild mushroom soup, salmon in parchment, and quail in raspberry sauce. An assortment of mousses set in crème anglaise are served for dessert. Children are welcome.

Crabtree's Kittle House (914-666-8044), Route 117, Mt. Kisco. ($$$) Open for lunch Monday through Friday, noon–2:30; dinner served daily 6–10. Sunday champagne brunch, noon–3. The American and Continental cuisine here has Italian, French, and Asian influences. The menu changes daily but the excellent cherrywood-smoked Norwegian salmon is always available. Other house specialties are the venison and the sweetbreads of milk-fed Hudson Valley veal. The pastry chef suggests the Alsatian cheesecake—one of his favorites. Live jazz Friday and Saturday nights.

L'Europe (914-533-2570), Route 123, South Salem. ($$$) Lunch (11:30–2:30) and dinner (5:30–9:30) served daily except Monday. This attractive dining establishment reminiscent of an English club serves outstandingly good Continental cuisine. Specialties include fillet of sole stuffed with seafood mousse, fettuccine with prosciutto and smoked salmon, and galantine of halibut and salmon, as well as such tempting desserts as lemon and orange torte and délice (layers of chocolate and buttercream in a meringue). Not recommended for children. Dinner reservations suggested.

Fujinoya Seafood House (914-686-8854), 522 Mamaroneck Avenue,

White Plains. ($$) Open daily except Wednesday, for lunch at noon and dinner at 5. This tiny restaurant seats under 20 people, but it offers an outstanding selection of seafood, sashimi, and sushi. Dozens of dishes include deep-fried oysters, tempura, fried bean curd, and seafood rolls.

Hudson Café (914-591-9850), 63 Main Street, Irvington-on-Hudson. ($$) Open daily for lunch 11:30–4; dinner 5–11. The emphasis in all the cooking here is on fresh ingredients and healthful preparation. The cuisine is American and the atmosphere is intimate and informal. There is a beautiful antique bar, a tin ceiling, and many other lovely old-fashioned architectural details. The fresh fish and pasta dishes are highly recommended.

India House (914-736-0005), 199 Albany Post Road, Montrose. ($$) Open daily for lunch 11:30–2:30 and dinner 5–10. Lots of greenery surrounds this attractive restaurant. The dining rooms are decorated to resemble a colorful, handmade tent, with walls hung with antique tapestries. Tandoori lamb, chicken, and shrimp dishes are the specialty. The vegetarian entrées are excellent, and everything can be prepared from mild to very hot and spicy. Children welcome.

Inn at Pound Ridge (914-764-5779), 258 Westchester Avenue, Pound Ridge. ($$$) Open Tuesday through Friday for lunch, noon–2:30; dinner daily at 6. Sunday brunch served noon–3. Closed Monday. The American cuisine here includes rack of lamb, sautéed pork chops, and grilled tuna. The menu is contemporary yet familiar and all breads and desserts are made fresh daily on the premises. The proprietor enjoys the crème brûlée and the Bavarian chocolate cake—only two of the tempting selections offered.

Jillyflowers (914-835-1989), 309 Halstead Avenue, Harrison. ($$) Open for lunch Monday through Friday at noon; dinner Monday through Saturday at 6. Enjoy innovative French cuisine, candlelight, brick walls, antiques, and flowers. Some specialties include roast duck in cranberry wine sauce and crabmeat ravioli. Children over 13 permitted.

Main Street Café (914-524-9770), 24 Main Street, Tarrytown. ($$) Open for lunch Tuesday through Saturday, noon–3; dinner 5–10; Sunday brunch noon–3 and dinner 3–9. A casual stop for bistro food and jazzy entertainment, this restaurant features American cuisine including a wide variety of pasta entrées, steaks, fresh seafood, and an extensive wine list.

Mamaroneck Harbor Grille (914-698-1011), 136 Mamaroneck Avenue, Mamaroneck. ($$) Open Tuesday through Sunday from 11:30 AM. Sunday brunch is served. This American bistro offers an array of grilled seafood and pasta dishes, organic salads, and vegetarian entrées. The atmosphere is casual and there is patio dining in the summer.

Maxime's (914-248-7200), Old Tomahawk Street, Granite Springs. ($$$) Open Wednesday through Sunday for lunch, noon–4; dinner 6–10:30. Fine French cuisine is featured here, along with an excellent wine list.

There is a fireplace in the charming dining room, and the selections include unusual dishes like baby quail eggs, mousse of duck liver in pastry, medallions of venison, and excellent desserts like chocolate terrine. Not recommended for children.

Monteverde (914-739-5000), Bear Mountain Bridge Road, Peekskill. ($$) Open Monday, Wednesday, Thursday, and Friday for lunch, noon–2:30; and dinner 5:30–9:30; open Saturday 5:30–9:30 and Sunday noon–8:30. Closed Tuesday. This 18th-century stone mansion was built by the Van Cortlandt family and is now an outstanding restaurant. Great views of the river and a rural setting make this stop a treat in summer for fine Continental cuisine.

La Panetiere Restaurant (914-967-8140), 530 Milton Road, Rye. ($$) Open for lunch Tuesday through Friday, noon–2:30; dinner Tuesday through Saturday 6–9:30; Sunday 1–8:30. The building dates back to the 1800s and the Provençal interior features exposed beams, stucco walls, and a huge grandfather clock. Appetizer specials include warm oysters with leeks, duck terrine with truffles and pistachios, and fresh foie gras; entrées include squab, venison, and Dover sole filled with puree of artichokes. Six-course prix fixe menu. Children welcome.

Paul Ma's China Kitchen (914-962-7996), 2020 Crompond Road, Yorktown Heights. ($$) Open Tuesday through Sunday for lunch 11–3 and dinner 5–9. Paul Ma has created many of the specialty dishes based on his "hometown" favorites; they include chicken imperial, sea delicacy in a nest, and pan-fired flounder. Children welcome.

Provare Restaurant (914-939-5500), Anderson Hill Road, Rye Brook. ($$) Lunch Tuesday through Friday 11:30–2; dinner Tuesday through Thursday 5:30–9:30, Friday and Saturday nights until 11, Sundays 4–9. A cheerful trattoria-style restaurant, Provare is decorated in black and yellow from the wallpaper to the tile floors. The gourmet pizzas are baked in a wood-fired brick oven; the smoked pheasant pizza and the barbecued chicken pizza are two unusual varieties. The menu is extensive, and vegetarian lasagne and linguine with mussels are both recommended.

Rene Chardin (914-533-6200), Route 123, South Salem. ($$) Open Wednesday through Saturday for dinner at 6; Sunday brunch, noon–3. Set in a Victorian mansion, Rene Chardin serves French cuisine, with specialties that are a little unusual, such as ginger fragrance roast chicken and lobster Charlotte. Reservations are suggested.

The Roadhouse (914-693-6565), Saw Mill River Parkway, Ardsley. ($$) Open daily at 11:30 for lunch and dinner. A beautiful 100-year-old stone building houses this "restaurant in the park," which overlooks Woodlands Lake. Continental cuisine and fresh seafood are the specialties here. The Buffalo fajita (American bison) and Angus beef are among the more unusual entrées; steaks and pizza are served as well. Enjoy outdoor dining in warm weather. Children welcome.

Santa Fe Restaurant (914-332-4452), 5 Main Street, Tarrytown. ($$) Open daily for lunch and dinner 11:30–10. You can get steak, chicken, shrimp, and even shark fajitas at this colorful Mexican dining spot. For taco lovers, there is a make-your-own taco basket: Diners are served chicken or beef, beans, rice, peppers, and other fixings from which they can create their own meal. One of the most unusual and delicious dishes is the shrimp and crab enchiladas with blue corn tortillas.

Zephs' (914-736-2159), 638 Central Avenue, Peekskill. ($$$) Open Wednesday through Sunday at 5:30 for dinner. Set in a reclaimed factory building, Zephs' serves American cuisine with a fresh twist; choices may include Moroccan lamb, tomato tart, salt and pepper squid, fresh fruit cobblers, mud cake, and rich custards. Many of the herbs are grown by the owners, and summer diners can enjoy the outdoor patio area. Reservations are necessary.

EATING OUT

Horsefeathers (914-631-6606), 94 North Broadway, Tarrytown. ($$) Open daily except Sunday, for lunch and dinner at 11:30 AM. One of the first "grazing" restaurants in the county, Horsefeathers continues to offer great café food like hamburgers, steaks, and overstuffed sandwiches. The atmosphere is casual and comfortable, and children are welcome.

Louisiana Cajun Cafe (914-674-0706), 25 Cedar Street, Dobbs Ferry. ($$) Open for lunch Monday through Saturday, noon–2:30; dinner daily 6–10; Sunday brunch 11–3. The most flavorful Cajun and Creole dishes are served here: gumbo, red beans and rice, jambalaya, and blackened steak and fish are just some of the dishes that will be prepared to your taste. Live Dixieland band on Saturday night.

Silver Moon Ristorante and Pizzeria (914-962-4040), 2010 Saw Mill River Road, Yorktown Heights. ($$) Open for dinner Tuesday through Sunday 5–10. Enjoy Continental and Italian dishes including steaks, seafood, pasta, and pizza prepared to order at this informal eatery. You can choose a full dinner or a light meal.

SELECTIVE SHOPPING

In Westchester, shopping could be a full-time vacation activity. Dozens of boutiques, shopping malls, specialty shops, and antiques stores cater to discriminating buyers. Since many of the towns and villages are chock-full of interesting places to see, you may want to plan your shopping excursions around a visit to a nearby museum or gallery.

One mall worth mentioning is the **Galleria** (914-682-0316), 100 Main Street, White Plains. This mall has a food court, and more than 150 stores dazzle shoppers with their selections.

Another notable shopping area is **The Yellow Monkey Village** (914-763-5848), Route 35, Cross River. The shops are located in old-fashioned, Early American buildings and offer a wide range of paintings, jewelry, gifts, and gourmet foods.

Crafts lovers should visit **Somerstown Gallery** (914-277-3461), Route 100, Somers, which has changing art exhibits, a well-stocked crafts shop, and an annual print show.

The Animazing Gallery (914-478-7278), 549 Warburton Avenue, Hastings-on-Hudson, specializes in animation art. **Arctic Artistry Gallery** (914-478-7179), Spring Street, Hastings-on-Hudson, offers browsers a fine selection of Inuit, Northwest, and Southwest art.

At the **Empire State Flea Market** (914-939-1800), Boston Post Road, Port Chester, hundreds of dealers sell everything from designer accessories to housewares. Open weekends only.

Central Avenue, which runs through White Plains, Hartsdale, and Scarsdale, is lined with dozens of small stores, discount malls, and shops. In White Plains, off I-287, you can find classy standards like Bloomingdale's (on Bloomingdale Road) and Macy's (at Main Street and Mamaroneck Avenue).

BOOKSTORES

Westchester County is filled with fine bookstores; here's a worthy selection.

Good Yarns (914-478-0014), 8 Main Street, Hastings-on-Hudson, is the only full-line bookstore in town. It offers personal service; yarns—that is, wools!—and a separate children's room.

Galapagos Books (914-478-2501), 22A Main Street, Hastings-on-Hudson, offers foreign-language books, as well as books on language learning and on other cultures. Children's section.

For used books in Hastings-on-Hudson, try **Riverrun** (914-478-4307), 7 Washington Avenue, which has an extensive general collection. Or call for an appointment with **Gordon Beckhorn, Bookperson** (914-478-5511), 497 Warburton Avenue, an antiquarian bookseller who offers modern first editions and selected Americana.

The Bookstore (914-769-8322), 20 Wheeler Avenue, Pleasantville, located in an old train station, offers new books and a small selection of used.

In Rye, **Lighthouse Bookstore** (914-967-0966), 15 Purchase Street, and **Village Book Shop** (914-967-0031), 84 Purchase Street, both offer good general selections. **DiscoveRead** (914-921-2223), 81 Purchase Street, has books, CD ROMs, computers, and all kinds of games and toys for children.

Panacea Books (914-939-4500), 39 Main Street, Port Chester, is an interesting alternative bookshop emphasizing Hispanic and other cultures, as well as feminist works.

Second Story Bookshop (914-238-4463), 75 North Greeley Avenue, Chappaqua. A well-known general bookstore.

Call for an appointment at **Ben Chaney, Jr. Books** (914-941-1002), 73 Croton Avenue, Ossining. Modern first editions, mostly for collectors.

SPECIAL EVENTS

Crafts at Lyndhurst (914-631-4481), Lyndhurst Historic Site, Route 9, Tarrytown. Shows are usually held the third weekend of May and the third weekend of September, Friday 10–5, Saturday 10–6, and Sunday 10–5. Admission fee. This spectacular crafts fair has become a Westchester tradition over the past decade. Craftspeople from across the United States participate—potters, jewelers, fiber artists, and glassmakers, to name just a few. There's a children's tent with activities for the kids, so parents can shop in the huge tents unimpeded. A tour of the Lyndhurst mansion is available at a discount to those who attend the show. Food vendors offer an array of delicious treats. Be sure to get there early and beat the crowds.

General Index

Lodging Index

Books from The Countryman Press

Explorer's Guides
The alternative to mass-market guides with their homogenized listings, *Explorer's Guides* focus on independently owned inns, motels, and restaurants, and on family and cultural activities reflecting the character and unique qualities of the area.

Explorer's Guides are available for: Cape Cod and the Islands, Connecticut, Maine, Massachusetts, New Hampshire, Rhode Island, and Vermont.

A selection of our books about New York . . .
Canoeing Central New York
50 Hikes in Central New York
50 Hikes in the Hudson Valley, Second Edition
25 Bicycle Tours in the Hudson Valley
25 Bicycle Tours in the Adirondacks
25 Mountain Bike Tours in the Hudson Valley
Walks & Rambles in Westchester and Fairfield Counties
Good Fishing in the Catskills
Good Fishing in the Adirondacks
Walks in Nature's Empire

. . . and the Northeast
The New England Herb Gardener
Perennials for the Backyard Gardener
Full Duty: Vermonters in the Civil War
Fishing Vermont's Streams and Lakes
25 Bicycle Tours in Vermont
25 Mountain Bike Tours in Massachusetts
Waterfalls of the White Mountains
Elusive Quarry, by B. Comfort
    The latest in Comfort's Vermont Village Mystery series

We offer a variety of fiction and nonfiction, and outdoor recreation guides. Our books are available through bookstores, or they may be ordered directly from the publisher. VISA/MasterCard accepted. For ordering information, or for a complete catalog, please contact:

The Countryman Press
c/o W.W. Norton & Company, Inc.
800 Keystone Industrial Park
Scranton, PA 18512
http://web.wwnorton.com